A CHURCH FULLY ENGAGED

# A Church Fully Engaged

*Yves Congar's Vision
of Ecclesial Authority*

Anthony Oelrich

A Michael Glazier Book

**LITURGICAL PRESS**
Collegeville, Minnesota

www.litpress.org

A Michael Glazier Book published by Liturgical Press

Cover design by David Manahan, OSB. Photo courtesy of ThinkstockPhotos.com. Illustration by Frank Kacmarcik, OblSB.

Scripture texts in this work are taken from the *New Revised Standard Version Bible* © 1989, Division of Christian Education of the National Council of the Churches of Christ in the United States of America. Used by permission. All rights reserved.

All excerpts from the documents of the Second Vatican Council are taken from *Decrees of the Ecumenical Councils, Vol. II*, ed. By Norman P. Tanner (Washington, DC: Georgetown University Press, 1990).

© 2011 by Order of Saint Benedict, Collegeville, Minnesota. All rights reserved. No part of this book may be reproduced in any form, by print, microfilm, microfiche, mechanical recording, photocopying, translation, or by any other means, known or yet unknown, for any purpose except brief quotations in reviews, without the previous written permission of Liturgical Press, Saint John's Abbey, PO Box 7500, Collegeville, Minnesota 56321-7500. Printed in the United States of America.

1    2    3    4    5    6    7    8    9

**Library of Congress Cataloging-in-Publication Data**

Oelrich, Anthony.
   A church fully engaged : Yves Congar's vision of ecclesial authority / Anthony Oelrich.
      p. cm.
   "A Michael Glazier book."
   Includes bibliographical references (p.   ) and indexes.
   ISBN 978-0-8146-5797-3 — ISBN 978-0-8146-8042-1 (e-book)
    1. Congar, Yves, 1904–1995.  2. Church—Authority.  3. Catholic Church—Doctrines.  I. Title.

BX1746.O365 2011
262'.8—dc23

2011031995

# Contents

Acknowledgments   vii

Introduction   ix

Chapter One: The Life and Work of Yves Congar, OP   1

Chapter Two: Historical Foundations for the Understanding and Practice of Authority in the Church   11

Chapter Three: The Community or Life Principle of Authority   43

Chapter Four: The Hierarchical Principle of Authority   81

Chapter Five: A Trinitarian Logic of Authority   117

Conclusion   135

Selected Bibliography   143

Index of Names   159

Index of Subjects   161

# Acknowledgments

This work flows out of my doctoral dissertation completed at the Pontifical University of St. Thomas Aquinas. I am most grateful to Fr. Robert Christian, OP, who directed my work there. I have been inspired by the precision of his theological insight, the breadth of his knowledge of the theological sources, and, above all, by his truly fraternal concern for my efforts in research and writing.

Fr. Yves Congar offers an observation concerning the study of theology that highlights well the sentiments I would like to express: "A bishop who ordains one priest every two years and who nevertheless makes the effort of sending one of his seminarians or one of his young priests for training in a university or an institute is almost heroic."[1] It is certainly true that Bishop John F. Kinney of the Diocese of St. Cloud, Minnesota, has shown me great generosity in affording me very precious time for the study that has resulted in this book. For this I am most grateful. I am grateful, as well, for the sacrifices made every day for the sake of the People of God by my brother priests of the Church of St. Cloud. They are generous and faithful stewards of the mysteries of God and a source of inspiration for my priesthood. It is necessary to say as well that the faith of the People of God in my local church of St. Cloud has given rise to and continually nurtures my faith. I am thankful for the gift of faith they enkindle in me.

---

1. Yves Congar, *Fifty Years of Catholic Theology*, ed. Bernard Lauret, trans. John Bowden (Philadelphia: Fortress Press, 1988), 29.

Finally, to my family and friends who have been a source of goodness and encouragement to me, let me say that I love you and am grateful for all you are to me. In particular, my dear friend Don Lane read every word of my dissertation in all its drafts and gave me much valuable insight. I dedicate this present work to his memory.

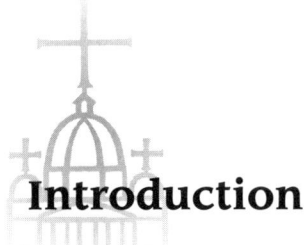
# Introduction

Since the Second Vatican Council the various currents within the discussion concerning ecclesiology have moved increasingly around the notion of *communio*, or communion. Indeed, the German theologian Walter Kasper has even said that this idea concerning the church is "perhaps *the* guiding idea" of that council.[1]

In *Novo Millennio Ineunte* Pope John Paul II laid out what might be called a "pastoral vision" for the church at the beginning of the new millennium. There, as often during the course of his pontificate, the pope placed this image of *communio* before the people of God, saying that *"the domain of communion (koinonia) . . .* embodies and reveals the very essence of the mystery of the Church" (n. 42).[2] He went on to say that the church must become *"the home and school of communion"* and to this end *"promote a spirituality of communion."* This demands, according to the pope, "the contemplation of the mystery of the Trinity" in the "brothers and sisters around us," seeing that they are in fact "part of me" and "gift for me" (n. 43). To this end, John Paul placed a striking call before the church, without which such ideas concerning the church

---

1. Walter Kasper, *Theology & Church*, trans. Margaret Kohl (New York: Crossroad, 1989), 19, 152.

2. John Paul II, *"Novo Millennio Ineunte,"* Acta Apostolicae Sedis [hereafter: AAS] XCIII (3 May 2001): 266–309; emphasis in original. English translation: *Apostolic letter of Pope John Paul II: novo millennio ineunte. At the beginning of the new millennium, to the bishops, clergy and lay faithful at the close of the great jubilee of the year 2000* (Boston: Pauline Books & Media, 2001).

as communion could very easily remain only in the domain of theory. "[T]he new century will have to see us more than ever intent on valuing and developing the forums and structures which, in accordance with the Second Vatican Council's major directives, serve to ensure and safeguard communion. . . . Communion must be cultivated and extended day by day and at every level in the structures of each Church's life" (n. 44, 45).

Within the broad discussion of communion, the "structures" of the church have certainly been the topic of much theological and other discussion. In particular, those structures that surround the expressions of authority within the church—specifically the papacy, the role of the local bishop and national episcopal conferences, indeed, the entire hierarchical reality within the church and the place of the lay faithful in relation to it—have been at the center of seemingly endless debate. My intention here is to engage this "call" to "ensure and safeguard" the structures of communion by reflecting on the nature of ecclesial authority. This will be done by developing a synthetic treatment of the monumental theological writings of the French Dominican Fr. Yves Congar as they are addressed to this question of ecclesial authority. To do so, I will develop Congar's conviction, based on his work of theological *ressourcement*, that the church is "built up" by Christ and the Holy Spirit from within, by what Congar calls the community or life principle, and from above and outside by what he calls the hierarchical principle.

To begin, I will offer an overview of the person and monumental work of Fr. Yves Congar. This will reveal the enormous significance of the contribution he has made to theology in general and to ecclesiology in particular. In chapter two I will present a general survey of the historical development of the understanding and practice of authority throughout the church's two-thousand-year history. This historical outline will provide the foundation for the more specifically theological work of chapters three and four, in which I will systematically explore the various aspects of the "principles" of authority, which will make possible their synthetic definition. An essential aim of this work, then, will be to present a systematic understanding of the community or life principle and the hierarchical principle of authority as they are found within the writings of Congar.

Chapter five will present an analysis and critique of these theological insights articulated by Père Congar. In order to express faithfully the authentic tradition of the church regarding its nature, Congar found it necessary to speak "dialectically" of authority—thus of a hierarchical principle *and* a community or life principle. I will indicate how this approach effectively expresses the richness of the church's tradition regarding the nature of authority. Nonetheless, it is my conviction that speaking of authority dialectically does not adequately show the essential unity of God's action in building up the church in an authentically *theological* way. Though Congar clearly saw the need to speak of the church as a communion of persons flowing essentially from the trinitarian communion of Persons, the "occasional" nature of his writings on the topic of authority did not lend itself to an essentially trinitarian understanding of authority in the church. Beginning from the profound theological insights into the nature of authority as they appear in the writings of Congar, and as articulated in chapters three and four, I will be able to offer the first intimations of an authentic trinitarian understanding of authority. This will serve as a critique of Congar's dialectical approach and also as a synthesis of his works on authority. I believe that this trinitarian synthesis is a natural outgrowth of the essential trajectory of Congar's theological labors. Some specific implications for the understanding and practice of ecclesial authority in the church today will be offered in the conclusion.

Some words on my approach to the topic might be useful. The bibliography of Yves Congar contains a remarkable 1,856 entries.[3] Granting that this list includes reprints, translations, and books of collected articles already noted, it remains an astonishing theological production. In addition to the sheer size of Congar's opus, his work ultimately lacks fundamental systematization. Congar saw his role as a theologian to be one of service to any and all needs of the contemporary church upon which he would attempt to shed the light of the most authentic sources of the tradition. This profound openness to the demands made on his time for various projects ultimately prevented the completion of the systematic work on the church that was his lifelong ambition.[4] The size of Congar's theological corpus and its fundamental lack of systematization demands a very intentional approach to the topic of authority in the works of Congar.

---

3. For the most comprehensive bibliography of Congar's works see Pietro Quattrocchi, "General Bibliography of Yves Congar," 189–241 in Jean-Pierre Jossua, *Yves Congar: Theology in the Service of God's People*, trans. Mary Jocelyn (Chicago: Priory Press, 1968); Aidan Nichols, "An Yves Congar Bibliography 1967–1987," *Angelicum* 66 (1989): 422–66; Gabriel Flynn, "Appendix: An Yves Congar Bibliography 1987–1995, with Addenda: 1996–2002," 229–33 in idem, *Yves Congar's Vision of the Church in a World of Unbelief* (Burlington, VT: Ashgate, 2004).

4. Jossua, *Yves Congar*, 30, 49, 22.

I will seek to offer an authentic expression of the nature of ecclesial authority as it appears in the theological work of Père Congar. This will demand drawing forth from the body of Congar's work those texts that possess implications for the nature of authority. In order to systematically treat his articulation of authority, it will be necessary to gather his various theological observations under his most prominent themes. These in turn will serve as various *aspects* of the more general principles—regarding life and hierarchical principles—that flow from the dialectical methodology—structure and life—found throughout the whole of Congar's ecclesiology. When we survey the texts that touch on the topic of ecclesial authority certain dominant themes present themselves as aspects of the overall reality of authority and serve as an effective means for the systematization of Père Congar's theology of ecclesial authority.

In an examination of Congar's contribution to the understanding of ecclesial authority, certain questions of interest and significance must be set aside. First, what one finds here is not a full articulation of the present status within theology as a whole of the questions surrounding ecclesial authority. Clearly, these questions are multiple and the theological discussion of them extensive. Nonetheless, reference will be made to the positions of other authors as a means of clarifying Congar's position or when a significant critique of his position demands it. In this process the articulation of the French theologian's position will find its place within the larger discussion on authority without providing a complete exposition of that discussion.

Second, though Congar's theological career spanned more than five decades, no attempt will be made to give a detailed articulation of the evolution of his thought. Such development, which is inevitable over the course of such a long period of work, will certainly be noted in those instances where it proves necessary for an authentic presentation of his position. With the theological enterprise of Père Congar, the Congarian scholar Joseph Famerée makes clear, "all is in profound continuity."[5] Over the course of Congar's writings one discovers a development that is deeply organic; what is found in seed early on grows consistently throughout to maturity.

Finally, the various ecumenical dialogues are of profound significance. Clearly, issues surrounding the understanding and practice of authority have been much discussed within these various groups. More-

---

5. Joseph Famerée, "Formation et ecclésiologie du 'premier' Congar," 51–70 in *Cardinal Yves Congar, 1904–1995*, ed. André Vauchez (Paris: Cerf, 1999), 52. [Unless otherwise noted, all translations are the author's.]

over, the importance of ecumenism for a greater understanding of the theology of Congar cannot be neglected. Still, the complexity and nuance of these varied ecumenical dialogues raise a cautionary flag when one is already attempting a rather large project. In this regard I have taken something from Congar's own approach to the matter and applied it to the present study.

> My services to ecumenism have been far from exclusive to other tasks, largely because of my conviction of the inseparable connection between the massive process of denudation which ecumenism demanded and the ecclesiological, pastoral, biblical and liturgical movements. It very soon occurred to me that ecumenism is not a specialty and that it presupposes a movement of conversion and reform coextensive with the whole life of all communions. It seemed to me, also, that each individual's ecumenical task lay in the first place at home among his own people.[6]

This rather narrow focus on the enormous contribution to the topic of ecclesial authority made by the French Dominican, who sought to bring forth the great tradition on all matters of ecclesiology from within the Roman Catholic tradition, may nevertheless aid the dialogue between the various ecclesial communions. In order to articulate Congar's contribution effectively I will make little attempt here to address the present status of the question of authority within the ecumenical dialogue. Within these limits I offer in this book a systematic articulation of the theological fruits of Père Congar's work as they contribute to an understanding of ecclesial authority.

---

6. Yves Congar, *Dialogue between Christians*, trans. Philip Loretz (Westminster, MD: Newman Press, 1966), 21.

Chapter One

# The Life and Work of Yves Congar, OP

In an article exploring trends in ecclesiology since Vatican II, Avery Dulles highlights their foundations in preconciliar theological history.

> The ideas that surfaced at the Council, to be sure, were not produced out of nothing. Practically all these ideas had been discussed at some depth in the theological literature of the preceding decades, especially in the circle of theologians in contact with Yves Congar. Without this *previous theological reflection* on episcopacy, collegiality, ecumenism, Church reform, the role of the laity, religious freedom, and liturgical renewal . . . the achievements of Vatican II would not have been possible.[1]

A simple review of Congar's major theological contributions prior to the Second Vatican Council shows that Dulles's comment, placing him at the center of a circle of theologians instrumental in the achievements of that council, was without the slightest hint of exaggeration. As early as 1937 Congar published his *Divided Christendom*, in which "for the first time, with this book, an effort was made, from the Roman Catholic side, to situate ecumenism theologically."[2] In 1950 Congar published a

---

1. Avery Dulles, "Catholic Ecclesiology since Vatican II," *Concilium* 188, ed. Giuseppe Alberigo and James Provost, 3–13 (Edinburgh: T & T Clark, 1986), at 3; emphasis in original.

2. Joseph Famerée, "Y. M.-J. Congar: Un théologien de la catholicité," 15–31 in *Le christianisme: Nuée de témoins—beauté du témoignage*, ed. Guido Vergauwen, OP (Fribourg: Editions Universitaires, 1998), at 23.

work on intraecclesial reform, *Vraie et fausse réforme dans l'Église*, historically and theologically articulating the way in which reform in the church might be considered and its authentic character expressed.[3] The future Pope John XXIII, while papal nuncio in Paris, reportedly wrote on the inside of his own copy of this text, "A reform of the Church—is it possible?"[4] In 1953 Congar's influential *Lay People in the Church* showed the relationship of the laity to the priestly, prophetic, and kingly functions of Christ. In this work he offered a more substantial and integral vision of the position occupied by the laity within the very life of the church. The book *Sainte Église* (1963) brought together previously written influential articles on the full range of ecclesiological questions, most significantly those on the nature of the collegiality of the episcopacy and the fundamental conciliar nature of the church. In *Tradition and Traditions* (1960 and 1963), the later part of which was composed in the very midst of the proceedings of Vatican II from notes used in conferences he gave to various groups of bishops, Congar put forth a remarkable historical and theological synthesis of the dynamic character of the living faith carried within the life of the whole church. Among these pillars of Congar's literary efforts are a remarkable number of smaller books and articles dealing with topics of ecumenism, the laity, reform in the church, the nature of faith, ecclesial structure, and ecclesiology more generally. Clearly, even this rapid survey of Congar's preconciliar labors shows that "[t]he great wonder of his contribution to the council is that his life-long program for theological research matched the theological program of Vatican II."[5] Congar acknowledges, with uncharacteristic boldness, "All the things to which I gave quiet special attention issued in the Council: ecclesiology, ecumenism, reform of the Church, the lay state, mission, ministries, collegiality, return to the sources and Tradition. . . ."[6]

---

3. See Jean-Pierre Jossua, *Yves Congar: Theology in the Service of God's People*, trans. Mary Jocelyn (Chicago: Priory Press, 1968), 28, who considers this to be Congar's "finest work," and Étienne Fouilloux, "Friar Yves, Cardinal Congar, Dominican: Itinerary of a Theologian," trans. Christian Yves Dupont, *U. S. Catholic Historian* 17 (Spring 1999): 63–90, at 75, who says that this work "is perhaps the most structured and, historically speaking, certainly the most important work by Congar."

4. Jean Puyo, *Yves Congar: Une vie pour la vérité* (Paris: Le Centurion, 1975), 117; William Henn, *The Hierarchy of Truths according to Yves Congar, O.P.* (Rome: Editrice Pontificia Università Gregoriana, 1987), 14–15 n. 21.

5. Paul J. Philibert, "Yves Congar: Theologian, Ecumenist, and Visionary," *U.S. Catholic Historian* 17 (Spring 1999): 116–20, at 119.

6. Yves Congar, "Reflections on Being a Theologian," trans. Marcul Lefébure, *New Blackfriars* 62 (1981): 405–9, at 405.

In order to appreciate these theological accomplishments it is important to gain some sense of the man himself. For Congar, all is vocation. Every fruit of his labor has its basis in a profound sense of having first been called. Congar is clear: "I have no plan for myself; I have only tried to do what God wanted of me."[7] As far as it concerns his vocation, Congar is explicit. "[M]y vocation has always been at one and the same time and for the same reason priestly and religious, Dominican and Thomistic, ecumenical and ecclesiological."[8] The remarkable continuity of theological endeavor in the life of a man who claims to have "never had a plan"[9] finds its basis in this profound awareness of and sensitivity to the call of God expressed in the exigencies of his personal history.

There are two aspects of Congar's self-described vocation that serve to influence the whole of his theological work and therefore require particular attention: his call to ecumenism and his emphasis on questions of ecclesiology. Congar experienced these two calls as profoundly intertwined. Prior to his ordination to the priesthood in July 1930, while making his retreat, he reflected on the Eucharist and the Gospel of John. "It was in meditating particularly on chapter 17 of St. John that my ecumenical vocation was clearly revealed to me, coming along on top of a certain ecclesiological vocation. A double, profoundly interior revelation that could come before my eyes only from God."[10] John's "High Priestly Prayer" (John 17), in which Jesus expresses his desire that his disciples share in the unity of the Father and Son, set Congar on a lifelong journey to theologically promote Christian unity.

Congar's ecclesiological project crystallized when he was invited in 1935 to write the conclusion to a three-year series on the contemporary causes of unbelief for the influential journal *La Vie Intellectuelle*.[11] Within this article he concluded that in significant part modern unbelief resulted from the church's own presentation of itself, a presentation almost entirely legalistic, triumphalistic, and defensive toward modern thought. In this article Congar proposed the need for a renewal of the

---

7. Patrick Granfield, "Yves Congar," 243–62 in *Theologians at Work* (New York: Macmillan, 1967), at 252.

8. Yves Congar, *Dialogue between Christians: Catholic Contributions to Ecumenism*, trans. Philip Loretz (Westminster, MD: Newman Press, 1966), 5.

9. See Congar, "Reflections," 405.

10. Puyo, *Une vie*, 75.

11. "Une conclusion théologique à l'enquête sur les raisons actuelles de l'incroyance," *La Vie Intellectuelle* 37 (1935): 214–49.

church's presentation of its life and nature if it was to evangelize the modern world effectively.[12]

What might be called the *milieu* of Congar's thought was created by the life he lived as a Dominican. *Veritas* being the motto of the Friars Preachers, Congar insists that he developed a "cult of Truth."[13] "The Order of Friars Preachers is dedicated to the service of the Gospel, especially under its aspect of truth. I've consecrated my life to the service of the truth. I've loved it and still love it in the way one loves a person. I've been like that from my very childhood, as if by some instinct and interior need."[14]

Certainly the grand influence on this sense of truth in the life of Congar was his theological master, St. Thomas Aquinas. Specifically, he owed to Thomas "a certain spiritual structure"[15] or way of framing the theological task. In Thomas, Congar discovered, one finds a clarity of ideas constructed by means of precision in language and in the stating of questions. Thomas possessed a very distinct openness and spirit of dialogue in his approach to the most profound questions of his day, seeking always to apply to these questions new texts and new translations from all the possible sources of knowledge.[16]

In 1926 Congar entered the Dominicans and began his studies at Le Saulchoir, then located in Belgium. There, he came into contact with Père Marie-Dominique Chenu, who would begin as Congar's professor and then become his confrère and dear friend.[17] Congar's understanding of revelation as a profoundly historical reality played a central role in the development of his understanding of ecclesial authority, and he acquired that historical awareness in large part from Chenu.[18] Through this pioneer in medieval studies[19] Congar encountered an approach to St. Thomas profoundly different from what he had previously known, one that sought to place Thomas within the historical context from which his theology arose. A further dimension of Chenu's influence on Congar was how he instinctively drew the ancient tradition into a living dialogue with contemporary life and questions. Congar made contact

---

12. Congar, *Dialogue between Christians*, 23.
13. Puyo, *Une vie*, 38.
14. Congar, "Reflections," 406.
15. Congar, *Fifty Years*, 70.
16. See ibid., 70–71; Granfield, "Yves Congar," 247–49; Puyo, *Une vie*, 39–42.
17. Puyo, *Une vie*, 45.
18. Jossua, *Yves Congar*, 17.
19. Paul J. Philibert, "Introduction," v–viii in Marie-Dominique Chenu, *Aquinas and His Role in Theology* (Collegeville, MN: Liturgical Press, 2002), at v.

as well with the Catholic Youth Movement and the Worker Priest Movement through Chenu.[20] In his course on the history of doctrine Chenu spoke to his students of the Faith and Order Movement and the Lausanne Conference, the first movements of modern ecumenism.[21] Clearly, Chenu's influence on the life, thought, and work of Congar cannot be overstated. Chenu profoundly shaped Congar's approach to theological science, initiated his first contacts with the trends in ecumenism, and placed him in touch with important pastoral developments in the life of the contemporary French church.

The enormous energy and amazing pace of writing, conferences, teaching, preaching, editing, and significant ecumenical contacts that engaged Congar came to a sudden stop with the outbreak of the Second World War. In the fall of 1939 he began a brief time of combat in defense of France against the Nazi regime, only to become very quickly a prisoner of war. Though he attempted to keep himself busy—studying Russian and giving at least nineteen talks against national socialism to his fellow captives—"he experienced intensely the disastrous impression that he was losing some of the best years of his life without any hope of recovering them."[22] The relationships Congar developed with his fellow prisoners were significant for his life as a theologian, giving him added perspective on the profound alienation of the church from the lives of contemporary people. The captivity, he would reflect later, added a dimension of "realism" to his preaching and teaching.[23] In this epoch of his life Congar was given concrete experience to add to his earlier insight concerning the need for theology to speak more explicitly to the modern person's situation and mentality.

Upon his return at the end of the war, Père Congar found himself in the midst of a church filled with vitality spurred by the biblical and liturgical renewals. "Anyone who did not live through the years of 1946 and 1947 in the history of French Catholicism has missed one of the finest moments in the life of the Church."[24] A new pastoral dimension was added to this revitalization of French Catholicism by the very experiences of many priests who had suffered imprisonment in labor camps during the war. In these camps they encountered modern labor personally and in the process found a unique ability to offer their priestly services to

---

20. Puyo, *Une vie*, 41.
21. Congar, *Dialogue between Christians*, 3.
22. Fouilloux, "Friar Yves," 72.
23. Puyo, *Une vie*, 87–92, 94.
24. Congar, Dialogue *between Christians*, 32.

those with whom they worked side by side. This gave rise, after the war, to the Worker Priest Movement when priests went to work in factories.[25] Congar engaged in these renewed theological and pastoral endeavors by "providing new theological foundations for their extensive dialogue and engagement with society."[26] He became "a 'theologian of service,' that is, a skilled theologian ready to respond as a theologian to every call coming from the various groups and movements among the Christian people."[27]

This period following the war, dominated by "an ecclesial climate of recovered liberty" and "of marvelous creativity on the pastoral plane,"[28] was soon to be tempered for Congar and many of his colleagues. By 1947 there were already indications that questions were being raised concerning his writings and associations, in particular those connected to ecumenism and the Worker Priest Movement. "As far as I myself am concerned, from the beginning of 1947 to the end of 1956 I knew nothing from that quarter [Rome] but an uninterrupted series of denunciations, warnings, restrictive or discriminatory measures and mistrustful interventions."[29] Indicative of the sorts of aggravations he faced in this period is his attempt at publishing a revision of his *Divided Christendom*. After more than a half year of work on the manuscript he submitted it for approval to the Dominican Master General, who kept it without response for the next two years. When the manuscript was finally returned Congar was told that it needed revision, though without details of the necessary alterations. At this same time certain Roman theologians began to criticize the theological approach taken by those like Congar, which they deprecatingly labeled *théologie nouvelle* (the new theology). Congar began keeping a file of those critiques, which he provocatively entitled *La tarasque*, after a very dangerous animal that is only imaginary.

In 1950, Pope Pius XII issued the encyclical *Humani generis*, broadly warning against dangerous tendencies in certain contemporary approaches in philosophy, theology, morals, apologetics, ecumenism, and pastoral practices. It was made clear to Congar by his superiors that, though no particular theologians were named, the warnings in this docu-

---

25. Thomas O'Meara, " 'Raid on the Dominicans': The Repression of 1954," *America* 170/4 (5 February 1994): 8–16, at 9.

26. Mark Wedig, "The Fraternal Context of Congar's Achievement: The Platform for a Renewed Catholicism at Les Éditions du Cerf (1927–1954)," *U. S. Catholic Historian* 17 (Spring 1999): 106–15, at 113.

27. Fouilloux, "Friar Yves," 74.

28. Puyo, *Une vie*, 98.

29. Congar, *Dialogue between Christians*, 34.

ment were indeed directed, at least in part, at his theology.[30] The year 1954 served as the culminating point of these pressures on Congar. On February 8 of that year the Dominican Master General, at the insistence of the Vatican, arrived in Paris to take action, the result of which was the unprecedented dismissal of the three French provincials. Congar was also called to Paris, where it was decided that he would remove himself from the "French scene" and go to Jerusalem. After returning from there in the fall he was summoned to Rome, a stay that lasted four months just as he was about to begin a new teaching assignment. The result of this time in Rome was his assignment to Cambridge in England, where he spent ten months under "odious restrictions" to his priestly ministry and his interactions with houses of study and ecumenical gatherings.[31] The darkest of these clouds over Congar lifted in December 1955 when, at the explicit request of Jean Weber, the bishop of Strasbourg, he was assigned to a monastery in that diocese. Here he enjoyed a great deal of freedom to preach, to participate in conferences, and to engage in a great variety of pastoral activities, though he did not teach in an academic faculty.

The deep, personal suffering and, at times, real frustration that suspicion and censorship of church leaders evoked in Congar reveal something truly profound. As he reflected later: "I only succeeded in overcoming all this, both spiritually and at the level of ordinary human sanity, by complete resignation to the cross and to reduction to insignificance."[32] This experience of conflict with the church he loved so deeply also gave rise to a profound sense of the need within the Christian for what he came to call an "active patience," which "is something quite different from merely marking time. It is a quality of mind, or better of the heart, which is rooted in the profound, existential conviction, firstly that God is in charge and accomplishes his gracious design through us, and secondly that, in all great things, delay is necessary for their maturation."[33] This active patience is a reality lived in view of the truth of the paschal mystery. "The cross is a condition of every holy work. God himself is at work in what to us seems a cross."[34] Here again Congar's profound sense of his life as vocation is evident. He possessed such conviction concerning God's guidance of his life that he viewed

---

30. Puyo, *Une vie*, 99, 106.
31. Congar, *Dialogue between Christians*, 42–43.
32. Ibid., 43.
33. Ibid., 44.
34. Ibid., 45.

even the misunderstandings and injustices he faced in the light of God's abiding, faithful presence.

"When Pope John XXIII summoned an ecumenical council in January 1959, it was recognized that a new climate was stirring in the Vatican."[35] This also meant a new "climate" for the theological work of Père Congar. Pope John XIII appointed him a consultor to the preparatory theological commission for the council on July 20, 1960. After a brief initial period of marginalization in his efforts he soon became deeply immersed in the heart of the work of the council. In the end his contribution was enormous. He expended great energy on multiple council commissions and subcommissions as well as in many workshops on theological questions organized by various groups of bishops. Congar's contribution to the conciliar documents includes aspects of *Lumen gentium*, *Gaudium et spes*, *Dei Verbum*, *Unitatis redintegratio*, *Dignitatis humanae*, *Ad gentes*, and *Presbyterorum ordinis*.[36] There is no better example of the French Dominican as a "theologian of service" than in the availability and openness he maintained to whatever was asked of him during the course of the Second Vatican Council. Congar expressed the enormity of the work: "I do not think that I had more than two days' rest in the four conciliar sessions of three months each."[37] Clearly, the contribution of Père Congar bore concrete fruit in the conciliar documents. "Without the contribution of Yves Congar, . . . one of the most influential minds at Vatican II, the process of renewal initiated there would have been seriously impeded, and the battle for a 'real council,' a council capable of substantial reform, might not have been fully realized."[38]

In the years following the council "Congar became *the* theologian of Vatican II *par excellence*, and its interpreter throughout the world to the degree that his declining energies permitted him."[39] Already in 1964 the Dominicans named him a Master of Sacred Theology, "the traditional crowning of the career of a professor in the Order, the recognition . . . of a brother's theological knowledge and teaching."[40] He received appointments to the International Theological Commission and the International

---

35. Gabriel Flynn, "Book Essay: *Mon journal du Concile*: Yves Congar and the Battle for a Renewed Ecclesiology at the Second Vatican Council," *Louvain Studies* 28 (2003): 48–70, at 48.

36. In his *Mon journal du Concile* 2: 511, Congar provides a specific outline of his contribution to the various documents of the council.

37. Congar, "Letter," 215.

38. Flynn, "Yves Congar and the Battle for a Renewed Ecclesiology," 49.

39. Fouilloux, "Friar Yves," 83.

40. Jossua, *Yves Congar*, 34.

Catholic-Lutheran Dialogue. He traveled extensively, attending various theological gatherings and giving talks at conferences. "It was precisely during one of these exhausting trips, to Chile in 1967, that an old neurological illness suddenly awakened." As the disease progressed Congar was forced to use first a walker, then a wheelchair, until finally, in 1984, he had to enter Les Invalides, a military hospital in Paris. Throughout this period of declining energy Congar continued to interact with the theological questions of the day, especially those regarding the crisis within the church following Vatican II. "He read a lot, a book a day at least,"[41] the means by which he remained in touch with the theological world. The enormous number of published reviews by Congar during this period is evidence of just how remarkably engaged he remained. He continued to publish significant works of theology, including *L'Ecclésiologie du haut moyen age* (1968), *L'Église de saint Augustin à l'époque moderne* (1970), *Mysterium salutis: l'Église une, sainte, catholique, apostolique* (1971), *L'Église catholique et France moderne* (1978), and his last great work of dogmatic theology, *I Believe in the Holy Spirit*, in 1979 and 1980. In 1994, just a year before Congar's death, Pope John Paul II raised him to the cardinalate, a much-delayed honor,[42] crowning a life of faithful, generous, and abundant service to the church.

Clearly the importance of Père Yves Congar in not only the theological thought but also in the very life of the church of this recently past century justifies the effort made here to highlight one aspect of his vast theological corpus. His central place in the profound renewal of ecclesiology, and in particular his explicitly stated intention to move the presentation of the church beyond mere "hierarchologies," makes his theological treatment of ecclesial authority particularly worthy of investigation. His perspectives on issues of authority are made even more compelling in light of his own deeply personal experiences with certain aspects of ecclesial authority, often at great personal cost.

---

41. Fouilloux, "Friar Yves," 83, 86.
42. See Avery Dulles, "Yves Congar: In Appreciation," *America* (15 July 1995): 6–7.

Chapter Two

# Historical Foundations for the Understanding and Practice of Authority in the Church

## *Introduction*

In the preface to *A History of Theology* Congar identifies the return to the sources as the primary nourishment for the theological renewal of the twentieth century. This return to the biblical and patristic sources carried with it, among other things, the vivid awareness that "[r]evelation takes place in the framework of history or of an 'economy.'"[1] For Congar this recognition emphasizes that history is the very place of revelation. History is, therefore, an authentic *locus theologicus* where the understanding of the nature of God's saving revelation in Jesus Christ is unfolded.

This profound appreciation for the importance of history drew Congar to an equally profound awareness of the role of the Holy Spirit in the life of the church. The action of the Holy Spirit sustains and moves the revelation of the Father in his Son throughout the course of history. It is precisely because the history of the church is a locus of the action of the Holy Spirit that its history is truly a sacred history.

The importance of the history of ecclesial authority is emphasized in Congar's deeply held conviction, as Dennis M. Doyle describes it,

---

1. Yves Congar, *A History of Theology*, trans. Hunter Guthrie (Garden City, NY: Doubleday, 1968), 12.

that "the Church's engagement with history is a defining characteristic, such that the particular questions encountered by Christians living in the world and the manner in which the Church responds help to shape the Church's very contours."[2] The general survey of the history of ecclesial authority in this chapter will serve to underscore and to identify the many theological dimensions of the question of authority in the church.

## *Historical Foundations:*
## *The History of Authority according to Congar*

Almost without exception Congar's writings on the subject of authority "deal with the history of the idea of ecclesiastical authority" and "with the way in which authority has been exercised" throughout that history.[3] Thus it is important to undertake a historical survey here in anticipation of the more theological synthesis to follow in chapters three and four. While it is not possible to highlight all the nuances of that history found within Congar's works on authority, I will examine the major trends and movements, dividing them into five successive periods: (1) The New Testament and the apostolic age; (2) The time of the martyrs and monks up to Gregory VII; (3) The Middle Ages; (4) The Reformation and the Council of Trent up to the twentieth century; and (5) The twentieth century and the Second Vatican Council.

### Preliminary Definition of Authority

First, it is necessary to ground the historical variety and development of the understanding and exercise of authority in a general understanding of authority as Père Congar uses it within his writings. The historical "flow" of the living Christian community will then bring breadth to this general notion, reveal the inherent difficulties in its exercise, and show what is intrinsic and what is extrinsic to the practice of Christian authority.

For Congar it is the very reality of God that grounds the whole of the church's life, specifically in the church as "from end to end . . . built on

---

2. Dennis M. Doyle, "Communion, Mystery, and History: Charles Journet and Yves Congar," 38–55 in idem, ed., *Communion Ecclesiology* (Maryknoll, NY: Orbis Books, 2000), at 50.

3. Yves Congar, "The Historical Development of Authority in the Church: Points of Christian Reflection," 119–56 in *Problems of Authority*, ed. John M. Todd (London: Helicon Press, 1962), at 119. [Hereafter "Historical Development"]

the image of the Three-in-One."[4] Congar highlights the significant implications this has for the proper understanding of the reality of authority in the life of the church: "The gospels show Jesus as having *authority over* his Church . . . but they also show him as the *life* of his Church, dwelling in her by his Spirit. . . . The one Christ is both transcendent to his body the Church by his power and immanent by his life; the one body is both fellowship in the reconciled life of sonship and means, ministry or sacrament of that life."[5] What this implies, for Congar, is that within the church there are "two authorities," the one hierarchical and possessing power from above to structure the community, the other of life and unity flowing from the interior action of the Spirit in the life of God's people.[6] "In life as it is lived, the hierarchical principle (determinant for structure) combines with the communal principle (which calls for all to be associated together according to their order) for a work which is the work not of the hierarchs but of the Church."[7] Essential to Congar in this vision of authority is that in the church is found

> an earthly order that follows the pattern that exists in God himself, in whom the Father is Principle, but he is not alone. The witness that God has raised up on the earth, the Church, is also many and one, a concord, literally a symphony. The fatherly and fertilizing voice of apostolic authority is echoed by the voice of the faithful people, in such a way that the second voice, while in exact agreement with the first, does not repeat it mechanically: it amplifies it, carries it further, enriches it and corroborates it.[8]

To speak of "two authorities" in the church, as Congar does, calls for a note of clarification concerning the use of terms for authority. "*Auctoritas* designates moral superiority, power founded in right, *potestas*, the public power of execution."[9] *Authority* is, then, the larger reality that, in the case of the church, designates a spiritual authority possessed "by

---

4. Yves Congar, *A Gospel Priesthood*, trans. P. J. Hepburne-Scott (New York: Herder & Herder, 1967), 165. See also idem, "The Council as an Assembly and the Church as Essentially Conciliar," 54–56 in *One, Holy, Catholic, and Apostolic*, ed. Herbert Vorgrimler (London: Sheed & Ward, 1968).

5. Yves Congar, *Lay People in the Church*, trans. Donald Attwater (Westminster, MD: Newman Press, 1957; repr. Westminster, MD: Christian Classics, 1985), 167.

6. Ibid. See also pp. 234, 246–47, 279–85, 290, 327–28.

7. Ibid., 282.

8. Ibid., 294.

9. Yves Congar, *L'Église: de saint Augustin à l'époque moderne* (Paris: Cerf, 1997), 32–33.

right" by the individual within the community. This "right" may be based in the office one holds (*ex officio*), such as for the hierarchical authority, or in the charisms or holiness of a person (*ex spiritu*), such as in the community or life principle of authority, though the two cannot always be precisely separated.[10] *Power* in the church designates the public authority to pronounce laws, define dogma, implement discipline. In this sense power refers solely to the hierarchical principle of authority.

Within the church there exist these two principles or aspects of authority, both flowing from the *auctoritas* of God, who is the ultimate *auctor* in the construction of the church, the Body of Christ.[11]

## The New Testament and the Apostolic Age

Congar, repeating the words of St. Irenaeus, says that the Holy Spirit "continually rejuvenates the apostolic tradition preserved in the vessel of the Church and communicates its youth to the vessel which contains it."[12] This highlights the importance of the church's foundational era. Regarding the question of authority, Congar spends considerable effort investigating the New Testament and apostolic teaching, dealing with both the "literary" and the "theological" aspects of the question as it is encountered within the New Testament texts.

In his treatment of the "literary aspect" Congar observes, "The New Testament avoids or rarely uses the words which signify authority or power in classical Greek."[13] The word "hierarchy" is never used, while the word for power, *arche*, is found twelve times and refers to the power of secular rulers and to those "powers" or "forces" overcome by Christ; never does it refer to authority within the church. *Time*, meaning honor or dignity, is used rarely and then only of Christ and the priesthood of Aaron. *Taxis*, or order, is found ten times, seven in reference to the orders of Aaron and Melchizedech and never applied to the church. The significant word *exousia* is found ninety-five times within the New Testament, of which, for Congar, seven hold significance. "In five, Jesus

---

10. Yves Congar, *Power and Poverty in the Church*, trans. Jennifer Nicholson (Baltimore: Helicon, 1964), 87; idem, *Vraie et fausse réforme dans l'Église*, Unam Sanctam 72, 2d ed. (Paris: Cerf, 1968), 190. All translations from the latter source are my own. For an English translation, see Yves Congar, *True and False Reform in the Church*, trans. Paul Philibert (Collegeville, MN: Liturgical Press, 2010).

11. Yves Congar, *Tradition and Traditions*, trans. Michael Naseby and Thomas Rainborough (Needham Heights, MA: Simon & Schuster, 1966), 312.

12. Congar, *A Gospel Priesthood*, 74.

13. Congar, "Historical Development," 120. For this entire section on "literary aspects" see also idem, *Power and Poverty*, 37–39.

gives his disciples authority to drive out devils (Mt 10:1; Mk 3:15; 6:7; Luke 9:1; 10:19). In two passages, the reference is to authority invested in the Apostle as a minister of the work God does in the Church, and this is the building up of the Body of Christ or of the Temple built of living stones (2 Cor. 10:8 and 13:10). In both cases, St. Paul declares that he has received *exousia* in order to build and not to destroy."[14] Finally, in the writings of St. Paul we find the term *epitage*, which means the "authority to command." Paul clearly understands himself as possessing this authority (Titus 2:15) but he also speaks of his preference not to use it (1 Cor 7:6; 2 Cor 8:8). Though Paul is very much aware of his authority as an apostle, still "[h]e prefers to appeal to the gifts he has received, rather than to his authority."[15]

When "particular functions or offices" within the Christian community are highlighted in the New Testament they "are indicated by terms which refer to a task or activity viewed as a service to be done in the community."[16] These are cases of "particular ministries" such as those of apostles, doctors, prophets, evangelists, teachers, pastors, bishops, overseers, priests, elders, deacons, leaders, chiefs, officials in charge, stewards, bailiffs, managers.[17] Further, all these various functions possess "one and the same end: the building up of the Body of Christ, which is both temple and sacrifice, by the service of the gospel."[18]

This "literary" investigation focuses the idea of authority on the centrality of service in the Christian understanding of the church's life. "All these offices are included in the *diaconia*, even that of the apostle. All of them are forms of service; or better, 'service' or the '*diaconia*' transcend and involve these offices. It is a universal value coextensive and identical with Christian life itself."[19] The centrality of the notion of "service" is borne out by the gospels as well. There, Jesus defines the very nature of authority within the community of the disciples by its character as service (see Mark 10:42-45; Matt 20:25-28; John 13:1-20). Leaders within the Christian community are servants (*diakonoi*) or even slaves, common workers (*douloi*).[20]

---

14. Ibid., 120.
15. Yves Congar, *Christians Active in the World*, trans. P. J. Hepburne-Scott (New York: Herder & Herder, 1968), 13. See also idem, "Historical Development," 121, and *Power and Poverty*, 33.
16. Congar, "Historical Development," 120.
17. See Congar, *Power and Poverty*, 39.
18. Congar, *A Gospel Priesthood*, 76.
19. Congar, "Historical Development," 120–21.
20. Congar, *Power and Poverty*, 25, 32–33.

The writings of the apostles express this same understanding of authority. "All the Apostles repeat the Gospel teaching that identifies superiority of rank with the maximum degree of humble and loving service. Not only do they call themselves *douloi*, slaves, servants, labourers, of Jesus Christ, but they also teach that they do not wish to 'domineer' over the faithful, to be their masters or lords. On the contrary, they are their servants for the sake of Jesus (2 Cor 4:5; cf. 1 Cor 9:19) in virtue of the very fact that they are the servants of God."[21]

The "literary analysis" points to important theological implications for a proper understanding of authority in the apostolic age. Authority is decidedly based in Christ. All authority within the church exists within the nature of religious relationships as witnessed to in the Gospel and as an organizational element for the life of discipleship.[22] The relating of authority essentially to service reveals the ecclesiological "shape" of authority. In Christianity "there is only one *dominus,* the Lord."[23] The call to service, whether through charisms or apostolic succession, is an overriding characteristic of the whole church, not simply of a few. Service is "identical and coextensive with the fact of being Christian." Service directed toward the formation of disciples united to Christ as one body reveals, as well, the anthropological nature of Christian authority.[24] Authority in the church is a service to which all are called, in various ways, from within the Body of Christ precisely for the vitality of the Body of Christ.

Congar's analysis of this period shows the profound unity existing within the community of Christians beyond whatever distinctions in roles there were. This unity was reinforced from the outside as well. The first Christians lived in a world that "was opposed to it, sometimes with great violence." The Christian movement was born in the time of the great Roman Empire, possessing its own strength of culture, history, and traditions. "Under these conditions clergy and laity, despite the strongly marked inequality of their positions, were more readily aware that they formed the people of God, on the march to its true country, the goal of its pilgrimage."[25]

---

21. Congar, "Historical Development," 121.
22. See Congar, *Power and Poverty*, 83, 98; Congar, *A Gospel Priesthood*, 75.
23. Congar, "Historical Development," 122.
24. Congar, *Power and Poverty*, 86, 98–99, 83. See also idem, "Historical Development," 123.
25. Congar, *Christians Active in the World*, 4.

What stands out in this period of the New Testament and the apostolic age is a deep sense of the unity of the people of God under the one lordship of Jesus Christ, in whom the fulfillment of sacrifice, priesthood, and temple resides. In his ministry, death, and resurrection Jesus reveals a radically new notion of what it is to possess power and authority. Indeed, the very way to life is the path of self-giving service. This "new way" was for all who would call themselves Christian. All shared, through faith, in the fullness of Christ. Authority within the community was precisely a service, most often designated by functions and accompanied by spiritual gifts for the building up of the one Body, the one living Temple of the Spirit, thus enabling people to unite themselves with Christ by means of living faith. Authority is service that functions to bring about this profound unity with the one Lord, Jesus Christ. Essential to this age is the profound unity of christology, ecclesiology, and anthropology.

## The Time of the Martyrs and Monks

The epoch to be considered now is in fact two distinct periods divided by what is known as the "peace of Constantine." There is the age of the martyrs, which is the time of the second and third centuries up to Constantine's peace, and the age of monasticism, from this peace to the eleventh century. Nonetheless, Congar insists, the two are very much linked "as regards the idea of authority," for "they both belong to the same ecclesiological world."[26]

Congar identifies three distinctive "features" or "values" within the age of the martyrs that have significance for the topic of authority. First, Congar states, "The insistence upon authority has never been greater than in the writings" of this period. Citing Ignatius of Antioch, Cyprian, Irenaeus, Hippolytus, and Origen, the dominant figures of this age all place a strong stress on the authority of the bishop in whom are united the spiritual and juridical aspects of authority. As examples of this Congar points to Origen, who addresses the bishop with the title "Prince," and to Ignatius of Antioch, who insists that "by being subject to their bishop, the Magnesians or the Trallians are subject to God himself or to Jesus Christ (*Magn*. III, 1-2; cf. VI, 1; *Tral*. II, 1). It is the Spirit who cries out in Ignatius: 'Cleave to your bishops, to the presbyterium and the deacons' (*Phil*. VII)."[27]

This emphatic stress on the importance of the bishop comes within the equally clear stress on the second feature of authority in this period,

---

26. Congar, "Historical Development," 124.
27. Ibid.

that is, the priority of the whole community. Here again we find that "for early Christianity, the primary reality is the *ecclesia*. This word . . . means the Church community, the assembly or the unity of Christians." This emphasis is found throughout the writings of this period, within its liturgy, which possessed "no 'I' distinct from the 'we' of the whole community," as well as in letters from one community to another, which were often written in the name of the whole community along with its head. Congar points to the example of St. Cyprian as an instance of the "union between the hierarchical structure and the communal exercise of all church activities."[28] Cyprian writes: "[I]t has been a resolve of mine, right from the beginning of my episcopate, to do nothing on my own private judgment without your [the priests and the deacons] counsel and the consent of the people."[29]

The third feature of authority within the period of the martyrs is the essentially charismatic or spiritual character of the whole church's life. Those possessing authority did not do so "according to purely moral qualities or to character, but according to 'pneumatic' or charismatic qualities."[30] This is witnessed in all the actions of the life of the church. This "period abounds in formulas in which the action of God and ecclesiastical activity appear to coincide and are identified with each other."[31] Congar points to a council held at Carthage in 252, which prefaced its canons with "It has pleased us, under the inspiration of the Holy Spirit and in accordance with admonitions given by the Lord in many manifest visions," as exemplary of this period's identification of the acts of those in authority as determined by inspirations and visions from the Holy Spirit.[32]

Authority within the time of the martyrs, then, is marked by a strong insistence on the continued presence and action of the risen Christ through his Spirit within the Body joined to him by faith. It is equally marked by the insistence that this presence is authenticated and assured for those who unite themselves firmly to their bishop who is, it might be said, the visible head of the now invisible head, Jesus Christ. The bishops are "princes" of a community "overshadowed by the Spirit of God."[33]

---

28. Ibid., 124–26.
29. Cyprian, "Letter 14," 4, *The Letters of St. Cyprian of Carthage*, ed. Johannes Quasten, Walter J. Burghardt, and Thomas C. Lawler; trans. G. W. Clarke, Ancient Christian Writers 43-44 (New York: Newman Press, 1984), vol. 43, p. 89. See also Cyprian, "Letter 34," 4.1, vol. 44, p. 43.
30. Congar, *Lay People*, 342.
31. Congar, *Tradition and Traditions*, 135.
32. Congar, "Historical Development," 127.
33. Ibid.

Congar identifies two influences that sustained continuity in the church's fundamental understanding and practice of authority into what he calls the age of monasticism. The first of these influences was that the primacy of the church, meaning all of the faithful, remained central. Examples of writings and homilies insisting on the faithful as the true *ekklesia*, rather than the "places" where they gathered for worship, were abundant during this period.[34] Further evidence is found in St. Augustine's repeated insistence that his being a bishop is a service for the people, while he himself still remains "a Christian," "a sinner," "a disciple and a hearer of the Gospel" together with his flock. Augustine, within his sermons, offers detailed accounts to his flock of his episcopal actions and decisions.[35]

Central for Congar, and flowing from this "ecclesiological" understanding, is the prominence of councils during this period. Indeed, "this time is one of national or provincial councils."[36] The reality of the council is a concrete expression of the fundamental conviction that the truth of revelation is preserved and lived within the unity of the whole people of God. The authority of the councils rested, not in the council as such but in "their expression of the faith of the Apostles and the Fathers, the tradition of the Church."[37] The assurance that they did indeed authentically transmit the *regula fidei* (the rule of faith), however, is based on the conviction that their teachings expressed the faith of the whole church and that "faith and tradition are born" precisely within the church as unity.[38]

A second influence that helped maintain continuity with the age of the martyrs was the influence of monasticism itself. Because of the growth of monasticism in this period "it was possible for a charismatic or spiritual authority to continue to exist, an authority which should be exercised when the aim is to form the spiritual [person]." For instance, beginning with the eighth century, and especially in the East, which most arduously confronted the monothelite heresy and the iconoclastic crisis, "the monks had been the champions of orthodoxy" and as a result "a real transfer to spiritual direction and of the exercise of the power of keys from the hierarchical priesthood to the monks" took place "because

---

34. Congar, *Christians Active in the World*, 29–31.

35. Congar, "Historical Development," 133–34.

36. Yves Congar, *L'ecclésiologie du haut Moyen-Age: De Saint Grégoire le Grand à la désunion entre Byzance et Rome* (Paris: Cerf, 1968), 133.

37. Yves Congar, "Reception as an Ecclesiological Reality," *Concilium* 77, eds. Giuseppe Alberigo and Anton Weiler (New York: Herder & Herder, 1972), 43–68, at 53. See also idem, *L'ecclésiologie*, 135.

38. Congar, "Reception as an Ecclesiological Reality," 54.

it was clear that they were genuinely spiritual men." Congar points to Celtic Christianity in the West as a further example of the influence of monasticism on the exercise of authority. Here, up to the twelfth century, there "was no diocesan pattern, that is, there were no specific territories under the authority of bishops, but a whole complex of spheres of spiritual influence" where particular areas came under the influence of monasteries and thus lived under the authority of abbots and, in at least one case, under that of an abbess. Significantly, many of the bishops of this period "were monks or at least men trained in a monastic setting and . . . ordered their lives on a similar pattern, often with a nostalgic longing for the religious life." Over the course of this period bishops were seen as possessing authority because they were filled with spiritual gifts as well as having a juridical mandate.[39] Thus the essentially spiritual character of authority was very much sustained during this period.

What has been highlighted here is the essential continuity of the church's understanding of authority from the age of the martyrs into the age of the monks following the peace of Constantine. Authority remained essentially both ecclesial and spiritual or charismatic. Nonetheless, the new relationship between the church and society in general had increasing impact on the way authority was conceived and practiced. Following the Peace of Constantine, the temporal world and the church were increasingly seen as forming a single reality, often called simply *Respublica Christiana*.[40] With the peace of Constantine the clergy were given important positions of secular jurisdiction, privileges, and honors.[41] This period marked the development of titles of honor, special dress, and an increased focus on celibacy for clerics.[42] Further, feudalism, which dates to the early Middle Ages near the end of this period, had its influence on the church in privileges associated with office and the importance attached to the "lands" of bishoprics, parishes, and monasteries. These many changes affecting the clergy, such as dress, political privileges, and the many insignias of office, brought a significant transition in how the relationship between ordained and lay persons was conceived. "[W]hilst in the Church of the Martyrs there was a tension, not inside the Church between the various categories of Christians, but between the ecclesia

---

39. Congar, "Historical Development," 128, 129–33.
40. Congar, *Lay People*, 358.
41. Congar, "Historical Development," 134–35.
42. For thorough discussion of these honors, insignias of office, and changes in vocabulary and rituals see Congar, *Power and Poverty*, 114–23; see also idem, "Historical Development," 135.

and the world, henceforth within a society entirely Christian, tension grew inside the Church or within Christian society between monks or priests on the one hand and laymen on the other."[43]

The move to a single Western society conceived as wholly Christian and its implications for authority in the church are made concrete by Congar's understanding of the influence of the *Donation of Constantine*, a forgery dating to the later part of this period that exerted enormous influence on the church's understanding of papal authority.[44] The *Donation of Constantine*, bequeathing to the church of Rome much of what was to become the papal states, extended imperial dignity and honors to the papacy and led, over time, to the "development of papal claims and the day to day administration of the Church along imperial lines."[45] The French Dominican considers the *Donation* to be "one of the most harmful pieces of forgery known to history" since it grounds the authority of the pope in a gift from the emperor rather than that of Christ to his apostles.[46] The *Donation* served to "turn" the discussion of ecclesial authority in a direction that would be accentuated in the next period of its development. This turn is the placing of the discussion of ecclesial authority within the framework of temporal power, and what is derived from temporal power, rather than from within an understanding of spiritual power derived from Christ.

To conclude, this period of the martyrs and monks was marked by an authority understood and commonly lived as essentially spiritual and still firmly grounded in an ecclesiology marked by the primacy of the entire people of God as truly the church. Yet the progressive assimilation of the temporal into the sacred as well as the growing distinctions between clergy and laity established the grounds for a certain transition in the way authority within the church was understood and lived.

## The Middle Ages

Most certainly, the period of the Middle Ages is, for Congar, full of significance for the understanding and practice of authority within the

---

43. Ibid., 135.
44. Yves Congar, *Fifty Years of Catholic Theology: Conversations with Yves Congar*, ed. Bernard Lauret, trans. John Bowden (Philadelphia: Fortress Press, 1988), 44.
45. Congar, *Power and Poverty*, 120. The questions surrounding the Donation of Constantine, its origins and timing, are dealt with here in some detail on pp. 118–21.
46. Yves Congar, *After Nine Hundred Years* (New York: Fordham University Press, 1959), 15.

church. It is a time marked by rich, complex, and conflictual developments in the spheres of ecclesiology, theology, culture, and society. Because of this reality there is a danger in any summary evaluation. Nonetheless, Congar consistently delineates a number of very broad and decisive characteristics of the period that highlight the transitions in authority. These include: the reform of Gregory VII and its outgrowth, the spiritual movements that appeared in the life of the church from the twelfth century onward, and the growth of the universities with a transition in the very concept of theology. Within these very broad developments one may discover the essential lines in which authority came to be understood and lived in the church on the eve of the Protestant Reformation.

The birth of Christendom following the Peace of Constantine led to a unified vision of society so firm that the very word for church, *ekklesia*, came to mean "both the mystical Body and the Empire with no distinction made between them."[47] This union, however, was not in all regards a happy one. Congar insists that "the whole medieval period is full of struggles between the priesthood and the empire—or the priesthood and the monarchies."[48] These struggles would prove to be decisive for the development of the practice and understanding of authority.

Congar is absolutely "convinced that the reform begun by St. Leo IX (1049–54) and continued with such vigour by St. Gregory VII (1073–81) represents a decisive turning-point from the point of view of ecclesiological doctrines in general and of the notion of authority in particular."[49] At the heart of what is known as the Gregorian Reform was the desire to purify the church, especially in the face of the problem of lay investiture. The popes who engaged in this reform believed that the "root of all the evils was lay investiture, by which the lay powers disposed of ecclesiastical offices and treated them in a secular fashion."[50] With the development of the feudal system, church property and the office of bishop and abbot were drawn into the system of benefices that made it possible for a ruler to bestow the office of bishop, with all its rights of ownership and administration, on the person he or she chose, bestowing on him the pastoral staff as the symbol of the office. This often involved a demand

---

47. Congar, "Historical Development," 136.
48. Congar, *Fifty Years*, 24.
49. Congar, "Historical Development," 136. See also idem, *L'Église: de saint Augustin à l'époque moderne*, 103.
50. Yves Congar, "Renewal of the Spirit and Reform of the Institution," trans. John Griffiths, 39–49 in *Ongoing Reform of the Church*, ed. Alois Müller and Norbert Greinacher (New York: Herder & Herder, 1972), at 43.

for payment from the one being invested (simony) and implied allegiance to the ruler.[51] Within this historical context of "the need to shake off the tutelage, if not the domination, of the temporal power,"[52] Gregory VII sought to confront the "confused notion of the Church which made the emperor its head" and he "began to formulate the idea of two societies."[53] He did this, specifically, by appealing to the sovereign rights of the pope over the church and the secular rulers.[54]

Gregory made his claim by engaging in a process of gathering the "maximum number of juridical texts in favour of" papal authority.[55] His own *Dictatus papae*,[56] which is made up of twenty-seven statements gathered from the tradition and affirming the rights of the papacy, stands at the beginning of this effort. It "gave a new impetus to the study of canon law . . . [which] culminated with the famous *Decretum Gratiani*, which is dated very precisely to 1140."[57] This document gave the church a collection of formulas from councils, popes, and the fathers of the church under common headings. The ascendancy of canon law is made clear by the fact that for the two centuries following Alexander III (1159–81), nearly all the popes were canonists.[58] This process included, as well, the development of a certain *mystique* of authority that identified the authority of the church, particularly the pope's authority, with the authority of God.[59] Connected to this "mystical" vision of authority was the tendency to exalt "obedience as *the* virtue of the good Catholic."[60]

The results of these attempts on the part of the popes to assert their authority in the face of the always-encroaching secular rule were crucial. Congar insists that "when the Church opposed the temporal power . . . it was led to adopt very much the same attitudes as the temporal power

---

51. See Hubert Jedin, ed., *History of the Church* (New York: Crossroad, 1982), 3: 276.
52. Congar, *Power and Poverty*, 105.
53. Yves Congar, *Laity, Church and World*, trans. Donald Attwater (Baltimore: Helicon Press, 1960), 52.
54. Congar, "Historical Development," 136.
55. Ibid., 137. See also Hugh Lawrence, "Spiritual Authority and Governance: A Historical Perspective," 37–57 in *Authority in the Roman Catholic Church: Theory and Practice*, ed. Bernard Hoose (Burlington, VT: Ashgate Publishing Company, 2002), at 49, where Lawrence asserts that "the chief vehicle in establishing papal supremacy proved to be canon law."
56. See Jedin, *History of the Church*, 3: 369–71, for a good summary of this document.
57. Congar, *Fifty Years*, 41.
58. Congar, *Power and Poverty*, 104.
59. Congar, "Renewal of the Spirit," 43. See also "Historical Development," 137.
60. Congar, *Laity, Church and World*, 32.

itself, to conceive of itself as a society, as a power, when in reality it was a communion, with ministers and servants."[61] Thus began a dramatic transition from envisioning authority in a spiritual and sacramental way to viewing it juridically or legalistically. In Gregory's *Dictatus papae*, for instance, "a simple papal delegate, a simple nuncio, even if he is not a bishop . . . has authority over bishops, archbishops and all the rest of the church. That shows how the legal has priority over the sacramental."[62] A further example is the papal title *Vicarius Christi*.[63] "Vicar of Christ" referred originally to a "religious recognition, more than an attribute of power."[64] However, in this period there was a move away from this more sacramental and "vertical" understanding of the presence of God's authority in the one who has authority to "[t]he idea of a 'power' given at the beginning by someone, by Christ, to his 'Vicar,' that is, to a representative who takes his place and who hands on to those who come after him, in a historical sequence of transmission and succession, the power thus received. The predominant feature is not a vertical movement, an actual presence, an iconological representation, but the 'horizontal' transmission of a power vested in the earthly jurisdiction."[65]

Throughout the Middle Ages the popes, faced with the continuous threat of coercion on the part of secular rulers, found it necessary to exert their own proper authority in the domain of the sacred. Their way of doing this, however, was to appeal to their rights and privileges, especially through the gathering of legal documentation, leading to an ever-increasing stress on papal authority understood as rights, privileges, and power.

Against this "encroaching legalism" Congar consistently refers to the importance of the spiritual movements that began in the twelfth century and ran throughout this period. He laments that these "movements of critique" have "never been taken seriously enough, either at the time or

---

61. Congar, *Fifty Years*, 42. See also idem, *Power and Poverty*, 97; Hermann J. Pottmeyer, *Towards a Papacy in Communion: Perspectives from Vatican Councils I & II*, trans. Matthew J. O'Connell (New York: Crossroad, 1998), ch. 4. Pottmeyer shows convincingly that this same tendency of deriving the forms of ecclesial authority from those of secular authority was operative in the development of the notion of "sovereignty" in the nineteenth century.

62. Congar, *Fifty Years*, 42.

63. Congar, "Historical Development," 139. See also idem, *Tradition and Traditions*, 179.

64. Ovidio Capitani, "Congar et l'ecclésiologie du haut Moyen Age," 41–50 in *Cardinal Yves Congar, 1904–1995*, ed. André Vauchez (Paris: Cerf, 1999), at 46.

65. Congar, "Historical Development," 139.

since, by the historiographers." What Congar is referring to are those protests "represented by the more or less anti-ecclesiastical spiritual movements so frequent in the twelfth century and which continued into the Franciscan spiritual movement down to the fourteenth century when it was succeeded by Lollardism and subsequently by the Hussite movement." Identified by Congar among these movements, besides those just mentioned, are the neo-Manicheans,[66] the "Friends of God" in the second half of the fourteenth century, *devotio moderna*, the Brothers of Life in Common,[67] Catharism,[68] the Petrobusians,[69] extending down to the figures of John Wycliffe (d. 1384) and John Hus (d. 1415)[70] among others. Though there are profound differences among these movements, they all share a fundamental orientation.[71] All are decidedly set in protest against an ever-increasing emphasis on structures of authority and the resulting alienation of the people from God's active presence in their lives.[72] A striking example of the "spirit" of these movements is found in the one headed by Peter de Bruys. The Petrobusians actually went about destroying church buildings in criticism of a church that had become "far too weighed down by the earthly and the temporal."[73]

From the heart of the church, too, voices reacted against the growing juridicism. St. Bernard and Hugh of St. Victor often held up the reality of charity as the true nature of the church.[74] Bernard frequently confronted popes about their attachment to privileges and their focus on the law rather than the spirit.[75] More important, the movements led by St. Francis and St. Dominic, while sharing many essential themes with the anti-ecclesiastical movements, were at the same time explicitly "in" the church. The movements of Francis and Dominic had the incredible ability to pierce through the pomp and growing rigidity of so much of the church of the day with their embrace of gospel poverty while holding to the institution with radical notions of obedience to the pope and

---

66. Ibid., 142.

67. Congar, "Renewal of the Spirit," 42.

68. Yves Congar, *The Word and the Spirit*, trans. David Smith (San Francisco: Harper & Row, 1986), 48.

69. Congar, *Christians Active in the World*, 32.

70. Congar, *Tradition and Traditions*, 97.

71. Congar, *The Word and the Spirit*, 48.

72. Yves Congar, *Ministères et communion ecclésiale* (Paris: Cerf, 1971), 83. See also idem, *Laity, Church, and World*, 32; *Tradition and Traditions*, 138.

73. Congar, *Christians Active in the World*, 32.

74. Ibid., 32–33.

75. Congar, "Historical Development," 142.

bishops.[76] But in doing so, these movements actually served to promote the growing centralization of papal authority. By special dispensation these orders were allowed to preach and hear confessions under the direct jurisdiction of the pope, freeing them from the supervision of local bishops. Though this special "protection" from the papacy was not entirely new—the monasteries of the Cluniac reform also came under papal jurisdiction—the fact that the Franciscans and Dominicans were not "rooted" in a monastery meant that they carried papal jurisdiction directly into the life of the local churches outside of Rome in an unprecedented way.[77]

The anti-ecclesiastical movements influenced the way authority was thought of and lived, flowing as they did from a reaction against the authority of the church. Within these movements are found the beginnings of a totally new understanding of the relationship between the *regula fidei*, most concretely Sacred Scripture, and the church. In reaction against the dominance of hierarchical authority these movements insisted on the supremacy of Sacred Scripture. For them Scripture stood outside the church, over and above it. In reaction to this, defenders of ecclesiastical authority insisted all the more on the place of the pope and bishops in defining doctrine, "defending unwritten traditions by arguing from the insufficiency of Scripture, and therefore, to a certain extent, by opposing them to it."[78] In short, the church and Sacred Scripture had become competing authorities.

This separation between the church and Scripture, and more broadly still the *regula fidei* itself, was accompanied by a further significant separation. The juridical insistence on the authority of popes and bishops led to an equal emphasis on obedience. Thus the public acts of faith came more and more to reside in the ecclesiastical authority, while all others in the church simply lived the faith by means of private acts of obedience. This in turn led, according to Congar, to "a tendency to see only the moral aspect of problems—or rather that part of their moral aspect deriving from intentions and purity of intentions." This has significant implications for the effectiveness of these spiritual movements on the vitality of the church. "Some strong and pure reformist currents failed to

---

76. Congar, *Christians Active in the World*, 33.

77. Cf. Yves Congar, "De la communion des Églises a une ecclésiologie de l'Église universelle," 240–48 in idem et al., eds., *L'épiscopat et l'Église universelle* (Paris: Cerf, 1962). See also idem, *L'Église: de saint Augustin à l'époque moderne*, 91.

78. Congar, *Tradition and Traditions*, 98.

be more effective because they stayed too much in a spiritual and private realm." They "had no effective impact on institutions."[79]

In short, the growing insistence on authority in its juridical and legalistic aspects led to many reform movements. The encounter between these two trends brought about fundamental changes in how authority was perceived and lived. First, the authority of Scripture was placed in competition with the authority of bishops. Second, faith itself was no longer understood as being lived and expressed primarily by the whole people of God. The result was a growing tension and opposition between hierarchy and community. As the hierarchical principle gained strength, the communal principle receded.

Congar highlights a third broad movement of this period: the growth of the universities in the urban centers. This development of the schools brought with it a new way of doing theology. "Indeed, while theology in the first thousand years of Christianity was the task of bishop-theologians who had frequently had an experience of religious life," increasingly the role of *magister* was transferred to professors of theology. Though this development existed in a "healthy balance" through the thirteenth century, there followed a growing division between "knowledge" and "power."[80] Out of this division arose an understanding that the *studium* possessed an authority within the church alongside those of the *regnum* and the *sacerdotium*. Congar points to the thirty-fourth session of the Council of Basel (25 June 1439) to show how dramatic a shift took place in this regard. At this session "there were 300 doctors but only thirteen prelates and seven bishops."[81]

Further, there were theological controversies, "particularly those conducted by certain Franciscans about the poverty of Christ and the beatific vision (Ockham against John XXII)" which "brought up all kinds of questions on the rule of faith and theological criteria."[82] In the writings of such men as Henry of Ghent (d. 1293) and William of Ockham (d. ca. 1349–50), working in this climate of controversy combined with the legalism introduced by the growing influence of the canonists, we can perceive a shift in the science of theology.[83] "This new mode of

---

79. Congar, "Renewal of the Spirit," 41–42.
80. Ibid., 214, 219.
81. Yves Congar, "Theologians and the Magisterium in the West: From the Gregorian Reform to the Council of Trent," *Chicago Studies* 17 (1978): 210–24, at 210, 214, 219, 220.
82. Congar, *Tradition and Traditions*, 179.
83. Congar, *Power and Poverty*, 106.

theological reflection, clearly different from that which prevailed in the monasteries, employed a rational method directed toward analysis, definition, construction, and systematization."[84] Congar summarizes the direction this change effected and its implications for the practice of authority. "The tendency to move from the 'reasoned' to the 'rational,' and from the 'rational' to doubtful or debatable explications was certainly not fatal, but it was dangerous. In this way, the theology of the masters evoked a reaction from the traditional Church." The reaction on the part of the hierarchy, and in particular the popes, was to intervene more and more on controversial matters, insisting increasingly on their authority —power and right—to do so as final arbiters in matters of faith.[85]

This third broad characterization of the Middle Ages identified by Congar reveals a further "split" beginning within the tradition. Essentially a growing gulf emerged between the church, particularly the church's pastoral-teaching office, and reason or knowledge, or between faith as proposed and defined by the popes and bishops and rational reflection on the nature of things, which belongs to the domain of scholars. Faced with the growing influence of and popular regard for this "reasoned" explication of theology, the church's teaching office often relied more heavily on its authority to define doctrine apart from reasoned explanation.

We have thus observed these major trends in the medieval period: In the face of endless struggles with the secular state the church sought to establish its own proper authority. The Gregorian Reform and the popes who followed it did this by insisting on their own rights and powers, often in a juridical and legalistic way.[86] This growing juridical understanding of the very nature of the church in turn resulted in the many anti-ecclesiastical movements that sought to restore the primacy of the active presence of God in the church. Doing so, however, resulted in opposition to the church, specifically its hierarchical element. As a result Scripture and the church came to be viewed as competing authorities and a certain division emerged between the public and private aspects of faith as lived. The growth of the universities and their claim to an authority based on knowledge as opposed to authority based on

---

84. Congar, "Theologians and the Magisterium," 214. See also idem, "The Magisterium and theologians—a short history," *Theology Digest* 25 (1977): 15–20, at 16.

85. Congar, "Theologians and the Magisterium," 215, 216.

86. Cf. Pottmeyer, *Towards a Papacy in Communion*, 30. Here Pottmeyer insists that "under Gregory VII a break with the previous paradigm of church and [papal] primacy occurred that could hardly be described as a logical or organic development. The Gregorian reform had revolutionary features."

power increasingly implied a division between pastoral authority and the authority of reason.

## From the Reformation and the Council of Trent to the Twentieth Century

The various ecclesiastical, spiritual, and sociological trends that marked the entire period of the Middle Ages came to full development, often violently and destructively, in the sixteenth century and the centuries that followed. "From crisis to crisis, from abortive reform to abortive reform on the part of the Church, from cultural advance to cultural advance, from demand for independence to demand for independence on the part of laity and sovereigns—and eventually the Protestant Reformation of the sixteenth century was reached."[87] What enabled the sixteenth-century reformers to advance their thought so successfully was Martin Luther's remarkable religious genius combined with the new willingness of princes to support the movements. The invention of the printing press, too, gave a new place to the printed word and allowed for the wide distribution of anti-ecclesial, anti-papal thoughts.[88]

For Congar the theological claims contained in the works of the reformers flow directly from the struggles of the Middle Ages, particularly those of the fourteenth and fifteenth centuries, which "unfortunately bequeathed" to the age of the reformers "the false option between the primacy of Scripture and the primacy of 'the Church.'" Again Congar would insist that this "false option" was "itself the fruit of excessive exaggeration of ecclesiastical machinery and especially of papal authority."[89] This tension was clearly witnessed in a remark made by Luther to Prierias: "I don't know what you mean by calling the Roman Church the rule of faith. I have always believed that faith was the rule of the Roman Church."[90] In this the opposition between the church and the *regula fidei*, on the part of both sides, is clearly highlighted.

Congar stresses the rejection of the mediating value of the church's authority as the basis on which the thought of the reformers such as Luther, Zwingli, and Calvin, and the movements flowing from their

---

87. Congar, *Laity, Church and World*, 53.
88. Congar, *Tradition and Traditions*, 139. See also Walter Ullmann, *A Short History of the Papacy in the Middle Ages*, 2d ed. (London: Routledge, 2003), 329.
89. Congar, *Tradition and Traditions*, 142, 146.
90. Quoted by Congar, "The Magisterium and theologians—a short history," 18.

theologies, was firmly grounded.[91] "The reformers substituted the Word of God for the Church in the functions, privileges and attributes which Catholic theologians recognized as belonging to it: and by the Word of God they meant Scripture."[92] As they did so, moreover, there was a growing tendency to place "in the personal, or even individual, religious subject, all the elements of this spiritual relationship." With the Reformation the growing separation between the church and the *regula fidei* and the division between public and private faith, with their foundations in the previous period, became radicalized and mutually exclusive.

The Council of Trent, in responding to the positions taken by the reformers, refused to set the church and tradition against Sacred Scripture by placing the church's magisterium above Scripture as its interpreter. Indeed, Congar would insist, "the council affirms first and foremost that there is but one source and that the Gospel as that source has full and complete value. The fountain-head of this vital force is the mouth of Jesus, the Son of God."[93] In practice, nonetheless, there was a renewed emphasis on the principle of authority, particularly papal authority, which was "strengthened by the theology of the Counter-Reformation." Congar claims that the

> progress of ideas was now taking a new course. For example, in the theology of Thomas Stapleton, the spirituality of St. Ignatius of Loyola, in the orientation of Robert Bellarmine's *Controversies*, possibly even in Suarez's theory comparing the definitions of the Church to new revelations, the force of the decisions taken by authority appears as unconditioned and truly divine. Instead of seeing tradition as having its reference to the past, there is a tendency to see

---

91. Congar, *Tradition and Traditions*, 142. Later, however, in his book *The Word and the Spirit*, Congar says (p. 48): "The Reformers did not exclude the foundation of the Church by Christ or the mediation of the word, the sacraments and the ministry. They did, however, emphasize very strongly the action here and now of God in justification and in the whole process of salvation." Certainly this evidences a development in Congar's thought in this regard. One might say even that it is more rightly nuanced. Nonetheless, the point made here about "mediation" is still appropriate. The conflict had forced the Reformers into what they came to see as a choice between God and the church or, as Congar puts it, "this option became with the Reformers a choice between submission to God and submission to some human bidding. Put in such a way, the issue was never in doubt" (*Tradition and Traditions*, 142); see also idem, *Lay People*, 38.

92. Congar, *Tradition and Traditions*, 481, see also 142.

93. Ibid., 157.

it in reference to the current magisterium of the Church expressing itself in the passing of time.[94]

This same tendency can be identified in the development of the notion of custom. "[B]eginning in the sixteenth century, canonists and theologians (especially the followers of Suarez) held the thesis . . . according to which custom only obtains the force of law by the approbation of the competent superior."[95] This general trend progressed throughout this period until the truths of faith find their value not so much because they are present within the tradition, a matter of revelation, as because they have been defined by the magisterium of the church. It is precisely this move that eventually made it possible for Pius IX to make "that almost incredible statement: 'La tradizione son'io!' " in a debate on the nature of tradition during the time of the First Vatican Council.[96]

The Catholic response to the Reformation's denial of hierarchical authority and its mediating role, a response that dominated its pastoral and theological efforts into the twentieth century, was to reassert its authority, emphasizing the role of the hierarchy to such a degree as to end "up seeing the Church as practically nothing more than a society in which some commanded and the rest obeyed."[97]

These trends have implications for the understanding of ecclesiology. This stress on authority, the defense of the church's rightful authority in fact, led to an ecclesiology that is nothing more than, in Congar's now famous terminology, a hierarchology. "Ecclesiology, as far as the instruction of clerics and of the faithful is concerned, became fixed in a set pattern in which the question of authority is so predominant that the whole treatise is more like a hierarchology or a treatise on public law. In this assertion of authority, the papacy receives the lion's share.[98]

As in the Middle Ages, various "spiritual movements" arose, many flowing directly from Protestantism, which produced "a fantastic burgeoning of initiatives, movements and even new 'churches.' " Congar highlights, specifically from Protestantism, George Fox (1624–91) and the Society of Friends or Quakers; the Pietist movement, in particular Philipp Jakob Spener (fl. ca. 1675); the Moravian Brethren of the eighteenth

---

94. Ibid., 176.
95. Ibid., 181.
96. Congar, "Reception," 54.
97. Congar, *Power and Poverty*, 109.
98. Congar, "Historical Development," 144. For the implications for how the pope came to be viewed, see pp. 144–45.

century; John Wesley and Methodism (eighteenth century); the Great Awakening in the United States, headed by Jonathan Edwards (1703–58); and the beginnings of the Pentecostal movement in Topeka, Kansas, on January 1, 1901.[99] These movements were all the "product of persons who were captivated by Christ and dedicated themselves to his cause with the object of converting the world to him, 'in this generation' as John Mott put it."[100]

Congar, again, insists on the important implications contained within such movements for an understanding of the nature of God's action in the world. These movements highlight for Congar both the "immediacy" of God's initiative and the importance of human initiative. "This is an indisputable reality which cannot be overlooked, and which is not expressed in a Catholicism consisting purely in organization and obedience."[101] Again, what is clear here is that God builds up his church not only by means of the "mediation" of the institution but also by the "immediacy" of his Holy Spirit acting in the lives of individuals.

The significance of the cultural shifts within this period cannot be overstated. At the very moment the church was insisting on the authority of the institution, "the modern world [was] attempting to build its life on the principle of the individual personality."[102] This entire epoch was marked as the moment "when men seized their independence in the various fields of politics, science, reflection and research, judgment and criticism, the organization of life and, in short, of the city, a real world was found—or refound—outside the Church and face to face with her."[103] This "turn to the application of personal reason" was in part a result, certainly, of the wars of religion that flowed from the spiritual rupture in Europe following the Reformation. "Unity proving impossible on the basis of faith, it was necessary to search for it on the basis of nature and of reason."[104] Faith, having become a source of division, then accelerated

---

99. Congar, *The Word and the Spirit*, 49–51.

100. Yves Congar, *Called to Life*, trans. William Burridge (New York: Crossroad, 1987), 82.

101. Congar, *The Word and the Spirit*, 53.

102. Congar, "Historical Development," 145. Clearly this cannot be separated from the Protestant Reformation and its turn to the subject, whereby the Spirit brings about the proper understanding of Scripture *within the personal subject*. Cf. Louis Dupré, *The Enlightenment & the Intellectual Foundations of Modern Culture* (New Haven: Yale University Press, 2004), 242.

103. Congar, *Christians Active in the World*, 7.

104. Yves Congar, *Église catholique & France moderne* (Paris: Hachette, 1978), 26. See also idem, *Sainte Église. Études et approches ecclésiologiques* (Paris: Cerf, 1963), 179.

the cultural drive for independence from ecclesial authority and toward the basing of all social structures on human reason.

All the forces of secularization that mark this period—the development of science, secular humanism and the turn to the subject, the Enlightenment, the push toward political independence, and industrialization—had the effect of leaving the church in a world in which it no longer felt at home, indeed one that was profoundly alien and in many ways hostile to it. For Congar, however, the church's response, though understandable in the context of history, did not always profit from its vitality.

> Involved in formidable attacks, sometimes even to the point where her very existence was threatened, the Church locked herself up as if in a besieged castle, all doors barred and drawbridges raised, while all the time carrying out a powerful restoration of her internal forces and an exceptional missionary expansion. She closed herself not only to antitheistic anthropocentrism but also to real problems, to genuine acquisitions in the realm of thought.[105]

In summary, then, the church faced two forces, each of which had enormous consequences for the understanding and practice of authority: the Protestant Reformation and secularization. The authority of Scripture was set against the authority of the church. The personal subject—and by extension, the community or life principle of the church—was placed in opposition to the institutional church—specifically the hierarchical principle. Reason came to be viewed as an enemy of faith. These trends, already present in the previous epoch, solidified and came to dominate the very life of the church on every level. The church, and specifically the hierarchy, was influenced by "a certain defensive mentality in which nothing must enter the citadel without being duly checked and carefully sifted."[106] Losing religious ground to the Reformation, intellectual ground to science and secular humanism, philosophical ground to the Enlightenment, and political ground to the often violent forces of democracy, the church found itself always on the defensive. In the end this led it to create a strong internal structure able to foster convictions that pushed the church outward in vast missionary expansions. Unfortunately, it also brought about an even greater separation from the culture in which

---

105. Yves Congar, *Challenge to the Church: The Case of Archbishop Lefebvre*, trans. Paul Inwood (Huntington, IN: Our Sunday Visitor Press, 1976), 54.

106. Yves Congar, "The Laity," 239–49 in *Vatican II: An Interfaith Appraisal*, ed. John H. Miller (Notre Dame: University of Notre Dame Press, 1966), at 247.

people lived and found meaning for life. Apart from the church there was now this "'complete' society which offers all the means of leading an earthly life that is at the same time both difficult and pleasant, and which leaves religion solely to the personal conscience of individuals."[107]

## The Twentieth Century and the Second Vatican Council

The historically complex and theologically rich period of the twentieth century has already been the subject of many books. Here again I will simply attempt to indicate, in summary fashion, the major trends of the period as identified by Congar. Three come up repeatedly in his work. First are the cultural realities affecting the understanding of authority, so many of which flow directly from the previous period. Second, the movements within the church herself that affect contemporary theological debates deserve consideration. Finally we will briefly examine the Second Vatican Council, as the great culmination of so many of these movements, and its implications for an understanding of ecclesial authority.

The secularization of the previous period created a social climate marked by antiauthority and anti-institutional sentiments. The scientific method had in effect transformed the very notion of truth, restricting it to the strictly observable and to those things that are perceivable as "facts." Spiritual and moral claims, values, and anything touching on the meaning of life as such are seen as subjective rather than as matters of truth.[108] There is, according to Congar, a quite clear personal principle within Christianity. Nonetheless, because of the "attitude of individual freedom and sincerity understood as spontaneity, people no longer tend to think or appreciate on the basis of principles proposed by authority . . . but on the basis of things themselves and following the bent of their personal tastes." The result is "the radical criticism of everything that is an institution, the 'Establishment,' that is, everything that wishes to impose itself without one having freely determined it oneself." [109] This has decisive ramifications for the way people see themselves living within the church, particularly in relation to the hierarchical authority of the church. The twentieth century is marked, in the Western world, by a radical resistance to authority, suspicion of the institution, and an

---

107. Congar, *Fifty Years*, 25.
108. Yves Congar, "What Belonging to the Church Has Come to Mean," trans. Frances M. Chew, *Communio* 4 (1977): 146–60, at 152.
109. Yves Congar, "The Church after the Council," *Christ to the World* 19 (1974): 57–65, at 60, 59.

explicit stress on the individual as the personal subject directing the course of one's own life.

As a direct result, and because the structures and institutions of democracy throughout the Western world have become so firmly established, the person of the twentieth century can be characterized, according to Congar, as "a democratic man."[110] Active engagement with the realities that affect his or her life in direct and at times not so direct ways within the spheres of politics, economics, and social life makes the person of today particularly "fitted for collaboration" within the framework of religious life as well.[111] People today expect to "have a say" and to be actively engaged in whatever it is that touches their lives.

The technological explosion that unfolded during this period also had enormous consequences for people in the twentieth century in terms of their experience of and relationship to authority. In the first instance technology sets the age decidedly toward the future. "In a technical universe, the truth is not in what can be received from the past, it is ahead; more will be known tomorrow, more will be able to be done tomorrow."[112] While the church can seem stuck in the past, insisting on its traditions, technology opens out to seemingly endlessly new possibilities. Technology likewise has a profound effect on the human imagination. The enormous quantities of images, sounds, and information communicated by new technological means both stimulate and serve to clutter people's inner worlds. This has left the church, once the source of much of culture's art and music, with an increasingly faint voice in a cacophony of voices.[113]

Significant currents of a theological nature also made themselves felt during this period within the church. The twentieth century was the great age of the return to the biblical and patristic sources, the liturgical, ecumenical, and lay movements. The return to the sources was on many levels a response to the inclinations and needs of the times. Congar was convinced that this generation of Christians had "rediscovered [the] dimension of History at the very heart of the Christian faith." The reason for this "rediscovery," according to Congar, was "the need which Christians [had] found, to return to their own sources in order to

---

110. Yves Congar, *Blessed Is the Peace of My Church*, trans. Salvator Attansio (Denville, NJ, 1973), 68; see also p. 69. See also Congar, *Fifty Years*, 67.

111. Congar, *Christians Active in the World*, 139.

112. Congar, "The Church after the Council," 59; see also, idem, *Blessed Is the Peace of My Church*, 39–40.

113. Congar, *Power and Poverty*, 130, 131.

drink from them afresh."[114] Indeed, within this period the church, most specifically theologians, "became bound up . . . with the inspirations of the period of the Fathers and those of the Bible."[115]

This return to the Christian sources was intimately connected to the extensive efforts directed to the study and reform of the liturgy. This, too, involved looking back in order to discover the source and significance of the church's liturgical rites. Congar insists that "the liturgical movement was a rediscovery of the meaning of things and of their anthropological dimension, a re-creation of a certain liturgical [person]," a restoration of the proper place of all the baptized in the liturgical action.[116] Furthermore, Congar points out that this movement resulted in an essential shift in our understanding of the church, from the church understood primarily as the hierarchy to the realization that all the baptized make up the church.[117]

This same trend found expression in the biblical movement's rediscovery of St. Paul's idea of the church as the body of Christ. This notion was taken up by Pius XII in his important encyclical *Mystici Corporis* (1943), which contained a significant "development of the idea of charisms in the sense of individual gifts for the benefit of all."[118] The recognition of charisms promotes the realization that every baptized person is empowered by the Spirit for the sake of the building up of the church, the body of Christ. Again, all of this marked the beginning of a vigorous and profound rethinking of the nature of the church and, specifically, the place of the lay faithful in it.

The movement toward unity exemplified in the many ecumenical endeavors of this period also had an enormous impact. Congar's own book, *Divided Christendom*, first published in 1937, could be considered a beginning point at which Catholics entered theologically into the ecumenical dialogue.[119] This movement had its foundations in the Protestant missionary conference held in Edinburgh (1910) and in the "Life and Work" and "Faith and Order" movements, which came together in 1948 to form the World Council of Churches. Congar stresses how the return to the sources at the foundation of the Christian faith inevitably

---

114. Congar, *Christians Active in the World*, 38, 39.
115. Congar, "The Church after the Council," 58.
116. Congar, "The Council as an Assembly," 53.
117. Congar, "Path-findings," 171.
118. Congar, *Fifty Years*, 66.
119. Cf. Joseph Famerée, "Formation et ecclésiologie du 'premier' Congar," 51–70 in *Cardinal Yves Congar, 1904–1995*, ed. André Vauchez (Paris: Cerf, 1999), 61.

led to a reconsideration of the Catholic Church's relationship to other Christian bodies.[120]

All the theological currents of the twentieth century came to fruition at the Second Vatican Council. To assess all that Congar has said concerning the council would be much beyond the scope of this work. Rather, a simple review of those aspects of the council that most directly concern the topic of authority will suffice.

For Congar the Second Vatican Council's teaching about the place held by the Word of God within the church was central. "The council's constitution on the liturgy has reinserted the Word into the liturgical celebration itself. Moreover the dogmatic constitution *Lumen Gentium* teaches us that the episcopacy is the fullness of the sacrament of Holy Orders. Therefore right there where the priesthood is most fully itself it is apostolic and pastoral . . . it includes also the prophetic function of the Word and the pastoral function of presiding over the Community."[121] The very direction of the bishop's ministry is viewed here as service to the Word. Indeed, Congar would claim that "the Council restored the traditional subordination of pastoral authority to the content of revelation. It affirmed that the magisterium itself is linked to the Word of God and is at its service."[122]

For Congar the council fathers' decision to place the chapter on the people of God in its constitution on the church before the chapter on the hierarchy "was one of the most important made."[123] The implications of this decision are crucial.

> The intention was, after having shown the divine causes of the Church in the Holy Trinity and in the incarnation of the Son of God: 1) to show this Church also in the process of constructing itself in human history; 2) to show this Church expanding and reaching various categories of men who are unequally situated in relation to the fullness of life that is in Christ and of which the Church is the sacrament; 3) to explain what all the members of the People of God hold in common on the plane of the dignity of Christian existence, prior to any distinctions among them based on office or state.[124]

---

120. Congar, *Dialogue between Christians*, 122.
121. Yves Congar, "Institutionalized Religion," 133–53 in *The Word in History*, ed. T. Patrick Burke (New York: Sheed & Ward, 1966), at 147.
122. Congar, "The Magisterium and theologians—a short history," 19.
123. Yves Congar, "The People of God," in Miller, ed., *Vatican II*, 197.
124. Congar, "The Church: The People of God," trans. Kathryn Sullivan, in *Concilium* 1, ed. Karl Rahner and Edward Schillebeeckx, 11–37 (New York: Paulist Press, 1965) at 11.

The placement of this chapter on the people of God in *Lumen Gentium* clearly has important implications for the place of history in the constructing of the church and its ecumenical relationships and reveals the primacy of grace through baptism over hierarchical and ecclesial structures. What was embraced by the council in the concept of the people of God, and its placement within the whole discussion of the church, was that "the first value is not organization, mediatorial functions, or authority, but the Christian life itself and being a disciple."[125]

Certainly this understanding of the church as the people of God carried with it many implications for the lay faithful, and Congar insists that this "Council was a council of the laity."[126] The most fundamental characteristic of the council's teaching on the laity was how it viewed them, first of all, as persons consecrated by baptism and confirmation, and then as consecrated, rightful participants in the church's mission. This speaks importantly of the nature of apostolicity. "[T]he apostolate is based, not on a reality of the juridical order, but in the supernatural ontology which makes a person a Christian, namely, in Christian existence itself . . . the basis of the right and the duty of the apostolate is membership in the body of Christ, the vitality and dynamism proper to this body into which the Christian is inserted and nourished by the sacraments of Christian initiation."[127]

Significant as well is the council's emphasis on the reality of "collegiality." For many, Vatican II was very much about the proper role of the bishop and a necessary "balancing" of the teaching on the role of the pope found in the First Vatican Council. Collegiality is the recognition of the responsibility of each local bishop in the maintaining and proclaiming of the Gospel of Jesus Christ for the sake of the universal church and in union with all other bishops. "The collegial act is above all one and the same action performed by a large number."[128] This teaching has "reopened the chapter on the conciliar or synodical life of the Church."[129] Ultimately, the reality of collegiality bases ecclesiology in the specifically Christian understanding of God as a communion of three persons. Communion, the unity of the church's life and mission, flows

---

125. Congar, "The People of God," 200.
126. Congar, "The Laity," 239.
127. Ibid., 242.
128. Yves Congar, "A Last Look at the Council," 337–58 in *Vatican II: By Those Who Were There*, ed. Alberic Stacpoole (London: Geoffrey Chapman, 1986), at 340.
129. Yves Congar, "Moving Towards a Pilgrim Church," 129–54 in ibid., at 141.

from a diversity of persons, charisms, and even locales that nonetheless remain a real unity.[130]

In Congar's mind the Second Vatican Council was above all a great event of theological and pastoral "integration."

> There was, for instance, no Scripture without Tradition and no Tradition without Scripture. There was no sacrament without the Word. There was no Christology without pneumatology and no pneumatology without Christology. There was no hierarchy without the people and no people without the hierarchy. There was no episcopate without the Pope and no Pope without the episcopate. There was no local Church that was not missionary and no mission that was not ecclesial. There was no Church which was not mindful of the whole Church and which did not provide universality within itself and so on.[131]

The twentieth century was decidedly marked by the fruits of secularization: democratic, focused on the personal subject, and influenced by technological advances. Individuals became increasingly focused on the personal pursuit of meaning and significance, which by then they were convinced they would not find in the institution. Within the church also, taking up the tools bequeathed to the world by the scientific method, many sought the purity, simplicity, and authentic meaning perceived in the early Christian communities by a dramatic return to the sources of the faith. This trend matured and bore exceptional fruit in the Second Vatican Council. This council firmly restated the priority of the relationship of each person to Christ by grace. It opened the church to a diversity of voices while pointing the way to communion as the proper outgrowth of the work of the Spirit in the variety of persons, charisms, and local churches. Authority was again seen, in its essence, as service to the Word and the building up of the Body of Christ. This service would be most fruitful if it honored the action of the Spirit of Christ in the diversity of charisms present within all the faithful.

## *Conclusions*

We can now summarize the historical trends emphasized and the central theological conclusions drawn by Yves Congar in his examination

---

130. See *Lumen Gentium* 4.
131. Congar, "A Last Look at the Council," 343–44.

of the historical development, in practice and in understanding, of authority within the church.

## Historical Trends in the Understanding and Practice of Authority according to Congar

The necessary place to begin a summary of the history of authority, according to Congar, is with the very reality of history itself. The historical nature of God's action with human beings is central. The understanding of the church as the people of God highlights the dynamic nature of the church. The church is certainly something given, instituted by Christ, but it is also something that is actively being "constructed" by the "two hands" of the Father, the Son and the Spirit, throughout the variety of places, peoples, and times through which the church moves.

The foundational period of the church, the apostolic age, showed forth the primacy of faith in the one Lord Jesus Christ and the call of all to share in his life of loving service to the Father and to neighbor. The reality of authority, apostolic and charismatic, is a function of service to the building up of the Body of Christ.

With the peace of Constantine came the growing identification of the secular world with the sacred, so that with time the very word *ekklesia* came to mean the whole of the secular and sacred world. The clear distinction that once existed between the church as sacred and the world as secular came increasingly to be transferred to a distinction within the *ekklesia* itself between clerics and laity. Nonetheless, Congar would maintain, through the powerful influence of monasticism and the conciliar expression of the church during this stage, the essentially spiritual and charismatic nature of authority and the primacy of the community were maintained.

Clearly, the Gregorian Reform marked a decisive transition in the Christian understanding of the nature of church and authority. As a result of the secular authority's ever-greater encroachment on the legitimate domain of the church, highlighted above all in the lay investiture controversy, the church's leaders, in particular the popes, were faced with the need to defend their rightful authority. This was done most decisively by collecting the canons that established the authority of the pope and bishops over the secular rulers and by the development of a strong mystique of authority. The unfortunate result of this battle was the establishment of a juridical understanding of the very nature of the church, defending its own proper authority in secular rather than sacred terms, on the basis of rights, privileges, and the obligations of obedience.

The ever-growing claims to power and privilege by those possessing hierarchical authority in the church were followed, from the twelfth century onward, by the reactions of many anti-ecclesiastical movements seeking freedom from the oppressive claims of authority and a return to a more "pure" living of the Gospel. The ongoing battles with secular encroachment throughout the medieval period, failed attempts at reform within the church, and the growing popularity and possibilities for success of the anti-ecclesiastical movements eventually culminated in the Protestant Reformation.

The Counter-Reformation brought about a growing centralization of power, focused on the papacy, in reaction to the Protestant denial of such authority. This same period witnessed the birth and development of secularization, a world, as Congar puts it, that is truly a world of its own, emancipated from any church tutelage. In reaction to this growing secularization—in science, industrialization, democratization, secular humanism, the Enlightenment—the church stressed the centrality of the institution and the absolute nature of its hierarchical authority. For Congar this time was marked by the defensive stance of the church toward the radically changing culture.

The twentieth century witnessed a remarkable renewal based on a return to the biblical and patristic sources at the foundation of the church's life. This turn to the sources led to the rediscovery of the place of Scripture in the church, the renewal of the liturgy, ecumenical endeavors, and dramatic changes in how the church saw itself, in its own life and in relation to the world. In the Second Vatican Council the reality of collegiality was affirmed, the role of the laity was examined and promoted, and the understanding of the church was transformed.

### Theological Conclusions from Congar's Historical Analysis of Authority

Throughout Congar's treatment of the historical development of authority he clearly identifies the theological implications. Above all, authority is christological, pneumatological with a strong trinitarian emphasis, and anthropological.

The christological emphasis highlights the primacy of Christ as the one Lord reigning over heaven and earth. Through faith all share in the kingly, priestly, and prophetic functions of Christ. Thus the primacy of the community of faith is firmly established. Still, the christological nature of authority also points to the reality that this faith comes as gift, from above and outside. The hierarchical principle of authority in the church rests here. The Word and grace are gifts from God, not generated from within the community. The hierarchical principle maintains the primacy of Christ, who stands over and above his people as Lord.

Authority is also pneumatological. Though Christ always stands over his people as their Lord, he also lives within his people by his ever-present Spirit. The Holy Spirit, through charisms and by inspiring initiatives, builds up the Body of Christ from within individuals and communities gathered in prayer. The "two hands" of the Father always build up the church. The pneumatological aspect of authority emphasizes the dynamic, living, growing aspect of the life of the people of God. From the theological perspective of Congar, a very real community or life principle of authority exists. The Holy Spirit is active in the lives of all who believe, drawing them into a living relationship with Christ in the very concrete dimensions of their day-to-day lives, for the offering of their lives in sacrifice to the Father.

The direction of all authority within the church is, finally, anthropological. Authority, according to Congar, has one purpose: service of the Word and grace of God for the sake of fashioning men and women, through faith and adherence to that Word and grace by the action of the Holy Spirit, into the living temple of Jesus Christ so that their lives may be beautifully offered to the glory of God the Father.

Authority within the church is clearly hierarchical and communal in that Christ reigns over his church and acts always within the church.

Chapter Three

# The Community or Life Principle of Authority

## *Introduction*

To appreciate the significance of the two principles of authority to be discussed in these next two chapters, we should first lay out clearly the dialectic of structure and life present in Congar's work overall. Congar shows the precise way he employs the terms "structure" and "life" by contrasting his use of these terms with that of Hans Küng.

> We spoke about structure in the singular, distinguishing it from structures, and we understood by that what gives to the Church its identity in the order of belief, the sacraments and the hierarchical functions. H. Küng spoke about structures in the plural (*Strukturen der Kirche*, Freiburg, 1962) in a sense which he did not define but which came out clearly from its developments. In the plural, it was not so much, as it is for us, the external forms . . . it was rather a question of challenging the identification of the structure with the hierarchical institutions and of asserting the membership to the structure or essential form of existence of the Church of these great realities which are the laity, charisms, councils, etc: things which we tend to classify only in the *life* of the Church.[1]

Distinct from those elements of the church that Congar places under the aspect of "structure," such as the *regula fidei*, the sacraments, and the

---

1. Yves Congar, *Ministères et communion ecclésiale* (Paris: Cerf, 1971), 47.

hierarchy, there are also those realities that have to do with the "life" of the church, such as the faith lived by the laity, charisms, and councils.

This distinction in the overall work of Congar carries a significant degree of ambiguity when applied to the question of authority. It is not always clear what the relationship between these two aspects is, whether the "life principle" is in fact an aspect of authority or simply a principle that works in strict dialectical fashion toward authority, itself simply hierarchical or structural. The struggle Congar faced in articulating the nature of these two principles and their relationship is seen in his groundbreaking book, *Lay People in the Church*. Here he endeavors to establish a theology that rightly places the lay faithful at the heart of the church rather than at its periphery where so many of the *De Ecclesia* treatises of his day had put them. In this work there are many indications that the two, though distinct, are in fact aspects of the one reality of authority through which Christ builds up the church, as when he speaks of the two working together as "warp and weft."

> We are also back again at the idea of the laity as the *pleroma* of the hierarchical priesthood and at that of "structure" and "life", of the Church as an institution making her members and in turn made by them as community . . . what Christ did once for all is woven with [people's] "living" and "doing" throughout history, the warp of the hierarchical ministry's part with the weft of what [people] contribute as religious subjects. In this way the Church is built together not only from above downwards but also sideways, or . . . in a way from below upwards.[2]

Frequently there are statements that highlight ecclesial authority as strictly part of the hierarchical, and therefore not the life principle, of the church. For example, in the conclusion of *Lay People* we find this exclusive regard for authority as strictly hierarchical: "The faithful are indeed living stones and are all part of the temple (1 Cor 3:16-17; Eph 2:21-22; 1 Peter 2:5; etc.); they are neither master-builders nor foundation, but rather are themselves built and based. There are gifts of authority and mediation in the Church, and they are accorded to some members only. This is the hierarchical principle."[3] Still, Congar's entire aim throughout his life's work is to articulate an ecclesiology that shows "the Church

---

2. Yves Congar, *Lay People in the Church*, trans. Donald Attwater (Westminster, MD: Newman Press, 1957; repr. Westminster, MD: Christian Classics, 1985), 313.
3. Ibid., 429.

essentially as a living organism" where "all share in the dignity of the whole, in the functions that compose it and in the activities of its life."[4]

This brief look at Congar's *Lay People in the Church*, while giving us an initial sense of his understanding of authority under the two principles of hierarchy and community, indicates a certain difficulty in perceiving systematic precision within his thought. As Congar points out, his "theology is occasional, related to events" as they presented themselves "from without" that impelled him to theological "efforts demanded more or less by the times."[5] Ultimately he was unable to fulfill his lifelong ambition of writing a systematic theological treatise on the church. The same can be said for the topic of authority within the subject of ecclesiology. Though Congar wrote enormous amounts on this topic, much of it is a matter, particularly in this area of authority, of historical surveys, reflecting his desire to "recover the sources, the roots."[6] Thus authority as hierarchical and communal is found within Congar's work of *ressourcement* and, as with *Lay People in the Church*, is discussed in connection with a particular theological theme, such as ecumenism, reform in the church, the role of the laity, or the pneumatological question, addressed when the occasion presented itself. The question of authority, however, cannot be restricted to any of these particular areas and incorporates some aspects of them all. Authority as hierarchical and communal is not simply a question of the place of the laity in the church, as if the two principles could be reduced to a clergy and laity dialectic, nor can it be reduced to questions of reform, implying perhaps that the status quo involves the hierarchical principle and reform of the community or life principle.

These two principles are found in Congar's overall ecclesiological vision and flow from various theological realities arising from the life of the church lived through the course of its history. It will be necessary to analyze the theological realities that illustrate these principles present throughout the range of Congar's writings. The purpose of this analysis is not to re-create "the particularity of the ancient situations," but to discover there "the inspirations, perceptions and deep motivations of the ancient tradition."[7]

---

4. Ibid., 430.

5. Yves Congar, "Letter from Father Yves Congar, O.P.," trans. Ronald John Zawilla, *Theology Digest* 32 (Fall 1985): 213–16, at 214–15.

6. Yves Congar, "My Path-findings in the Theology of Laity and Ministry," *The Jurist* 32 (1972): 169–88, at 170.

7. Yves Congar, "Les implications christologiques et pneumatologiques de l'ecclésiologie de Vatican II," 117–30 in *Les églises après Vatican II*, ed. Giuseppe Alberigo (Paris: Beauchesne, 1980), at 127.

Specifically, what I intend is first to highlight, under three headings, the overall theological framework out of which the community or life principle of authority flows. To begin I will look at Congar's ecclesiology and show how his growing appreciation for the role of pneumatology in ecclesiology led him directly into a greater understanding of the church as a historical expression of the trinitarian life of God. This trinitarian understanding, in turn, led Congar to speak of the church as a communion of persons. Second, the centrality of the "ontology of grace" highlights the need for ecclesiology to be linked to a solid Christian anthropology. Third, I will investigate the relationship between the church and world, underlining the importance of the church's mission to the world as marked by "apostolic responsibility" and an authority of "influence" rather than power.

Following this I will examine the theological realities discussed by Congar throughout his theological opus that speak to the community principle of authority, here again under three headings. First, the importance assigned to charisms and initiatives in the life of the church will show Congar's deep conviction that God builds up the church not only from outside and above it but from within it, through the lives of individuals and local communities. Second, attention will be given to councils in the life of the church; these will be shown to highlight the relationship between the hierarchical and community principles of authority. Finally, the notions of reception and *sensus ecclesiae* will be considered, underscoring the nature of faith as a reality held in and carried by the whole church.

From this analysis of Congar's articulation of the theological foundations and expressions of the community principle of authority we will be able to derive an explicit description of the community principle as understood by Congar. Though Congar did not offer a single, systematic theological articulation of this principle, all these various realities taken as a whole provide just such an articulation. In conclusion I will evaluate their impact on today's church.

## *Aspects of the Community or Life Principle of Authority*

### Church as Communion

Bradford Hinze highlights the implications of a renewal in pneumatology for ecclesiology: "During the second half of the twentieth century there was a growing realization that a revived pneumatology is needed to correct and complement a christomonist ecclesiology, but that this correction must not result in an excessive pneumaticism. To set up an opposition between a Spirit-centered and a[n] incarnational ecclesiology is false and fruitless. Instead, we need to develop a Trinitarian ecclesiology that can release and receive the full power of the Spirit."[8]

The trend identified here is most evident in the work of Congar, whose understanding of the church as a communion of persons sharing in the trinitarian communion of Persons became more highly developed as his pneumatology became more intentional and gained clarity. Congar also saw the need to integrate the pneumatological aspect into an ecclesiology that did not leave aside the christological reality.[9] It was his growing conviction that it is precisely the action of the whole Trinity that constructs the ecclesial reality: the Father by means of his "two hands," the Son and the Spirit. For Congar "the equivalence of action of Christ and the Spirit can only be explained ultimately by the profound Trinitarian concepts of the perfect consubstantiality of the divine Persons, their circuminsession and perichoresis."[10] This trinitarian perspective gives ecclesiology a true and profound *theo*-logical basis, that is to say, a consideration of the church from its divine causes and as an authentic participation in the divine, Trinitarian life.[11]

It is within this perspective that the church as communion has its significance. In trinitarian theology, particularly in the works of St. Thomas Aquinas, who was so foundational in Congar's intellectual formation, God is understood as a relational reality "identical to the divine substance."[12] In God the relations of the three divine Persons subsist in, and are in fact the essence of, the one God. How beautifully and succinctly this is expressed by St. Basil the Great in his treatise *De Spiritu Sancto*, where he addresses this same reality of the unity and plurality in the Godhead. He says simply that "in the case of the divine and uncompounded nature the union consists in the communion of

---

8. Bradford E. Hinze, "Releasing the Power of the Spirit in a Trinitarian Ecclesiology," 347–81 in *Advents of the Spirit*, ed. idem and D. Lyle Dabney (Milwaukee: Marquette University Press, 2001), at 366.

9. Cf. Yves Congar, *The Mystery of the Church*, trans. A. V. Littledale (London: Geoffrey Chapman, 1965), 18.

10. Ibid., 150–51.

11. Cf. Yves Congar, *L'Église: de saint Augustin à l'époque moderne* (Paris: Cerf, 1997), 465. See also idem, "Ecclesia de Trinitate," *Irenikon* 14 (1937): 131–46, at 141.

12. See Gilles Emery, "Essentialism or Personalism in the Treatise on God in Saint Thomas Aquinas?" trans. Matthew Levering, *The Thomist* 64 (2000): 521–63, at 535. See Yves Congar, "La Tri-unité de Dieu et l'Église," *La Vie Spirituelle* 128/604 (1974): 687–703, at 693.

the Godhead."[13] The communion, or relations as St. Thomas calls it, is the unity.

Unlike God, each human person is created as an individual substance grounded in a body, and therefore "it is only on the psychological and moral plane that he realizes himself, insofar as he is able to be *with, by, and for*." In other words, the trinitarian revelation affords the dramatic understanding that "the person fulfills himself, not in isolation but in relations of knowledge and of love with others." Because it is this very trinitarian life that the saving events of Christ's life, by the present action of the Holy Spirit, communicates to the church, "[t]he church appears, then, as a communion of persons, a mutual communication of various gifts, by which unity is built."[14]

For Congar, then, a thoroughly trinitarian understanding of the church shows it to be essentially a communion of persons wherein charisms, local initiatives, and diversity of cultures are communicated in a generous exchange of gifts in which its very unity is found. Within this understanding of the church as communion, the personal subjects who make up its members are recognized and honored while the call to charity that is at the heart of this communion directs all into a harmony of unity.

Congar's appreciation of the church as a communion is complemented by his frequent reflection on the church as the Body of Christ and the people of God.[15] The concept of the church as the Body of Christ implies, foremost, its nature as a deeply organic reality. "It is not only a unity of order or of co-operation, like a natural society, but a unity of life, rather like a living body." This nature as a "living body" comes from its having its principle of life from the Holy Spirit. As such, its law is interior, planted there in seed form, realizing itself from this seed. There is, as in all living things, growth and development. The organic nature of the church, as highlighted by this concept of the Body of Christ, shows forth the great diversity of its members while retaining its essential unity. The variety of gifts is directed toward the united work of the whole, single body. Further, Congar notes that the image of body also contains the advantage of highlighting the dual nature of the church as both visible

---

13. Basil the Great, *A Select Library of Nicene and Post-Nicene Fathers of the Christian Church*, 2d ser. VIII, trans. Blomfield Jackson (repr. Grand Rapids, MI: Eerdmans, 1968), 28.

14. Congar, "La Tri-unité," 693.

15. Regarding the relationship between these ecclesial understandings see the Sacred Congregation for the Doctrine of the Faith, "Litterae ad Catholicae Ecclesiae episcopos de aliquibus aspectibus Ecclesiae prout est communio," *AAS* LXXXV (9 September 1993), n. 1. English trans. Boston: Pauline Books & Media, 1993.

and invisible. It draws attention to the external, social structure of the reality of the church while maintaining the sense of the interior, spiritual principle which gives vitality to all that is exterior structure.[16] This internal spiritual principle, specifically the Holy Spirit, also allows the relationship between the head, which is the college of bishops united to the pope, and the body to be seen as marked by reciprocity and mutuality precisely because the Spirit dwells within the whole body.[17] The concept of the Body of Christ highlights the nature of the church as an organic, living communion whose vital principle is the Holy Spirit, containing a diversity of members working within a single unity and, like all living bodies, possessing an exterior structure enlivened by an interior principle.

Another central concept for Congar is the church as the people of God. In relation to the notion of communion, which can tend to an over-"spiritualization" or "conceptualization" of the church, the idea of the people of God roots the church firmly within history, specifically within the history of God's plan for his people beginning with Abraham and Israel.[18] This image introduces the reality of eschatology and history into our understanding of the church.[19] It distinctly relates the church not only *in* the world historically but *to* the world by its evocation of election by God for mission to the world as witness to God.[20] This view likewise incorporates what Congar calls the "anthropological value."[21] This image of the church as the people of God highlights what elevates the community of all the faithful, through election in the sacraments of baptism and confirmation, "over organizational structures and hierarchical positions."[22] While emphasizing the "ontology of grace," this concept does not deny the social reality of the church. As "the Israel

---

16. Congar, *The Mystery of the Church*, 90, 91, 36, 111. See also Congar, *L'Église: de saint Augustin à l'époque moderne*, 161.

17. Congar, "Les implications,"126.

18. Yves Congar, "The Church: The People of God," trans. Kathryn Sullivan, *Concilium* 1, ed. Karl Rahner and Edward Schillebeeckx, 11–37 (New York: Paulist Press, 1965), at 19. See also idem, "Richesses et vérité d'une vision de l'Église comme 'peuple de Dieu,'" 109–22 in *Le concile de Vatican II: son Église, peuple de Dieu et corps du Christ* (Paris: Beauchesne, 1984), at 114–17.

19. Congar, "Les implications," 123.

20. Cf. Congar, "The Church: The People of God," 19–21, and idem, "Moving Towards a Pilgrim Church," 129–54 in *Vatican II: By Those Who Were There*, ed. Alberic Stacpoole (London: Geoffrey Chapman, 1986), at 143.

21. Congar, "The Church: The People of God," 21.

22. Yves Congar, "The People of God," 197–208 in *Vatican II: By Those Who Were There*, at 198.

of old, it is a people of God with its own corporate life, its laws and its hierarchy."[23] Perhaps most significant for Congar, this image makes it possible "to speak of the Church dialectically: holy and imperfect, celestial and terrestrial."[24] Just as in the concept of communion, the church as people of God places a certain priority on the ontology of grace and the place of all within the church's reality. It complements the image of communion by rooting the church firmly in history and pointing to its eschatological character. While the church is already established as a communion, it is not yet fully realized as such.

In summary, we may say that Congar's pneumatological perspective led him increasingly to reflect on the *theo*-logical character of the church as both a construction of God who is Trinity and a sharing in the trinitarian life. From this arises the understanding of the church as a communion. The church exists as a communion, in a way analogous to how God, as Father, Son, and Holy Spirit, dwells from all eternity in communion. Communion expresses the deeply theological nature of the church. Its great gift is that it comes from God, lives in God, and is directed to God. Congar would not separate this understanding of the church from the notions of the Body of Christ and the people of God, which indicate the church's organic, social, historical, and eschatological character. In a more explicit way the church as Body of Christ and people of God draws its anthropological, sociological, and eschatological dimensions from the trinitarian concept of communion.

### Ontology of Grace

To see the church "as communion in divine life" is to see it as a "supernatural community consisting *first of all* of Christians."[25] For Congar, this truth was one of the great discoveries made in the return to the patristic sources. In the writings of the fathers one finds that "ecclesiology included anthropology." This significant insight was particularly highlighted by the fathers of the Second Vatican Council in the document on the church, *Lumen Gentium*. There, in chapter one, the church is first of all described in relation to its causes in the action of the divine Trinity. Chapter two, titled "People of God," shows how this work of God is held "in common on the plane of dignity of Chris-

---

23. Congar, *The Mystery of the Church*, 84–85. For further reflection on the reality of "hierarchy" in the Old Testament see Terence L. Nichols, *That All May Be One. Hierarchy and Participation in the Church* (Collegeville, MN: Liturgical Press, 1997), 23–38.

24. Congar, "The People of God," 207 n. 12.

25. Congar, "Les implications," 118.

tian existence, prior to any distinctions . . . based on office or state." "Thus, the highest value was given to the quality of disciple, the dignity attached to Christian existence as such or the reality of an ontology of grace, and then, to the interior of this reality, a hierarchical structure of social organization."[26]

In order to fully appreciate the emphasis Congar places on this "ontology of grace" and its significance for understanding the nature of ecclesial authority under this aspect of communion it is essential to examine a point from the history of ecclesiological treatises. Congar places great stress on the transition in the way the church was presented in the time immediately following the Reformation, and in particular the *Controversies* of St. Robert Bellarmine. With Bellarmine there appeared a new and decisive insistence on the visible, exterior nature of the church, the very aspect most emphatically rejected by the Reformers.[27] This is highlighted by Bellarmine's well-known definition of the church. "The one and true Church is the community of men brought together by the profession of the same Christian faith and conjoined in the communion of the same sacraments, under the government of the legitimate pastors and especially the one vicar of Christ on earth, the Roman pontiff."[28] Here the church is defined exclusively by external acts: *profession* of faith, *participation* in sacramental rites, and, most decisively, *submission* to the hierarchical authority of the Roman Church. The absence within the definition of the need for a vital, interiorly assimilated faith lived in charity is striking. Bellarmine says that, in belonging to the true church, "no interior virtue is required, but only exterior profession of faith and communion in the sacraments, things accessible to our senses."[29] Clearly, the church is here reduced to its external structure and, in the context of the antagonism toward Protestants, "the influence of Bellarmine was immense and lasting, felt up to the First Vatican Council."[30] The emphasis on external structures further served to remove from ecclesiology a true spiritual anthropology, which recognizes the church, with the patristic

---

26. Congar, "The Church: The People of God," 22, 11, 13. See also idem, "Richesses et vérité," 109.

27. Congar, *L'Église: de saint Augustin à l'époque moderne*, 372.

28. Robert Bellarmine, *De controversiis*, 2. 3, *De ecclesia militante* 2, "De definitione Ecclesiae," (Naples: Giuliano, 1857), 2: 75; trans. and quoted by Avery Dulles in *Models of the Church* (expanded ed. New York: Doubleday, 2002), 8. See Congar, *L'Église: de saint Augustin à l'époque moderne*, 372.

29. Ibid.

30. Congar, *L'Église: de saint Augustin à l'époque moderne*, 374.

authors as first of all a true communion of persons with God and one another.[31]

Bellarmine's defense of the church in the post-Tridentine period is simply a part of the much larger flow of the history of theological thought. A much earlier example, highlighted by Congar, is the eucharistic controversies of the eleventh and twelfth centuries, especially centered around Berengarius of Tours. "For St. Augustine, for the High Middle Age, the true body . . . was the body-Church. The sacramental body being realized was 'mystical.'" In the eucharistic controversies Berengarius resisted speaking of the "real body and blood" of Christ, preferring rather to speak of a "sacramental" presence. He sought in this way to avoid a sense of the Eucharist that stressed the physicality of Christ's presence.

What is central here for Congar is that this debate resulted in a growing analytical approach to the Eucharist, which sought to gain philosophical and theological precision regarding its nature. This led to "a certain loss of the sense of the unity of sacramental mystery and of dynamism." In this same context there arose treatises focused rather exclusively on the individual sacraments rather than on their place in the total sacramental economy.[32] The move here was decisive. It consisted in a transition from seeing and knowing the revelation of the living God in the celebration of the sacred mysteries within his holy temple, his Body the church, to a more objectified understanding of sacraments and grace as received in the ritual actions of the church.

This way of viewing the sacraments contains for Congar "a great and by no means imaginary danger," that of reducing sacraments to objects rather than places of true spiritual and personal encounter with the living God. Here, Congar makes a distinction in the approach to the sacramental acts that brings out the importance of the ontology of grace. That distinction is between sacraments approached as "system" and sacraments celebrated as "real spiritual acts." By "system" Congar means the risk of viewing sacraments as simply mechanical acts that lead to the automatic dispensing of "things." This leads to a vision of the church in terms of its structures and forms as the primary center of one's concern and energy. What is demanded by a spiritual act, however,

---

31. Yves Congar, *Sainte Église. Études et approches ecclésiologiques* (Paris: Cerf, 1963), 39.

32. Congar, *L'Église: de saint Augustin à l'époque moderne*, 167, 169–74. For a more complete theological discussion of the relationship between church, mystery, and sacrament see idem, *Un peuple messianique* (Paris: Cerf, 1975), Part One.

is the engagement of the person in the action.[33] The sacraments, of their nature, ought to engage persons in an encounter with the present and active Lord Jesus Christ. Spiritual acts, then, emphasize the personal and relational aspects of Christian faith.

For Congar one of the great moves flowing from the Second Vatican Council was a re-centering of the church, first, *vertically* from a focus on hierarchical authority to one centered on God, who is presently active in the life of the Christian community, and second, *horizontally*, focusing on the Christian faithful as the church rather than on the church's structures.[34] This is the significance of the notion of the "ontology of grace." Christianity has regained its human dimension and essence as relationship of persons with God, drawn together by Word and Sacrament into relationship with other human persons as well.[35] Thus belonging to the church "requires not only external loyalty to the visible institution but that people have the Spirit of Christ."[36]

This ontology of grace is foundational for an understanding of the community or life principle of authority. When Christianity is viewed from the primacy of discipleship based on election and new life gained in baptism, the place of charisms and initiatives is amplified. All the Christian faithful must be seen in light of their assimilation to the one Lord Jesus Christ in his Body the church.[37] This assimilation depends on the instituted structures of the church, but specifically as service to the one work of Christ in which all share (Eph 4:11-16), the building of the temple of God, the gathering of all persons into the fellowship of the divine communion of the Father, Son, and Holy Spirit.

## The Relation between the Church and the World

The lack of a vibrant anthropology connected to ecclesiology was deeply intertwined with a low regard for the world and its legitimate autonomy. This has often been the result of emphasis on an "otherworldly" spirituality that stresses the ends for which the human person is made

---

33. Yves Congar, *Christians Active in the World*, trans. P. J. Hepburne-Scott (New York: Herder & Herder, 1968), 12. See also idem, *Christ, Our Lady and the Church*, trans. Henry St. John (Westminster, MD: Newman Press, 1957; repr. Eugene, OR: Wipf and Stock, 2001), 63–64.

34. Cf. Yves Congar, *Called to Life*, trans. William Burridge (New York: Crossroad, 1987), 66; idem, *Ministères*, 32–33.

35. Yves Congar, *Faith and Spiritual Life*, trans Aelfric Manson and Lancelot C. Sheppard (New York: Herder & Herder, 1968), 189.

36. Congar, "The People of God," 204.

37. Yves Congar, "The Laity," 239–49 in *Vatican II: By Those Who Were There*, at 244.

54   *A Church Fully Engaged*

with little or no regard for the actual life of the human person as it is lived and experienced in the here and now.[38] This lack of anthropology and the consequent absence of what might be called an appropriate "secularity" was the natural outgrowth of what Congar would regard as the "sacralization of Western society in the Middle Ages."[39] As we saw in chapter two, this sacralization was evidenced by the growing identification of the world with the church and a tendency for culture to be increasingly in the hands of the clergy. The result was "a Christian society, all of which [had] become the Church, [where] there is no longer true tension between a Church purely the Church and a world truly the world."[40]

For Congar one of the exceptional accomplishments of the Second Vatican Council was a "reframing" of the question regarding the church's relationship to the world. Congar discusses the schema on the church presented to the theological preparatory committee before the council containing a chapter titled "On the relations between Church and State." Its treatment of the topic was basically limited to a collection of citations from the writings of the popes over the previous four centuries, which served to center the whole topic under the aspect of power with "the religious duty of the civil power conceived as a paternal sort of guide."[41] The interventions of the council fathers near the end of the first session clearly manifested a desire to move the understanding of this relationship in another direction. They wanted to see this topic spoken of in terms of apostolic responsibility rather than of power. Here, in a way Congar found so characteristic of Vatican II, the fathers insisted on moving away from a purely juridical and political understanding of the church in its relationship with the world to a vision marked more by the aim of communicating the kingdom values of Christ to the world.[42]

That this conception of the church-world relationship is something deeply integral to Congar's own thought can be seen in a most striking comment he recorded in his journal in the very early stages of the council. When approached by someone who told him of the possibility

---

38. Congar, *Christians Active in the World*, 14–16, 74.

39. The title of an article by Congar in *Concilium* 47, ed. Roger Aubert (New York: Paulist Press, 1969), 55–71.

40. Congar, *Christians Active in the World*, 6.

41. Yves Congar, "Église et monde dans la perspective de Vatican II," in *Vatican II: L'Eglise dans le monde de ce temps* (Paris: Cerf, 1967), 3: 15–41, at 26.

42. Ibid., 27. See also Yves Congar, *Église catholique et France moderne* (Paris: Hachette, 1978), 47–48.

that Pope John XXIII would beatify Pope Pius IX to show the connection between the two Vatican councils, Congar reacted pointedly. He commented in his journal on Pius IX's response to the fall of the Papal States to Italian unification in 1870. Pius IX, according to Congar, "was invited by the events to leave the awful lie of the 'Donation of Constantine' and to come finally to adopt an evangelical attitude, [but] he perceived nothing of this call and, rather, drove the Church in its claim to temporal power."[43] Clearly the move within the council itself in reframing this question was one that Congar recognized as profoundly central to the demands of the Gospel in the world of today.

Commenting on the Second Vatican Council's pastoral constitution *Gaudium et spes*, Congar writes that the world is "the totality of [people's] earthly activities and could be just as well called civilization or history, provided earthly values or realities are understood to be included." Notable is that the world possesses an autonomy over and against the church. The temporal sphere is not subordinate to the church but exists in its own right as history and culture developing alongside the church. The two distinct realities are related precisely in human persons as such and in the central importance of anthropology. The human person is the basis of the relation between church and world precisely because the "world is both the scene of human history and the realization of God's saving plan."[44]

Elsewhere Congar uses a helpful description of the "middle" of things and their "beginning and end" for understanding this relationship between world and church. By the "middle" Congar intends the world and all its activities that engage the life of human beings. Science, art, technology, labor, family life, commerce, and working the land are all things done in the world and for their own sake. They possess, in other words, values integral in themselves. They are activities in the middle, or in the heart of the created order and form the basic structure of the human person's day-to-day life. This middle is the world. Yet these realities possess at the very same time an ultimate purpose, a significance that exists beyond them and fills them with a transcendent meaning. This meaning is found in the "beginning" and the "end" of things, from which they come and to which they are ultimately directed. There is, in other words, an eschatological significance to all that is.

---

43. Yves Congar, *Mon journal du Concile* (Paris: Cerf, 2002), 1: 1, 115.
44. Yves Congar, "The Role of the Church in the Modern World," in *Commentary on the Documents of Vatican II*, ed. Herbert Vorgrimler (Freiburg: Herder, 1969), 5: 211, 206.

Here is the place of the church, which always points to the ultimate meaning of things.[45]

This has important implications for the mission of the church to the world. *Gaudium et spes* situates this mission within the Trinity itself, flowing from the missions of the Word and the Spirit, which are simply a continuation of their processions from the Father.[46] In its Decree on the Missionary Activity of the Church the council also located this activity within the "new framing" of the question of the church's relationship to the world. "For by the very fact of revealing Christ, the church reveals to people their real situation and the truth about their total calling" (*AG* 8).[47] Presenting Christ to the world reveals the authentic source and end of all that concerns the human person in the "middle," in the heart of daily life.

Though the "Church exists in herself, as a sacred thing in the midst of the world . . . she does not exist *for* herself: she has a mission to and a responsibility for the world."[48] Because of this the church possesses a distinct *munus* or function in relation to the world that exists on two planes. "The first duty of the Church in regard to the world clearly consists in converting it to the gospel."[49] The second level, which specifically results from the integrity and autonomy the world possesses, consists in influencing the structures and activities of the world so as to enable them to be receptive to and directed toward the kingdom of God. In short, the "Church reigns *directly,* by her jurisdiction, over the baptized, but over the world as such she has only an influence."[50]

For Congar it is essential to connect the implications of this latter aspect of the church's mission with the royal mission of Christ over the world. Christ's royal reign over the world, until the time he establishes the fullness of that reign in the *parousia*, is essentially *priestly* rather than kingly. The church, then, "follows Jesus, not in his condition of power, which he will reveal at his return, but in his coming in humility."[51] It is to be for the world a sign and instrument of reconciliation, peace, and life offered to and lived in view of God. As the church shares in Christ's kingship over the world in an essentially priestly way, so its prophetic ministry is marked by the character of *influence* as she lives and speaks

---

45. Yves Congar, *The Wide World, My Parish*, trans. Donald Attwater (Baltimore: Helicon Press, repr. 1962), 50–51.
46. Congar, *Un peuple messianique*, 15; *Gaudium et spes* 40.
47. Congar, "The Role of the Church," 212 n. 24.
48. Congar, *The Wide World, My Parish*, 21.
49. Congar, "The Role of the Church," 203.
50. Congar, *Christians*, 50.
51. Ibid., 49–50. See also idem, *Lay People*, 67–69.

the word of God, directing the attention of the world to the truth of its ultimate end and meaning in the reign of God.[52]

The essential link between the world and the church is the human person. This has immense implications for the church's mission to the world. "We have seen that 'Church' here means the social body which owes its origin to the incarnation and which has received a mission for the world; but what is active in the world is the People of God in the midst of all humanity."[53] If the church's mission is "the penetration of the temporal order in a Christian way,"[54] the absolute centrality of the lay faithful in this mission becomes clear. "Lay people exist, not in order to constitute the Church as a sacral organism, but to enable her to accomplish her mission fully; to recapitulate, to 'sum up in one' all the values of humanity in Jesus Christ. That is something the Church cannot do without the laity. So the laity are necessary, not that the Church may be a power of salvation, but that she may carry out the fullness of her mission."[55]

Congar sees the church as the Messianic People of God as the concept most helpful for understanding the nature of the church in its relation to the world. It is unfortunate that "we find that *Gaudium et Spes* has not taken up the expression 'messianic people' which is twice employed in *Lumen Gentium* (art. 9)."[56] The concept's usefulness is found in the implications contained in the term "messianic." "A people, a movement is called messianic when they are carriers of a hope for liberation and a better future involving the destiny of a large number." Jesus' messianic nature is not that of a revolutionary or even a reformer of institutions, but "[i]t is of an eschatological-prophetical kind."[57] The church as the Messianic People of God points to its proper stance toward the world as the bearer of a message of hope and liberation based on the truth of the human person and responding to the longing in humanity for ultimate meaning and fulfillment. It addresses the hoped-for "end" toward which humanity's efforts in the "middle" of the world are ultimately directed.

In summary, the reframing of the relationship of the church and the world by the council in terms of "apostolic responsibility" rather than that of two powers in confrontation has enormous consequences for

---

52. Cf. Congar, *Mon journal du Concile*, 1: 157; idem, "Path-Findings," 187–88.
53. Congar, "The Role of the Church," 214.
54. Congar, "The Laity," 242.
55. Congar, *Christians Active in the World*, 52.
56. Congar, "The Role of the Church," 215.
57. Congar, *Un people messianique*, 93, 94–95.

how the church's authority is viewed. Its authority in relation to the world is not that of power but of influence through the living and proclaiming of the reign of God, a work essentially tied to the whole people of God. It is the life lived by all God's faithful people in the "middle" of the world that serves to shape the world toward this ultimate end. The implication for the community or life principle of authority is striking. Indeed, through the actual living of the faith the Body of Christ is built up in disposing the world to its ultimate end, which is recapitulation in Christ. The hierarchical principle, by implication, exerts its own proper authority as "power" over the Christian faithful precisely as a service that equips them for this task, not of exercising power over the world but of bringing the influence of the Gospel into the midst of the world. For Congar the notion of the church as Messianic People of God speaks of this active presence of God's faithful living in the midst of all people as a sign and influence of the saving, reconciling, liberating end for which humanity longs and for which it is ultimately destined.

## Expressions of the Community or Life Principle of Authority

### Charisms and Initiatives

In an attempt to articulate the aspects of what Congar refers to as the community or life principle of authority we have highlighted the theological foundations of the church considered as a communion, which underscores a certain "ontology of grace" and its relation to the world. It is now time to examine the "particular" and "concrete" expressions of the life principle of authority in the church by looking first to charisms and initiatives, then to the reality of the council in the life of the church, and finally to the notions of reception and *sensus Ecclesiae*.

From the time of the Council of Trent in particular, Catholic ecclesiology had focused on the historical founding of the church by Jesus Christ as a hierarchically constituted institution. This ecclesiology lacked a significant pneumatological influence. Because of this the overwhelming tendency was to locate everything necessary for the building up of the church in the institution and, in particular, the clergy.[58] God the Father sent Christ, Christ sent the apostles, and the apostles established the episcopacy. Everything, then, is found within the hierarchical reality of

---

58. Yves Congar, *The Word and the Spirit*, trans. David Smith (San Francisco: Harper & Row, 1986), 48; idem, "Autonomie et pouvoir central dans l'Église," Irènikon 53 (1980): 291–313, at 298.

the church or, as Johann Adam Möhler stated and Congar often repeated, "God has created the hierarchy and so has shown more than enough care for the church until the end of the world."[59]

Flowing from the liturgical and biblical movements of the first half of the twentieth century, the development of a growing sense of the action of the Holy Spirit in the building up of the church opened the way for "[o]ne of the most striking aspects of the contemporary scene [with] a rediscovery of the charisms in our theology *de Ecclesia*," beginning with Pius XII's encyclical *Mystici Corporis* in 1943.[60] This "contemporary rediscovery" underlines the reality of God's action building up the church through all its members by means of the gifts each has received.[61] The transition highlighted here by Congar is from having "too exclusively conceived the unity [of the church] in the line of 'sub uno'" to seeing it more clearly "as a community where all have received the gifts of the Spirit so that this Church is constructed also from the base."[62] Thus the Second Vatican Council stated: "[The Spirit] leads the church into all truth (see Jn 16,13), and he makes it one in fellowship and ministry, instructing and directing it through a diversity of gifts both hierarchical and charismatic, and he adorns it with his fruits" (*LG* 4).

Congar's own understanding of the nature of charisms is very precise. "Charisms are gifts or talents which Christians owe to the grace of God" and that they "are called to put . . . at the service of the Body of Christ, for its building up."[63] Two aspects in particular are noteworthy in the definition he offers. First, it highlights the charisms referred to by St. Paul that are "less striking charisms, such as exhortation and acts of mercy (Rom 12:8), service (Rom 12:7), teaching (Rom 12:7; 1 Cor 12:28ff.), the utterance of wisdom and knowledge (1 Cor 12:8), faith (1 Cor 12:9), discernment of spirits (1 Cor 12:10), helping and administration (1 Cor

---

59. Johann Adam Möhler, review of Theodor Katerkamps, *Das erste Zeitalter der Kirchengeschichte 1: Die Zeit der Verfolgungen* (Münster: Theissing, 1823), *Theologische Quartalschrift* 5 (1823): 497, trans. Elizabeth Teresa Groppe, *Yves Congar's Theology of the Holy Spirit* (New York: Oxford University Press, 2004), 175 n. 14.

60. Congar, *The Word and the Spirit*, 79.

61. Yves Congar, "The Need for Pluralism in the Church," trans. Honor Rynne and Austin Flannery, *Catholic Mind* 73 (April 1975): 35–43, at 40.

62. Yves Congar, "Initiatives locales et normes universelles," *La Maison-Dieu* 112/4 (1972): 54–69, at 64.

63. Yves Congar, *I Believe in the Holy Spirit*, trans. David Smith (New York: Seabury, 1983), 2: 116. See also idem, *Esprit de l'homme, Esprit de Dieu* (Paris: Cerf, 1983), 58–60.

12:28)."[64] Congar views charisms as gifts of the kind that normally flow from the natural capacities and abilities of the person, strengthened and made useful for the building up of the Body of Christ.

Second, Congar's definition shows charisms to be ecclesial realities:

> It is, in other words, God who builds up his Church. In order to do this, he instituted, through Jesus Christ his faithful servant, the structures of that Church. At the same time, he continues to build it up, at all periods in history, by the gifts, (*charismata*), the services or ministries (*diakoniai*) and the various *energemata* or "ways of working" to which Paul refers in 1 Cor 12:4-6. He does this by distributing talents and gifts to all believers.[65]

The charisms, then, are moved from the strictly personal, spiritual sphere in which they were so often placed before the Second Vatican Council[66] and are to be viewed rather as "dynamic principles" within the church[67] by which God himself is ever "molding" it.[68]

Congar's study of the nature of the prophetic charism in *Vraie et fausse réforme dans l'Église* is most helpful in understanding the role of charisms and their presence in both the hierarchical and the community principles of authority.[69] Prophecy is the charism that allows one to "judge the times and the things that exist in time in the light of their truth in relation to the Absolute and to the end towards which they are directed." Prophecy exists, Congar further insists, as a permanent function within the whole people of God either as a hierarchical charism or as one found within the *life* of the church. As a hierarchical charism it serves to maintain and explain the faith given once and for all in the prophets, Jesus, and the apostles. This charism also functions in the *life* of the church and by it that life is connected explicitly with the historical movement of the world. Prophecy is the ability, considered under the aspect of the life principle, of scholars and saints to penetrate the things of God, with a truly personal dimension, by the very wisdom of God in the light of the "signs of the times." Though this charism func-

---

64. Congar, *I Believe in the Holy Spirit* 2: 163.
65. Ibid., 162.
66. Congar, *Called to Life*, 63.
67. Congar, *The Word and the Spirit*, 80.
68. Congar, *Called to Life*, 68.
69. For an extensive treatment of the topic of prophecy in the work of Congar see Victor Dunne, *Prophecy in the Church: The Vision of Yves Congar* (Frankfurt: Peter Lang, 2000).

tions from within the *life* of the church, Congar insists that "it supposes the given structure of [the church] and is exercised only in the limits of that structure." Its validity flows from the ability to express the truth of things in the light of that faith given once for all to the church in Christ through the apostles. In his treatment of prophecy Congar shows that charisms can be spoken of in connection with the *ex officio* teaching of the church, which is "the assistance linked to a charge," and that there is a charism of teaching "*ex spiritu,* the inspiration unforeseeably given."[70]

The role of *initiatives* is linked to this appreciation for the place of charisms in the life of the church. To get a sense of what is meant by "initiatives," consider Congar's description of the contemporary religious situation in France. Despite the rapid decline in the number of priests, diocesan structures lacking their former vitality, the ever-increasing numbers of inactive Catholics, all marked by a nation of Catholics "slipping gently into calm indifference," the "Church is being constantly refashioned as the Gospel makes fresh springs rise again in the lives of men and women."[71] These "fresh springs" are various prayer groups, gatherings for the study of Scripture, and movements based on the church's social doctrine. Small groups are rising up, more or less spontaneously, and apart from the direct intervention of the hierarchy, for the support of its members and in order to promote some aspect of faith to the wider community.[72] Initiatives, by their nature, are local—at least in their beginnings—and come "in response to concrete needs and often possessing a great density of evangelical meaning."[73]

These movements or initiatives are often minimized by the hierarchy in their significance and their ability to affect the lives of people and spheres within the church.[74] Historians have often failed to appreciate their importance to the church's life. This reality of initiatives, in fact, is at the heart of what professional historians today regard as "social history." Social history is the attempt to document "the history of practicing Christians,"; it refers to "the study not of great bishops but of

---

70. Yves Congar, *Vraie et fausse réforme dans l'Église*, Unam Sanctum 72, 2d ed. (Paris: Cerf, 1968), 198, 189, 206, 195, 190–91, 183, 199.

71. Congar, *The Word and the Spirit*, 82.

72. Cf. Congar, "Initiatives locales et normes universelles," 59–61. See also idem, Preface to Karl Delahaye, *Ecclésia Mater chez les Pères des trois premiers siècles*, 7–32 (Paris: Cerf, 1964), at 22–23, where Congar speaks of a "milieu" of faith created by such small groups.

73. Ibid., 57.

74. Congar, *The Word and the Spirit*, 48; idem, *L'Église: de saint Augustin à l'époque moderne*, 198–209.

communities of ordinary persons, to history 'from below,' to the social history of Christianity in the various guises in which it flourishes today."[75] Increasingly historians are finding that the authentic telling of history demands an appreciation of the initiatives of those who, although not great personal figures and not engaged in great historical happenings, have in fact had an impact on the very life of the church.

Central to Congar's understanding of initiative is that it highlights and gives due regard to the proper "personal principle" found within Christianity. "[E]very [person] is a subject who responds freely and who is always a source of free initiative, self-expression and invention. . . . It inevitably goes together with an ecclesiology based on the idea of the church as a communion of persons."[76] Again, the "ontology of grace" is key, granting due regard for the person in the church and viewing each one as an authentic disciple of Christ, truly capable of and needing to contribute to the building up of the whole body, the church.

Within this context of charisms and initiatives Congar highlights the importance of the relationship between the local and the universal church. Charisms and initiatives cannot be viewed exclusively in their "personal dimension"; they also imply the particular gifts and initiatives flowing from local communities. The Second Vatican Council clearly expressed the realization of the one church in the local church: "A diocese is a section of the people of God whose pastoral care is entrusted to a bishop in cooperation with his priests. Thus, in conjunction with their pastor and gathered by him into one flock in the holy Spirit through the gospel and the eucharist, they constitute a particular church. In this church, the one, holy, catholic and apostolic church of Christ is truly present and at work" (*CD* 11).

This expresses "the idea that the whole mystery of the Church is realized in the particular Church."[77] "In this vision of the local churches one can also give a fully positive value to diversities and originality. This vision of the local church is based, for Congar, on the patristic understanding, particularly that of Augustine, Jerome, and Gregory the Great, of the importance of respecting the diversity of local churches for the good of the unity of faith. Indeed, this tradition insists that "diverse

---

75. John W. O'Malley, *Trent and All That: Renaming Catholicism in the Early Modern Era* (Cambridge, MA: Harvard University Press, 2000), 99. See also Yves Congar, "Théologie historique," 233–62 in *Initiation à la pratique de la théologie, Tome I: Introduction*, ed. Bernard Lauret and François Refoulé (Paris: Cerf, 1994), at 240–52.

76. Congar, *I Believe in the Holy Spirit*, 2: 153–54.

77. Yves Congar, *Église et papauté* (Paris: Cerf, 1994), 212.

costumes represent a richness." In view of the community principle of authority, a church understood as a unity that exists through the diversity of local charisms and initiatives must be marked by mutual exchange of information and the need for communication.[78]

In summary, Congar views charisms and initiatives as of central importance. They flow from the truth of the "ontology of grace" that recognizes the reality of God's active presence in building up the church not only from above and outside through the hierarchical structures but indeed from within the Body of Christ by the gifts and talents given by the Holy Spirit to each Christian and in the Spirit's inspiration of initiatives arising from the actions of the faithful to promote the living out of the Gospel. Charisms and initiatives are concrete expressions of the authentic personalism of Christianity. The church is made up of free subjects capable of giving authentic expression to the demands of the Gospel in the very concrete situations of social, ecclesial, and personal life. Initiatives and charisms are based not simply in persons but in local communities that build up the universal church by their own particular and diverse gifts and initiatives in proclaiming and living the faith.

## Conciliarity

Councils, as "realities" or simply "facts" in themselves, are gatherings of bishops, either regionally or universally, held to address issues before the church such as doctrine, morals, liturgical practice, or pastoral concerns. Viewed in this narrow sense councils would seem to be related primarily to the hierarchical principle of authority. Indeed, they most certainly do engage authority on the hierarchical plane. For Congar, councils, when viewed in the fullness of their reality, are aspects first and foremost of the community and life of the church. Because of this, councils have great import for understanding the nature both of the community and of the hierarchical principles of authority.

It is necessary to begin by providing an ample description of the fullness of the reality of the council. Such a description is made easy, on a certain level, by the profound theological thought and writing Congar contributed to this topic, flowing from his ever-present desire to show the church in its "living reality" and from his personal experience of the Second Vatican Council.

Councils belong to the *life* of the church because they are not divinely instituted and therefore do "not belong to the structure which the Lord

---

78. Congar, "Autonomie et pouvoir central dans L'Eglise," 301, 291–94, 312.

gave his church."[79] Further, "there is no form of council which is given by divine right, nor even by apostolic right."[80] Councils flow from the very *life* of the church because they "are an expression of the conciliarity which derives from the very nature of the Church, which is to be a communion, *koinonia*."[81] Congar frequently points to Matthew 18:20, "For where two or three are gathered in my name, I am there among them," and the Pentecost event in which the Spirit came upon all the disciples who were "all together in one place" (Acts 2:1)[82] as foundational for understanding the conciliar nature of the church.

In light of what Congar refers to as the "covenantal presence"[83] of Christ and the Spirit in the midst of those gathered, councils are viewed as "events" of a "doxological and eucharistic" character. The members of a council come together not in conference, but in prayer, with the celebration of the Eucharist being central. Out of this arise the articulation, defining, and proclamation of faith.[84] It is Christ who presides, mystically, at the council, "represented visibly by placing an image of Christ in the middle of the basilica, or more often the book of the gospels open, on a throne."[85] The unity, the common sharing of the council fathers in the proclamation of the truth, is a unity attributed time and again to the action of the Holy Spirit, who is the "decisive character" of the council.[86]

Councils, besides being characterized by the "covenantal presence of God" in the midst of the church, also have the essential character of assemblies. "A council is an assembly of the Church, called by the spiritual heads thereof, in which individual communities are incorporated, personalized, and in this sense represented."[87] What is underlined in the council's aspect of assembly is the anthropological reality of the church. This aspect shows why it is not possible to have a "council by

---

79. Yves Congar, "The Council as an Assembly and the Church as Essentially Conciliar," 44–88 in *One, Holy, Catholic, and Apostolic*, ed. Herbert Vorgrimler (London: Sheed & Ward, 1968), at 72.

80. Yves Congar, "The Council, the Church, and the 'Others,'" trans. Elizabeth Hughes, *Cross Currents* (Summer 1961): 241–54, at 247.

81. Yves Congar, "The Conciliar Structure or Regime of the Church," trans. Francis McDonagh, *Concilium* 167 (New York: Seabury, 1983), 3–9, at 3.

82. Cf. Congar, *Sainte Église*, 303; idem, "Conciliar Structure," 6; idem, "The Council as an Assembly," 58.

83. Ibid., 73.

84. Congar, "Conciliar Structure," 5.

85. Congar, "The Council as an Assembly," 64.

86. Congar, *Sainte Église*, 311.

87. Congar, "The Council, the Church, and the 'Others,'" 246.

correspondence,"[88] for in the very act of gathering, praying together, deliberating, exchanging information and ideas, the awareness of the truths of faith, present in the lived faith of the whole people of God, is opened up and disclosed in a common consciousness.[89] This flows directly from the "particular dynamism or grace" resulting from the gathering together of people.[90] This "dynamism" highlights the importance, in Congar's thought, of a certain liberty that must mark the deliberations of a council for it to authentically reach a common consciousness of faith.[91] Underlined in the very reality of the "gathering" of the council, for Congar, is the anthropological truth of the human person created in the image and likeness of God who is a Trinity of persons. Indeed, the council "imitates the council of the divine persons"[92] and reveals the profoundly theological roots of the reality that the "Church's concrete regime is traditionally one of councils, not of solitary personal decisions."[93] In short, councils, though not part of the structure of the church, are a profound expression of the essentially conciliar nature of the church, underlining the anthropological reality of human persons created to live in and for communion. Councils highlight the profound reality that authoritative proclamation and definition of faith are done within the communion of the whole people of God.

The nature of this assembly is explicated by an understanding of who participates in councils and the nature of "voting" within them. The members by right of an ecumenical council with deliberative and therefore voting rights are, most customarily, bishops who are local ordinaries, cardinals, certain abbots and religious superiors, with titular bishops also often participating in this capacity. Canonists and theologians may participate, though with no deliberative voice, as consultants. In this

---

88. Congar, "The Council as an Assembly," 50–51. "Council by correspondence" refers to the actions of Popes Pius IX and Pius XII in obtaining input from the world's bishops by letter concerning the feasibility of defining the Marian dogmas of the Immaculate Conception and the Assumption.

89. Congar, "Conciliar Structure," 7.

90. Yves Congar, "The Council in the Age of Dialogue," trans. Barry N. Rigney, *Cross Currents* (Spring 1962): 144–51, at 146.

91. Cf. Congar, *Mon journal du Concile* 1: 114. Here, Congar speaks of the first act of the Second Vatican Council as the delaying of a vote on episcopal membership of the various conciliar commissions at the intervention of the council fathers. This was an initiative on the part of the fathers to treat matters freely and thus to afford themselves the "space" in which a common consciousness of faith might be achieved.

92. Congar, "The Council as an Assembly," 58.

93. Congar, *Lay People*, 237.

same capacity lay people of a variety of expertise may be present for the purpose of consultation.[94]

"The bishops represent their churches, not in the manner of delegates, but in the ancient sense of the representation or personification of a body by its head."[95] The Orthodox theologian John Zizioulas, emphasizes this same point. "The fact that in this case [of the council] it was the bishop that became essentially the sole participant in the councils should be seen in the light of his position in the community and not in terms of individual authority."[96] This "ancient sense" is captured by St. Cyprian, who speaks very clearly of the mutual interiority of the bishop and his church. "[T]he bishop is in the church and the church is in the bishop."[97] The bishops gathered in council, then, are there not as representatives "sent" by their communities but as organically linked to the community, as head, joined with the church throughout the whole world, from within which they identify the divinely revealed faith that is held and carried by the whole church.[98] The bishops gathered in council, then, express the *sensus ecclesiae*.[99] The *pleroma* or fullness of the bishops is found in the church in which the fullness of faith resides.

Congar distinguishes between "majority" decisions and decisions of "unanimity." Canons and decrees of councils are typically voted on by the council fathers, but this "vote" is to be seen simply as a means of elucidating the expression of faith on the part of the participants. "The conciliar law is not that of a majority, but that of unanimity," while the process of voting seeks to draw forth this unanimity from the whole. "So, the council is not the sum of the particular voices, but the totality of the conscience of the church having found its expression."[100]

The mutual relationship existing between the hierarchical and life principles of authority is significant. The council as a gathering in which

---

94. Congar, *Sainte Église*, 316.

95. Congar, "Conciliar Structure," 5. See also idem, *Sainte Église*, 308.

96. John D. Zizioulas, *Being as Communion: Studies in Personhood and the Church* (Crestwood, NY: St. Vladimir's Seminary Press, 1985), 241. He further says: "A tradition that survives up to now in the Eastern Orthodox Church—though unconsciously as to its rationale—provides that *only the diocesan bishops are allowed to vote in a synod*. This condition speaks loudly for the fact that a bishop is not a member of a council in himself but as the head of a community."

97. Cyprian, *The Letters of St. Cyprian of Carthage*, trans. G. W. Clarke, Ancient Christian Writers 46 (New York: Newman Press, 1986), vol. 3, letter 66.8.3, p. 121.

98. Congar, *Sainte Église*, 310–11.

99. Congar, "Conciliar Structure," 5.

100. Congar, *Sainte Église*, 311.

the presence of the living God is manifested so that the faith of the church might be proclaimed with clarity and decisiveness through the decisions of the bishops highlights, for Congar, the essential collegial or conciliar nature of the hierarchical principle of authority.[101] Councils, though not of divine origin as structures, are "happenings" or "events" flowing from the *life* of the church as it faces particular crises and challenges in a given time and place that reflect the very nature of hierarchical authority as communal. The concrete reality of a council shows the intrinsic relationship between the hierarchical and community principles of authority. Indeed, the hierarchical is in some way shaped by the community principle. The full nature of this relationship will be examined below and in light not only of this brief study on councils but also of the fuller development of the two principles. What is clear is that Christ works to build up his church, through the action of the Holy Spirit, within the very context and movement of its life as well as from "outside and above." As the church faces various moments of conflict the Spirit creates a place and a means by which, in the midst of struggle, it achieves greater vitality and insight into the plan of God. This "means," in the case of a council, shows the divine Trinity drawing God's people, in their heads the bishops, into a communion by which the whole is made to grow. The hierarchical principle, serving the plan of God by defining and proclaiming that plan revealed once for all in Christ to the church in a given historical context and moment, does so only by being in communion with the apostolic faith that is precisely recognized within the communion of bishops and faithful, bishops and local churches.

### The Realities of Reception and *Sensus Ecclesiae*

Integrally connected to the reality of councils is the notion of reception, which is, for Congar, an aspect of the full reality of the council,[102] precisely because the recognition of a particular council as "ecumenical," or of local synods as important, has not been a matter simply of their numerical makeup (how many bishops have taken part) or their juridical constitution (for instance, who has called them) but of the fact that in them the faith of the church is recognized and received by the universal church.[103] This notion of reception is important for understanding the import of the community principle of authority within the church.

101. Congar, "The Council as an Assembly," 61.
102. Yves Congar, "Reception as an Ecclesiological Reality," trans. John Griffiths, *Concilium* 77, eds. Giuseppe Alberigo and Anton Weiler, 43–68 (New York: Herder & Herder, 1972), at 47; idem, "Conciliar Structure," 5.
103. Congar, "Reception," 54.

Reception is the process by which an individual (such as the pope receiving conciliar decrees),[104] a group (bishops receiving a particular articulation of the faith in a council), or the whole church accepts, integrates, and lives from the various doctrinal statements defined by a synod, council, bishop, or the pope. Reception, as it concerns the lay faithful, is an act of obedience to the faith given expression by the teaching authority of the church. This obedience includes consent and adherence to that teaching in such a way as to make it effective in the living out of the faith expressed in the teaching.[105] The faithful are not merely passive in relation to the teaching authority of the church; in fact their very reception of a teaching by living it out in the concrete dimensions of life contains the possibility of a development of doctrine.[106] In this sense the faithful's reception of the teaching "adds" a certain note of authority to that teaching.

An important facet of this "development" that can involve reception is the question of "effectiveness" in the proclamation of the faith. Though clearly the definitive setting forth of doctrine belongs solely to the hierarchical principle of authority,[107] reception underscores the effectiveness or ineffectiveness of the doctrinal formulation.[108] In this may be seen how a certain "lack" of reception calls for a deeper expression of the faith, and therefore its development, on the part of the hierarchy. The "lack of reception" may even reveal the inapplicability of a certain doctrine. "When the sovereignty of the Popes in temporal affairs," for instance, "ceased to have the support of public opinion it became irrelevant." Another example is the doctrine "Outside the church, no salvation." In this case the actual life situation of the church has so dramatically shifted—from the relative unity of the Christian faith in the West to multiple Christian denominations—that the doctrine as once stated simply lacks coherence for the present life of the church.[109]

---

104. Yves Congar, *L'Église: Une, Sainte, Catholique, et Apostolique*. Mysterium Salutis 15 (Paris: Cerf, 1970), 249.

105. Congar, "Reception," 45.

106. See Yves Congar, *Tradition and Traditions*, trans. Michael Naseby and Thomas Rainborough (Needham Heights, MA: Simon & Schuster, 1966), 318, 322; idem, *Lay People*, 281. See also Hermann J. Pottmeyer, "Reception and Submission," *The Jurist* 51 (1991): 269–92, at 285, where Pottmeyer speaks of the "personal quality" of reception that necessarily implies "a maturing process and a deeper, penetrating understanding" of doctrine.

107. See Congar, *Tradition and Traditions*, 323–28.

108. Congar, "Reception," 48.

109. Yves Congar, "Magisterium, Theologians, the Faithful, and the Faith," *Doctrine and Life* 31 (1981): 548–64, at 556.

Congar is clear that the importance of the "fact" of reception is given its proper weight in the church only when the "life principle" is fully appreciated. As a juridical reality reception suffers from ambiguity. But the fact that there is such a reality is found within the historical movement of the church. It is only when history is properly regarded as a genuine *locus theologicus* that the theological depth of the notion of reception can be appreciated. The "fact" of reception is found, for Congar, throughout the life of the church. He points to the Council of Nicaea as an example that took fifty-six years, "punctuated by synods, excommunications, exiles, and imperial interventions and violence," before it was accepted by the church. Further, the "famous 'Peter has spoken through the mouth of Leo,' at the Council of Chalcedon (451), was an act of reception: the Council recognized Peter's declaration of faith in the pope's formulary."[110] The First Council of Constantinople (381) is recognized as the second ecumenical council of the church on the basis of its reception by the West despite the fact that there were no Western bishops present.[111] The Council of Orange (529) and its formulations on the nature of grace, though that council was attended by just fourteen bishops and remained in obscurity for a long time, came to be used by the Councils of Trent, Vatican I, and Vatican II.[112] These examples, which could be multiplied, underline the connection between the councils and reception and show reception as a fact within the historical life of the church.

Reception is broader than its conciliar expression. It is found in the first centuries of the church's life, when it was precisely the reception of certain texts that shaped what only later would definitively make up the canon of Scripture. Reception is seen in the liturgical life of local churches as one received certain ritual expressions from another, as well as in the development and spread of liturgical feasts. The place of reception in the recognition of saints is undeniable. The spread of laws and ecclesial disciplines from one part of the church to another is a further example.[113] In these instances, before even essential aspects in the life of the church were defined juridically by hierarchical authority they imposed themselves "authoritatively" on the church because it recognized in them some aspect of the authentic content of the *regula fidei*, and therefore they called forth the reception of the faithful.

110. Congar, "Reception," 60, 46, 47.
111. Yves Congar, "Church Structures and Councils in East-West Relations," *One in Christ* 11 (1975): 224–65, at 248.
112. Congar, "Reception," 52–53.
113. Ibid., 54–57.

70   *A Church Fully Engaged*

Congar also speaks of nonreception in the life the church.[114] For example, the Council of Ferrara-Florence (1438–1439) had active participation of bishops from both the East and the West in the decree *Laetentur coeli*, which restored the unity of the Eastern and Western churches after doctrinal agreements on papal primacy, the *filioque*, and purgatory. This agreement made in council soon failed as the bishops of the East began arguing over the specifics of the agreement. It encountered great resistance among the Orthodox faithful and was not immediately promulgated by the emperor.[115] In the case of the nonreception of this council of union Congar makes a significant point that possesses major implications for reception. "Florence failed because there was a lack of preparation of minds and a lack of evolution of mentalities."[116] Reception, or in this case a lack thereof, is a reality that demands and evokes greater clarity in the proclamation of the truths of faith and thereby a more profound articulation of the faith than had previously been presented. Further, it speaks of the organic reality of faith that both lives and grows within the whole church. This "lack of preparation of minds" and "evolution of mentalities" compels the hierarchy to be aware of the actual life of faith within the people of God that is an aspect of reception.

Congar also highlights the notion of a certain "re-reception." Dogmas, once received but lived out in isolation from other essential aspects of the tradition, demand a fresh reception that gives due regard to the cultural and historical situation into which the church has moved and the authentic expression of faith given within other Christian communities. "It is possible . . . to speak of a 're-reception' of Vatican I by Vatican II and, again, in a new context and by means of a renewed reading such as that which allowed the minority of Vatican I to be represented as the *avant-garde* of Vatican II."[117] This notion of re-reception has important ecumenical implications as well. There are doctrines and ecclesial disciplines expressed by and lived in the Roman Catholic Church, the various Protestant traditions, and Orthodoxy that each has received individually

---

114. Cf. ibid., 57–58.

115. See ibid., 57, and Congar, "Church Structures and Councils in East-West Relations," 234–35. See John Meyendorff, *Byzantine Theology: Historical Trends and Doctrinal Themes* (New York: Fordham University Press, 1979), 109–14, for a perspective on the Council of Florence from an Orthodox theologian. Meyendorff concludes (pp. 113–14) that whatever other results there might have been as a consequence of the council, "it actually bypassed the issues dividing East and West and, stiffening the positions of both sides, made the schism a much deeper reality than it had been."

116. Congar, "Church Structures and Councils in East-West Relations," 235.

117. Congar, "Reception," 49.

but would demand a "re-reception" if unity were to be achieved. They would have to be thought through and lived out together over time.[118]

In order to appreciate the deep theological reality of the notion of reception we must now articulate its foundation in the *fides ecclesiae* or *sensus ecclesiae*. The reality of *sensus ecclesiae*, as with reception, flows from the truth that the apostolic faith is held within the whole church. "It is in fact all believers, the whole People of God as the Body of Christ with the indwelling of the Holy Spirit, who preserve the Tradition of the apostolic faith, whereas it is the pastoral *magisterium* which interprets, teaches and authentically formulates that Tradition."[119] What is indicated by *sensus ecclesiae* is expressed succinctly by St. Thomas Aquinas. "The universal Church cannot err, since she is governed by the Holy Ghost, Who is the Spirit of truth: for such was Our Lord's promise to His disciples (John 16:13): *When He, the Spirit of truth, is come, He will teach you all truth.*"[120] For Congar the *sensus ecclesiae* relates both to the subjective aspect of faith, the *fides qua creditur*, which is "the spiritual disposition and energy by which one adheres" to the faith, and the objective aspect of faith, *fides quae creditur*, which is "the object or the content of belief."[121] *Sensus ecclesiae* speaks of that sense of the faithful to grasp the faith intuitively and live it instinctively.

This reality is referred to in a number of ways within the tradition; though they "are not exactly equivalent . . . they suppose a common basis": "*sensus* or *consensus fidelium, sensus ecclesiae, sensus catholicus, sensus fidei . . . christiani populi fides, communis ecclesia fides.*"[122] Congar's own articulation of this principle, though he uses all the various historical terms for it, inclines to the use of *sensus ecclesiae*. Here, *ecclesiae* serves to situate this *sensus* clearly within the whole community and thus avoids any possible tendency to see it individualistically. It speaks more clearly also of this sense of faith in a way that is truly catholic and apostolic, which is the faith as it has been recognized and lived over

---

118. Yves Congar, *Diversity and Communion*, trans. John Bowden (Mystic, CT: Twenty-third Publications, 1985), 171–72.

119. Congar, *The Word and the Spirit*, 81.

120. Thomas Aquinas, *Summa Theologiae*, II-II, q. 1, ad 9, *sed contra*, quoted by Congar, "The Council as an Assembly," 60.

121. Yves Congar, "Travail théologique et Communion," in *Communio Sanctorium* (Paris: Labor et Fides, 1982), 19–24. See also idem, *Lay People*, 288–89.

122. Congar, *Lay People*, 288. See also Francis A. Sullivan, "The Sense of Faith: The Sense/Consensus of the Faithful," 85–93 in *Authority in the Roman Catholic Church: Theology and Practice*, ed. Bernard Hoose (Burlington, VT: Ashgate, 2002).

the whole of space and time in which the church has lived its life.[123] The *sensus ecclesiae* is not, then, the "adding up" of each individual's understanding of the faith nor is it "simply the product of the present moment,"[124] but rather it is the faith in its "totality such as that of the memory of the Church."[125]

Both Pius IX and Pius XII appealed to this *sensus ecclesiae* in declaring the Marian dogmas of the Immaculate Conception and Assumption when they said that these dogmas flowed from the "outstanding agreement of the Catholic prelates and the faithful."[126] Indeed, "the extraordinary development of Marian doctrine has been carried on . . . by the people's faith and devotion, with the encouragement of their bishops."[127] Notice that this sense of the faith present within the church, here regarding Marian doctrine, contains within it an element of development.

Still, Congar insists that "[t]oo much not be attributed to the *sensus fidelium*," because history itself "tells us of widespread failures of faith in the Christian people."[128] For this reason it is crucial to recognize the "logically prior phase of obedience" as the first characteristic of a Christian in response to the faith authoritatively proclaimed.[129] At the same time Congar stresses that this order of belief cannot be taken in an exclusively passive way. Christian obedience carries "its own value as testimony, and, possibly, an element of development."[130] In light of this one can see the "dynamic" character of obedience within the Christian regime, which "is itself an activity of life and the Holy Spirit inspires it."[131] Obedience, then, is an act of the Spirit that enables one to receive the revelation of God as gift and to bring that revelation to expression in one's own life to build up the whole Body of Christ in faith.

---

123. See Congar, *Sainte Église*, 126–27; idem, *Tradition and Traditions*, 318; idem, "Reception," 63–64.

124. Congar, *Tradition and Traditions*, 320.

125. Congar, "Reception," 63–64.

126. Bull *Ineffabilis Deus, in Acta Pii IX* 1, p. 615. Apostolic Constitution of Pius XII, *Munificentissimus Deus, AAS* 42 (1950), 756: "*singularis catholicorum Antistitum et fidelium conspiratio. . . .*" For English translation see *Munificentissimus Deus: the definition of his Holiness Pope Pius XII, of the dogma that Mary, the Virgin Mother of God, was assumed body and soul into the glory of heaven issued November 1, 1950* (Boston: Pauline Books and Media, 1950).

127. Congar, *Lay People*, 274.

128. Ibid., 275.

129. Congar, *Tradition and Traditions*, 326; idem, *Lay People*, 278.

130. Congar, *Tradition and Traditions*, 327.

131. Congar, "Reception," 62.

*The Community or Life Principle of Authority* 73

This concept of the *sensus ecclesiae* again highlights the centrality of anthropology. The anthropological reality of the faith means that the "faith is lived out and expressed by human subjects. It is the faith not just of individuals but of human groups or particular churches characterized in their 'particularity' by a culture, a tradition, a language peculiar to them."[132] The reality of faith in both its unity and its diversity is found in the *sensus ecclesiae* because it is encountered within the human reality. The one faith is given diverse expression in the lives of individual Christians and local churches in such a way as to clarify the depth and breadth of the one essential faith.[133]

Within the church there exists an authentic relationship between the hierarchy and the community as a whole that is directed to the carrying of the faith "to the ends of the earth." It is marked, on the part of the community, which includes the members of the hierarchy,[134] by receptive obedience to the faith proclaimed authoritatively by the apostolic ministry. This obedience, however, is one that involves a certain creativity in application to life as it is lived, and in this it is further marked by a "teaching" character that involves "the actual unfolding of Christian truth."[135]

Congar's understanding of the notions of reception and the *sensus ecclesiae* highlights two important aspects of authority. First, reception and the *sensus ecclesiae* are not juridical realities as such but flow from the very life of the church. In this sense they are "facts" rather than "laws." It is precisely in their character as facts in the life of the church that they carry a real authority. The faith is indeed authentically carried within the whole people of God and, further, there is an aspect of "shaping" and "development" that takes place regarding the faith as it is lived by the church.

Second, the discussion of reception and the *sensus ecclesiae* illustrates the nature of the distinction between the two principles of authority, hierarchy and community. The hierarchy authoritatively proclaims the doctrine of the faith by an act of defining the faith, an act that belongs to it alone. The community, that is, the whole church, receives that faith as proclaimed in an obedience that cannot be considered simply passive. In their adhering to and living out the faith its authority increases as a

---

132. Congar, *Diversity and Communion*, 169.
133. Congar, *Lay People*, 280.
134. Ibid., 278.
135. Congar, *Tradition and Traditions*, 318. For this entire discussion on reception and the *sensus ecclesiae* see also Richard R. Gaillardetz, *By What Authority?* (Collegeville, MN: Liturgical Press, 2003), 115–17.

74    A Church Fully Engaged

word actually proclaimed and draws out multiple levels within doctrines of the faith that would otherwise remain obscure.

## *Defining the Community or Life Principle of Authority*

Having examined the community or life principle under the various aspects from which it is viewed in the work of Père Congar, we now address the important task of providing a succinct and useful definition of this principle while remaining faithful to the thought of the French Dominican. Defining the principle will also allow me to summarize all that has been said concerning this principle of authority. In concluding I will offer some thoughts on the implication, as I see it, of the insights of Congar's work.

### **The Community or Life Principle of Authority**

Although this definition is not found in Congar's own writings, a serious examination of the various theological proposals he set forth over the vast course of his writings can provide us with a formula that authentically reflects this aspect of authority as he saw it.

The community or life principle of authority is this: God the Father (always the ultimate "auctor" in the church[136]) acts from *within* the church by means of the Holy Spirit to build up the Body of Christ his Son. He does this by giving spiritual authority to his faithful people to receive, express, and carry forward the faith, in a communion of life and love with Him and with one another—in order to further the growth of his kingdom in the church and to proclaim the kingdom to the world— by means of charisms and initiatives. These charisms and initiatives, in the course of the church's historical existence, serve to amplify and give authority to the proclamation of the gospel and to move the world towards its ultimate goal, which is freedom to praise and worship the Father, creator of heaven and earth.

The community principle of authority as *God the Father acting within the church* expresses Congar's deep conviction that there is an interior principle in the life of the church. God does not simply build the church from outside and above but from within. The interiority of God's life, planted there as a seed in baptism in the hearts of God's people, cannot be underestimated.

The Father does this *by means of the Holy Spirit to build up the Body of Christ his Son*, which highlights Congar's insistence on the "two

---

136. Congar, *Tradition and Traditions*, 312.

hands" of the Father by which he established and sustains the church. The community principle is essentially linked to the action of the Holy Spirit, who works by means of a certain liberty over the course of the ages and in the diverse places of the church to accomplish the work of God. Still, Congar insists that the work of God is essentially related to the work of Christ and all that he established in his life, death, and resurrection. The Holy Spirit works, in short, to build the Body of Christ. Again, there is in the church structure and life.

This work of the Spirit is a *spiritual authority given to his faithful people to receive, express, and carry forward the faith*. This underscores everything said in the above section on the realities of reception and the *sensus ecclesiae*. The reception of faith cannot simply be comprehended as a purely "passive" reality, though it is characterized by a receptivity to the faith. In baptism and confirmation the faithful are given a capacity that allows them to fully embrace what is beyond them, to act on what is received, and to communicate it within the context of life as it is lived. Here, the designation of this authority or power as *spiritual* indicates the important distinction made earlier, that is, between authority as essentially a spiritual and moral reality and authority as power that has the nature of a public right in executing law and discipline.[137] There is obviously no power in this latter sense connected to the life principle of authority. It is an authority *ex spiritu* and *de facto*, not *ex officio* or *de jure*.[138]

This is done *in a communion of life and love with God and with one another*. This authority is particularly directed to unity in love. This again expresses what was said regarding the conciliarity of the church. The community principle of authority is one particularly directed to the conforming of mind and heart to the will of God, which is found most explicitly when God draws his people together in an exchange of faith, gifts, and insight. It is within communion that God's life abounds. Integral is the relationship alluded to here between this principle and the hierarchical principle of authority. The council is an example of the essential conciliar, communal nature of hierarchical authority.

This authority is directed toward *the growth of God's kingdom in the church and its proclamation to the world*. By means of this life principle of authority God does indeed fashion his church, and it is particularly

---

137. Cf. Congar, *L'Église: de saint Augustin à l'époque moderne*, 32–33.

138. For a discussion of the distinction made by Congar between *de facto* and *de jure* see his *Tradition and Traditions*, 323–38.

by the whole people of God that God reaches into the world, as world, to draw it to its proper end.

This authority takes the form of *charisms* and *initiatives* arising within individual members in the church and out of local communities, which *in the course of the church's historical existence serve to amplify and give authority to the proclamation of the Gospel and to move the world toward its ultimate goal*. The nature of this principle as "fact" and "reality" is stressed because it is precisely within the historical life of the church that these charisms and initiatives are encountered and are indeed experienced as possessing spiritual authority in contributing to the church's mission, both within the church and toward the world.

A point of clarification can now be added concerning the "naming" of this principle. Its character as "interior," flowing from the "communion" of the church in the trinitarian communion, and its marked "historicity" show the fundamental nature of this principle as an aspect of the life of the church. Therefore from this point on it will simply be referred to as the "life principle of authority."

This authority is directed to the *ultimate goal, which is freedom to praise and worship the Father, creator of heaven and earth*. Here is Congar's stress on the eschatological nature of the church. He is clear that though the church is a given reality it is also a task to be accomplished through time and fulfilled in the *parousia*. The church's mission to the world is to direct the world to its true end, and this it does most authentically by being church, by its own worship of God the Father in Jesus Christ through the action of the Holy Spirit. Congar insists that this can only be done if the life of the church becomes more and more one long epiclesis,[139] the prayer for and participation in the spiritual authority of God the Father that fashions and builds up the Body of Christ by the action of the Holy Spirit.

## Implications of the Life Principle of Authority

The very heart of Congar's theology of the church lies in his profound appreciation for and articulation of the ontology of grace. Congar finds the affirmation of the human person alongside that of God in Scripture, and as a result in the patristic authors.[140] This crucial rediscovery of the essential link between an understanding of the church and anthropology

---

139. Congar, *I Believe in the Holy Spirit*, 3: 267–72.
140. Yves Congar, "The Crucial Questions," 8–14 in *Problems Facing the Church Today*, ed. Frank Fehmers (New York: Newman Press, 1969), at 9.

## The Community or Life Principle of Authority 77

holds profound significance for the church's understanding and living out of its proper authority.

The importance of this "rediscovery" of the authentic personalism of Christianity for the church's life in the modern world cannot be overstated because, Congar claims, most forms of atheism have their basis in an affirmation of the human person.[141] The basis of modern atheism in humanism, in this affirmation of the human person, is given convincing articulation by the Yale professor of the philosophy of religion Louis Dupré.[142] He asserts that the atheism of Freud, Marx, and Nietzsche founded its ultimate claim not in antitheistic polemics, though certainly their works contain much of that, but rather in a radical immanentism, a thoroughgoing humanism that places all meaning and all value within the human subject. "To the extent that these attempts have succeeded, they have changed the perspective of our culture and have replaced religion in what used to be its unique function of integrating all of life. For many of our contemporaries, religion has been reduced to an experience, one among others, occasionally powerful, but not sufficiently so to draw the rest of their existence into its orbit."[143]

This radical "turn to the subject" of modernity has, as Dupré indicates, relegated religious truth to what can be discovered *within* the personal subject, and therefore to what corresponds to the interior experience of the personal subject. Dupré articulates the implications of this "turn" for the reality of religious authority.

> In the modern world, religion no longer exercises its integrating function—so essential to its survival—primarily by means of ecclesial power or discipline, or even by means of doctrinal authority. Increasingly the basis of authority has come to lie in the personal decision to *adopt* a traditional doctrine and to *use* it for guidance and integration of the various aspects of social and private conduct. It is not that believers have replaced doctrine by an eclectic *choice* of symbols. An arbitrary choice of signs of ultimate meaning is indicative of an advanced secularism, not of a serious religious attitude. Yet even genuine religion today differs from the past in that it integrates from *within* rather than from without, even when it continues to uphold the commitment to a particular doctrine and cult. Their

---

141. Ibid.
142. Louis Dupré, *Religious Mystery and Rational Reflection* (Grand Rapids, MI: Eerdmans, 1998), 131–43.
143. Ibid., 133.

authority, however, becomes operative only after and to the extent that they have been personally accepted and interiorized.[144]

Congar was keenly aware of this radical rejection of any authority exerting itself from the outside over the personal subject and outlined its development, rooted in the anti-ecclesiastical movements beginning in the twelfth century and resulting in the Protestant Reformation of the sixteenth.[145] Further, he showed the response of the Catholic Church to this development, most especially from the time of the Reformation, to have been the radical reassertion of its authority over the personal subject, resting its claims, of course, on certain authentic aspects of the tradition. Still, Congar insisted that the return to the sources of the Christian faith reveals a richer and more complete understanding of ecclesiology in general and authority in particular.

A central aspect of this *ressourcement* is a profound appreciation for the interior principle of the church. The authentic Christian tradition shows that God does indeed work within human persons, by his grace, to draw them to life and positive contribution to the building up of the Body of Christ. The church in the modern world, Congar insists, demands that this principle of interiority be given its full import. Indeed, it is his conviction that this is precisely the implication of the Second Vatican Council's placement of the chapter on the people of God before that on the hierarchy. The very ordering of the chapters of *Lumen Gentium* shows this restoration of the priority of the ontology of grace in the Christian life. This is the foundation on which is firmly grounded the authentic appreciation of charisms and initiatives and the active role of each person in the church in the living out and proclamation of the faith as expressed in the realities of reception and the *sensus ecclesiae*. In the life principle of authority, as a genuine aspect present in the fullness of the tradition, one discovers the authentic personalism of Christianity and, as a result, the evangelical call to all to become fully engaged in the mission of Jesus Christ to the world as authentically human subjects, placing their talents and gifts at the service of the plan of God for all humanity.

Congar's articulation of the wider and more authentic tradition as contained in his life principle of authority possesses great advantages for the life of the church in today's world. It opens the church to a deeper appreciation for and engagement of the human subject, which stands at the center of the contemporary worldview. After more than four cen-

---

144. Ibid., 136–37.
145. See chapter 2 above.

turies of the church confronting this radical turn to the subject with an ever-increasing emphasis on its hierarchical authority over the personal subject, it is time for a constructive address to modernity's philosophical basis in the personal subject. I believe this to be the conviction of Congar and, more centrally, I believe that Congar's lifelong investigation of the church's tradition is capable of doing just that.

## Chapter Four

# The Hierarchical Principle of Authority

## *Introduction*

The church as a communion of persons is socially constituted. It is a society, Congar insists, in which "there must be . . . a certain arrangement of powers and functions corresponding to the kind of co-operation and unity demanded by its own special nature and the well-being of its members."[1] The particular distinction of this society is that it is a "posited" reality. Specifically, its nature as "posited" rests on the fundamental claim that "[i]t is God who constructs his Church, God who calls us. . . . It is God who distributes the gifts of service . . . God who gives increase. . . . It is from Christ that the whole body is coordinated."[2] That the church possesses a hierarchical constitution flows precisely from within this essential structure of the church as a reality "given," first and foremost, from above and outside itself.[3] The hierarchical principle of authority is fundamentally a reflection of this nature of the church as institution, as a *given* reality, established by God the Father in his Son and the Holy Spirit.

---

1. Yves Congar, *The Mystery of the Church*, trans. A. V. Littledale (London: Geoffrey Chapman, 1965), 88.
2. Yves Congar, *Called to Life*, trans. William Burridge (New York: Crossroad, 1987), 89, 66.
3. Congar, *The Mystery of the Church*, 90.

This "givenness" of the church, so much emphasized within the Catholic tradition, provides what Congar refers to as an "objectivism" to faith.[4] It is because the revelation of Christ is held within a divinely given structure that there is a divine assurance that what was once given can be confidently received from one generation to the next. The grace and truth of Christ are not lost amid the weakness and fallibility of human inconsistency but are faithfully transmitted via the structures of apostolic authority, sacraments, and the *regula fidei*.

This "leaves almost intact the questions which are raised by the system of institution on the level of concrete behavior. . . . History and the facts show that the mediations not only take the necessary determined historical forms, but tend to develop in an autonomous fashion."[5] Again the historical dimension serves to concretize the intrinsic principle, the hierarchical principle, in ways that may indeed be simply relative to a particular time and place. In view of this the task at hand, so fundamental to the theological labors of Père Congar, becomes clear: a *ressourcement* regarding the hierarchical structure of the church.

Turning, then, to the question of the essential nature of the hierarchical principle of authority, we need to inquire into what, from the tradition, show themselves to be the constitutive aspects of this principle. To begin, the concept of apostolicity is absolutely foundational. Congar articulates apostolicity as a polyvalent reality in its New Testament roots in the Twelve, the apostolic succession, the collegial nature of the church's apostolicity and that of the successors to the apostles, the role of Peter and his successor within the apostolic college, and the power or *potestas* particular to the apostolic college revealed in the giving of the keys of the kingdom to Peter first and then to all the Twelve. After this discussion of apostolicity we will pose the specific question of the hierarchy's magisterial function. The nature of the hierarchy as service and ministry will need to be examined in more detail as it is a concept Congar returns to repeatedly. The sacramental nature of the hierarchical principle is to be explored first by addressing the wider sacramental reality of the church in general and then by drawing forth its significance for this principle. Finally, the nature of the *sacra potestas* found within the hierarchical principle is highlighted and clarified by a brief examination of the question of order and jurisdiction.

---

4. Yves Congar, "Institutionalized Religion," 133–53 in *The Word in History*, ed. T. Patrick Burke (New York: Sheed & Ward, 1966), 138.

5. Ibid., 135.

Clearly there is much that one might address, such as the historical development of the papacy, the nature and authority of national episcopal conferences, the concept of infallibility, and other particular hierarchical structures and theological realities pertaining to the hierarchy. The point here, however, is to speak of the various expressions of hierarchical authority insofar as they reveal the essential theological "content" of that authority.

## Aspects of the Hierarchical Principle of Authority

### Apostolicity

Within the enormous theological contribution of the French Dominican, the writings that focus on the nature of apostolicity stand out. His individual articles on this topic, as well as the frequent references to it throughout his other works, reveal the truly remarkable richness and depth of this theological reality. Apostolicity, under Congar's discerning eye, shows itself to be a polyvalent reality with significant implications for an understanding of authority under its hierarchical aspect.

In brief, the reality of the apostles or "the Twelve," apostolic succession, collegiality, and the Petrine ministry are all intermingled within the one theological reality of apostolicity. It will be important to investigate Congar's thought on each of these dimensions progressively while keeping in mind that in the end they must be held together, constituting different facets of the one reality. Rather than articulate a full theology of each of these complex realities, we will seek to glean from them Congar's understanding of the essential nature of hierarchical authority.

#### Apostolicity in general

Foundationally, apostolicity is that property of the church by which it sustains, through the course of history, the truth of the Gospel it has received from the apostles. The Gospel itself is none other than Jesus Christ, "the Reality and the Fullness of God's gift," and in light of this "[a]ll Revelation, the whole of Scripture, is relative to Jesus Christ."[6]

Apostolicity speaks of an "'authenticity' of content [and] conformity to the faith of the Apostles and the ancient Church." As Congar points out, "the theory of apostolicity had been accompanied by the fixing of the Canon of Scripture, the insistence on Tradition, and the formulation

---

6. Yves Congar, *L'Église: Une, Sainte, Catholique, et Apostolique*, Mysterium Salutis 15 (Paris: Cerf, 1970), 181–82, 196–97.

of the Apostolic Symbol."[7] Its concurrence with Scripture, tradition, and creed shows apostolicity to be essentially constituted by the faith and, further, to be that principle by which the faith is maintained in its authenticity and sustained as a living reality throughout the course of the church's life.[8]

### The apostles or "The Twelve"

Apostolicity as a theological reality is concretely rooted in and related to the apostles.[9] The apostles, in turn, draw the discussion of apostolicity back to its scriptural foundation. The word "apostle" appears seventy-nine times in the New Testament. The vast majority of these are found in Luke's gospel (six times), his Acts of the Apostles (twenty-eight times), and in the letters of St. Paul (thirty-four times).[10] Though modern exegetes disagree on whether or not Jesus himself used the term, there is nearly universal agreement that "Jesus certainly had, from among the first disciples, discerned and chosen a group of twelve" (cf. Mark 3:13-19).[11] During the course of his ministry Jesus sent the Twelve out on mission and gave them authority over unclean spirits and to heal (Mark 6:7-13; Luke 9:1-12).[12] For Luke, what distinguished this group, as illustrated in the selection of Matthias to replace Judas, is that they were associated with Jesus throughout his earthly ministry and were witnesses of the risen Lord (Acts 1:22).

"St. Luke tends to identify the apostles and the Twelve." Nonetheless, there is the fact of Paul himself, who was made an apostle "as to someone untimely born" (1 Cor 15:8); Acts applies the term to Barnabas and Paul (Acts 14:4); and it is used of those who are delegates of the church (2 Cor 8:23) or of those who possess a ministry for the building up of the church (1 Cor 12:28; Eph 4:11).[13] This is well summarized by Joseph Ratzinger (now Pope Benedict XVI): "Today exegetical research has brought forth two concepts: 'the twelve' and 'the apostles,' of which the first is older and the latter must be regarded as originating after Pentecost. Further-

---

7. Yves Congar, *Ministères et communion ecclésiale* (Paris: Cerf, 1971), 60, 69.
8. Congar, *L'Église: Une*, 190.
9. Yves Congar, *I Believe in the Holy Spirit*, trans. David Smith (New York: Seabury, 1983), 2: 39.
10. Congar, *L'Église: Une*, 183.
11. Ibid., 182. See also John P. Meier, *A Marginal Jew: Rethinking the Historical Jesus*. Vol. 3, *Companions and Competitors* (New York: Doubleday, 2001), 125–97.
12. Congar, *L'Église: Une*, 183.
13. Ibid., 183–84.

more, the two concepts were not related to each other in the beginning, but were identified only in the relatively late Lucan theology."[14]

Congar notes two points to be taken from this New Testament witness. First, the gospel accounts testify to the fact that Jesus called in a unique way a group, the Twelve, from the midst of his disciples and that he sent them out on mission with the same authority he possessed to heal and overcome evil spirits. Second, the New Testament does not provide a clear ministerial structure for the church.[15] The clarity of such a structure comes only in connection with the succession to the place of the apostles.

## Apostolic succession

With the death of the apostles and the beginning of certain doctrinal challenges to Christianity, in particular that of the Gnostics in the second century, the idea of apostolic succession emerged.[16] As early as Clement (ca. 96), in his letter to the Corinthians, the sense of the authority of Christ passing to the apostles and from the apostles to the bishops is expressed.[17] There is also the classic expression of Irenaeus (ca. 180) in his famous defense against the Gnostics, *Against All the Heresies*. "Wherefore it is incumbent to obey the presbyters who are in the Church,—those who, as I have shown, possess the succession from the apostles; those who, together with the succession of the episcopate, have received the certain gift of truth, according to the good pleasure of the Father."[18] For Congar the fundamental idea expressed here is that of "a sort of cascade of missions,"[19] beginning with the Father's sending of the Son, the Son's sending of the apostles, and the apostles establishing bishops and presbyters in the local churches.

The intrinsic link between the apostolic succession and apostolicity is found in the charism of truth, as is already made clear by Irenaeus when he speaks of bishops and presbyters "having received the certain gift of truth." "The bishops, in particular, were always selected from among the faithful being endowed with charisms, that, in particular, of

---

14. Joseph Ratzinger, "The Pastoral Implications of Episcopal Collegiality," *Concilium* 1 (New York: Paulist Press, 1964), 39–67, at 39–40. Congar himself refers to this article in "The Laity," 249 n. 21.
15. Congar, *L'Église: Une*, 184.
16. Ibid., 184–85.
17. *1 Clement* XLII.
18. Irenaeus, *Against All the Heresies* IV.26.2.
19. Congar, *L'Église: Une*, 185.

making known the truth."[20] The recognition of the "charism of truth," for Congar, illuminates the integral connection between the structure, here the hierarchical apostolate, and the action of the Holy Spirit. The Holy Spirit is the interior principle of the church, leading and guiding it in the fullness of truth. One way the Spirit does this is by raising up men filled with this charism of truth.[21] Central to the tradition, Congar insists, is that all hierarchical power is measured by the truth.[22] Here, too, he highlights the distinction between apostolicity as such and the apostolic succession. "Apostolicity in the confession of faith is grounded in the whole, believing community while apostolic succession in the strict sense is due to ministers ordained to continue the pastoral function of the Apostles."[23] The apostolic faith resides in all who believe, while the responsibility for its public proclamation and definitive definition belongs to the apostolic succession of bishops.

## Collegiality

Congar's understanding of apostolicity is very much "gathered together" within the rich concept of collegiality, toward the understanding of which he contributed much.[24] Indeed, for him "[c]ollegiality is, in its foundation, the very form of apostolicity."[25] "Collegiality," strictly speaking, "is a consequence of the existence of a college of bishops, i.e., a body of pastors responsible for a church composed of local churches."[26] It is only in this strict sense that the Second Vatican Council spoke of

---

20. Congar, *Ministères*, 67. See also Yves Congar, *Tradition and Traditions*, trans. Michael Naseby and Thomas Rainborough (Needham Heights, MA: Simon & Schuster, 1966), 177, where Congar points out that for Irenaeus "the *charisma veritatis* is not a power by which the hierarchy defines doctrine, it is the doctrine itself. . . . The bishops, by their agreement, were the sign indicating that a doctrine had always been held. . . ." See *Dei Verbum*, n. 8.

21. Cf. Congar, *The Mystery of the Church*, 161–74.

22. Congar, *Ministères*, 81, 82, 86.

23. Yves Congar, "The apostolic college, primacy and episcopal conference," *Theology Digest* 34 (Fall 1987): 211–25, at 215.

24. Cf. Yves Congar, *Blessed Is the Peace of My Church*, trans. Salvator Attanasio (Denville, NJ: Dimension Books, 1973), 74, where, in a rare display of taking credit to himself, Congar says that in his work *Lay People in the Church* he himself "restored the word 'collegiality' to currency."

25. Jean-Pierre Jossua, *Yves Congar: Theology in the Service of God's People*, trans. Mary Jocelyn (Chicago: Priory Press, 1968), 108.

26. Congar, "The apostolic college," 213.

collegiality,[27] yet there is a wider sense of this concept that Congar insists on, a sort of "collegiate spirit" that "is a fruit, an expression of the conciliarity essential to the church and to the image of the Trinity."[28] Placing the understanding of hierarchical authority within this broader sense of the word is a natural outgrowth of the Second Vatican Council's intentional description of "the church in a trinitarian light."[29]

It is necessary to examine the theological implications of Congar's analysis of collegiality, particularly in terms of this concept of apostolicity. To begin with, collegiality takes on greater clarity by turning again to the reality of the Twelve. Within the New Testament the Twelve serve theologically as the foundation not simply of the hierarchy but of the church itself.[30] This is given expression by the Second Vatican Council's document *Ad Gentes*.

> From the very beginning, the lord Jesus "called to himself those whom he desired . . . and he appointed twelve to be with him, and to be sent out to preach" (Mark 3:13). So the apostles were at the same time the seeds of the new Israel and the origin of the sacred hierarchy. Then, when once and for all, by his death and resurrection, he had achieved in himself the mysteries of our salvation and of the renewal of all things, the Lord who had received all power in heaven and on earth, founded his church as the sacrament of salvation, before being taken up into heaven. (n. 5)

There is within the concept of the Twelve a certain "mutual interiority" of the church in its leaders and the leaders in the church.[31] Here again Cyprian expresses it precisely: ". . . the bishop is in the Church and the Church is in the bishop."[32] This implies that "[t]he apostolic succession is inseparable from the apostolicity of the whole *ekklesia*." This insistence on viewing collegiality in its widest theological sense places the bishops profoundly within the church as those who "guard, profess and hand on

---

27. Though the word "collegiality" itself was never used in the conciliar documents. Rather, this reality was expressed in the phrase "college of bishops" (cf. *Christus Dominus* 4).

28. Congar, "The apostolic college," 214.

29. Yves Congar, "Autonomie et pouvoir central dans l'Église," *Irènikon* 53 (1980): 291–313, at 306. See also idem, "The apostolic college," 212–13.

30. Congar, *L'Église: Une*, 186. See Ratzinger, "The Pastoral Implications of Episcopal Collegiality," for a thorough evaluation of this reality.

31. Congar, "Autonomie et pouvoir," 304. See also idem, *L'Église: Une*, 214.

32. Cyprian, *The Letters of St. Cyprian of Carthage* 3, 121.

that which is accepted by the whole Church."[33] The "mutual interiority" of bishops and the church speaks of a certain "collegial" holding and professing of the apostolic faith.

Here it is important to indicate briefly the significance of the concept of *sobornost*, which was certainly dear to Congar.[34] The notion of *sobornost* came into the West via the emigration of Russian Orthodox theologians at the time of the Communist revolution. Though Congar thought the concept untranslatable, he would nonetheless insist that it "expresses or connotes everything that our tradition, social and political as well as theological and canonical, puts into that fine word *collegium*."[35] *Sobornost*, essentially, is "the idea of a relationship of a number of persons to a same principle of life, to a same work; a relationship through which persons were associated in such a way that each and every one of them had his part in the work, each according to his degree and resources, all being really necessary to one another, joined to one another, thus forming together a veritable transpersonal unity."[36] *Sobornost*, then, speaks of an ecclesiology that *begins* with the notion of the whole church united in faith and love rather than one that starts with the reality of hierarchical power. It does not inherently deny hierarchical power, though at times it has been employed in a polemical way, with the result that it seemed to do just that. Rather, it emphasizes that such power is not to be "considered separately from the Body."[37] The rich notion of *sobornost*, like collegiality, expresses for Congar the profound and fundamental unity that exists within the whole church in the one apostolic faith and mission. What the concept of *sobornost* adds to collegiality is the emphasis on the "collegial ontology" of the church as such.[38]

Further, collegiality underscores the succession of bishops from the apostles as itself a profound collegial reality. In this regard Congar points out the equivalency of the terms *ordo* and *collegium*. *Ordo*, in its contemporary usage, often carries the sense of a certain individualistic

---

33. Congar, *Ministères*, 66.

34. Congar's most inclusive treatment of *sobornost* is to be found in the French edition of *Lay People in the Church* (*Jalons pour une théologie du laïcat* [Paris: Cerf, 1953]), 380–94, of which a significant portion, particularly the extensive notations, is omitted from the English translation.

35. Yves Congar, *Lay People in the Church*, trans. Donald Attwater (Westminster, MD: Newman Press, 1957; repr. Westminster, MD: Christian Classics, 1985), 279, 283.

36. Ibid.

37. Congar, *Jalons pour une théologie du laïcat*, 382.

38. Congar, *L'Église: Une*, 205. See also idem, "The apostolic college," 214.

reception of the power to confect the sacraments. "However, in its ancient usage, *ordo* signifies, not a personal power possessed but the situation or the role of a minister, interdependent with others in the building of the *ekklesia*."[39] Ordination to the episcopacy is a succession from the college of apostles and insertion into the college or *ordo* of bishops.[40] This reality of an *ordo* into which a bishop is brought when ordained is precisely why the tradition has always insisted that "the witness of several neighboring bishops is required, and indeed that of the community of the faithful, in the case of an election and an ordination."[41] The bishop never stands in isolation from the full college of bishops or, indeed, from the whole of the faithful in whom the apostolic faith lives and by whom it is borne.

Here again Congar points to the New Testament use of "the Twelve" as highlighting this essentially collegial nature of the episcopacy. "[T]he Apostles themselves were not twelve individuals but 'The Twelve'; they formed a body, a college; they were organically united."[42] This indicates that it is clearly within the whole of the episcopacy as a college that care for the church and authentic proclamation of the faith are grounded.[43]

On the basis of this ancient understanding of the "collegial regime" of the church as such and the episcopacy in particular, Congar shows apostolicity and the apostolic authority of bishops to be essentially communal realities, just as the church itself is essentially a *corpus* or a communion.[44]

### The primacy of Peter and the keys

Within the apostolic college Congar identifies two poles, one of a certain *cephality* and the other of *synodality*.[45] What is significant in this distinction is the question of Peter's role in the apostolic college and its implications for Rome, the apostolic see of Peter. Having examined the *synodality* pole under the title of collegiality in the above section, I will

---

39. Congar, *Ministères*, 97.
40. Cf. Congar, *L'Église: Une*, 196, 203.
41. Yves Congar, "Reception as an Ecclesiological Reality," trans. John Griffiths, in *Concilium* 77, ed. Giuseppe Alberigo and Anton Weiler, 43–68 (New York: Herder & Herder, 1972), at 54.
42. Yves Congar, *After Nine Hundred Years* (New York: Fordham University Press, 1959), 80.
43. Congar, *L'Église: Une*, 196.
44. Cf. Congar, "The apostolic college," 213.
45. Ibid., 211. "Latin fathers and medieval writers linked *cephality* to Peter's name (Cephas) to show the special position of his successor."

turn now to a brief articulation of Congar's theological observations on this *cephality* pole.

In reflecting on the New Testament accounts Congar identifies what might be called a principle of priority or primacy given to the person of Peter. "Peter appears to us . . . as having received first and particularly that which after is given to the others." The first testimony to this priority given Peter is connected to the resurrection, "a constitutive element of the quality of an Apostle," found in Paul's first letter to the Corinthians: "[H]e appeared to Cephas, then to the Twelve" (1 Cor 15:5). The apostolic charge also demands a call and a being sent; the New Testament shows Peter to be the first so called and sent (Mark 1:16-20; Matt 4:18-22; 10:2; Luke 5:1-11). Further, Peter's name comes first in all the lists of the Twelve (Matt 10:2-4; Mark 3:16-19; Luke 6:14-16; Acts 1:13). Congar also points out the significance of Jesus' changing Peter's name from Simon. Three times such a change of name by God occurs in the Old Testament: Abram is given the name Abraham (Gen 17:5), Sarai's name is changed to Sarah (Gen 17:15), and Jacob is given the name Israel (Gen 32:29). Each of these changes contains the promise of a formation of a new people. This changing of Peter's name by the Lord, as well as the preeminence given Peter as witness of the resurrection, the first to be called and sent, and the testimony of the apostolic lists all reveal that "in the new people of God, in the church that God will build, Simon-Peter will have a role of premier solid foundation."[46]

An instance of this "priority principle" of particular significance is to be found in the giving of the keys. In Matthew 16:19 Jesus, speaking directly to Peter, entrusts the keys of the kingdom to him, saying, "I will give you the keys to the kingdom of heaven; whatever you bind on earth will be bound in heaven; and whatever you loose on earth will be loosed in heaven." Later, in Matthew 18:18, what has already been given Peter is now given as a promise to the Twelve as a whole when Jesus addresses them all, saying, "Truly, I tell you, whatever you bind on earth will be bound in heaven, and whatever you loose on earth will be loosed in heaven."[47]

---

46. Congar, *L'Église: Une*, 227–29.

47. This conferral of power for binding and loosing in Matt 18:18 is typically interpreted by biblical scholars today as a conferral of authority on the "community of disciples" as such, not simply on the Twelve. Cf. Rudolf Schnackenburg, *The Gospel of Matthew*, trans. Robert R. Barr (Grand Rapids, MI: Eerdmans, 2002), 176–78. A similar "tension" exists with the conferral of the forgiveness of sins in John 20:23, where the author of the gospel says that the disciples were gathered together (v. 19) while Thomas, "one of the twelve" (v. 24), was not with them.

Based on these two passages the tradition has followed three crucial theological lines identified by Congar. The first is that the entrusting of the keys to Peter directly follows his confession of Jesus as the messiah and Son of God.[48] This illustrates again the intrinsic link between power conferred and the authentic expression of faith.

A second point is the significance of the nature of this power as expressed in the conferral of the keys. Through the prophet Isaiah, God declares his intention to replace the master of the palace Shebna with Eliakim (Isa 22:21-22). "The keys designate . . . the power the master's lieutenant receives to manage his domain in his name and place."[49] Entrusting the keys to Peter, and later to the Twelve as a group, inaugurates a true "priesthood of pastors."[50] This priesthood, following on rabbinic interpretations of the Isaiah passage, contains a magisterial power to bind and loose the consciences of the faithful regarding matters of faith and an administrative power of excommunication for the safeguarding of the integrity of the community.[51]

Finally, the Matthean texts on the conferral of the keys, revealing the "priority principle" regarding Peter's role among the Twelve, raise the question not of a simple priority, but a primacy of Peter. Here, Congar again identifies two distinct emphases within the tradition. The first sees in the prior conferral of the keys on Peter alone a witness to the unity of the church, and in particular of the episcopacy.[52] The conferral of the keys on Peter alone before the other apostles indicates not the primacy of Peter but the unity of the episcopal ministry he symbolizes.

In Rome, however, a second emphasis was brought to bear on this note of unity in the conferral of the keys to Peter in Matthew 16:19. It was crystallized in the Carolingian period, which was marked by "a very strong sense of the universal sovereignty of Christ." All of society was one, the *respublica christiana*, encompassing the secular as well as the

---

48. Yves Congar, *The Mystery of the Temple*, trans. Reginald F. Trevett (Westminster, MD: Newman Press, 1962), 162.

49. Congar, *L'Église: Une*, 232.

50. Congar, *L'Église: de saint Augustin à l'époque moderne*, 58. Congar adds in connection to this the importance of excommunication in the life of the church from the first centuries; excommunication being an explicit expression of this "priesthood of pastors" safeguarding the integrity of the flock of Christ.

51. Congar, *L'Église: Une*, 233.

52. See Congar, "Notes sur le destin de l'idée de collégialité épiscopale en Occident au Moyen Age (VII–XVI Siècles)," 99–129 in *La Collégialité épiscopale: Histoire et théologie*, Unam Samctam 52 (Paris: Cerf, 1965), at 100. For an example of this emphasis, see Cyprian, *De Lapsis*, and *De Ecclesiae Catholicae Unitate*, 63–65; Letter 59 n. 14.

sacred domains in one organic whole. In this atmosphere the bishops of Rome began to see and describe themselves as the guardians of the unity of the whole *respublica christiana*.[53]

This same period saw the compilation of what is known as the *False Decretals* of pseudo-Isidore. Though, Congar insists, this document did not unduly exalt the power of the Roman Church, it did have a powerful influence in advancing the idea of the intrinsic requirement that the Body, the *corpus*, to be authentically one, must possess one head, one *caput*, an understanding the *Decretals* attributed to the martyr bishops of the first centuries of Christianity. Thus increasingly the view came to be held that "the body that is the church depends for her whole life on the *caput* which is the Roman Church."[54] As the Middle Ages unfolded this grand idea of universality was increasingly absorbed into the notions of order and hierarchy, ideas particularly alive to the medieval mind. Steadily the notion of the *plenitudo potestatis* of the bishop of Rome comes to be attached to the primacy of Peter, who came then to be seen less as the vicar of Peter and more as the vicar of Christ.[55]

For Congar it is a clear conclusion of the great tradition that all the apostles were given the power of the keys directly by Christ, and thereby they, as a college, had jurisdiction over the whole church.[56] It is in the nature of the church that such jurisdiction, power, and authority are found in one man, the pope, who "bodies forth" the inner unity of all things in Christ. In this way the position of the pope is viewed as being both *over* the church and decidedly *within* the church. "[Catholic theology] on the subject of the pope, does not affirm a power *over* that is not also a power *in*. The ecclesiology of pontifical power, as an 'episcopal' power qualitatively superior over the unity of the Churches and the faithful, must be expressed in union with a theology of communion."[57]

In summary, Congar's evaluation of the tradition shows that to Peter belongs not simply a priority but a primacy within the apostolic college. The giving of the keys confers pastoral power within the community of Jesus' disciples. This power, which is one of magisterium and jurisdiction, is clearly one in its source, which is Jesus Christ, and is shared equally by all

---

53. Congar, *L'Église: de saint Augustin à l'époque moderne*, 52, 61–62.
54. Ibid., 63.
55. Congar, "Notes sur le destin," 113–15.
56. Cf. Congar, *L'Église: de saint Augustin à l'époque moderne*, 58–60.
57. Yves Congar, "De la communion des Églises à une ecclésiologie de l'Église universelle," 227–60 in *L'épiscopat et l'Église universelle*, ed. Yves Congar and Bernard-Dominique Dupuy, Unam Sanctum 39 (Paris: Cerf, 1962), at 260.

the apostles. Its unity is given concrete expression in the primacy of magisterium and jurisdiction entrusted to Peter as head of the apostolic college.

### Summary of apostolicity

Apostolicity in its most general sense is that quality of the church by which God sustains it in faithfulness to the apostolic tradition, the *regula fidei*. This apostolicity is marked by a distinctively collegial spirit in that it is lived by and carried within the whole community of faith, progressing in fidelity throughout history from its origins in Christ (the *Alpha*) to its fulfillment in the *parousia* of Christ (the *Omega*).[58]

Within the people of God, Jesus established an apostolic college, specifically the Twelve, by entrusting the keys of the kingdom first to Peter and then to all the Twelve. The keys show that to the apostles was given a call and a mandate—with corresponding powers and charisms—to safeguard the authenticity of the faith (a magisterial function) and the faith community itself (a jurisdictional function).[59]

This call and mandate, as well as the corresponding powers, continue in the faith community by means of a "cascade of missions" whose principle is in God the Father's sending of the Son, the Son's sending of the apostles, and the apostles' sending of the bishops. The mandate and powers are profoundly collegial realities flowing from the college of the apostles into the *ordo* of the episcopacy.

Within the college there is a decided principle of primacy given to Peter, who is both the symbol and the guarantor of the essential unity of faith and life of the new people of God. This primacy, like the reality of apostolic succession in general, is handed on in the person of the pope, the bishop of Rome, and likewise contains the powers of magisterium and jurisdiction necessary for fulfilling the task of guarding and directing the unity of the whole church.

## Magisterium

In light of the apostolicity of the hierarchical principle of authority, the nature and role of the church's magisterium can be properly situated. Congar's efforts in this regard are notable, in particular his study focusing on the historical development of the word *magisterium* itself[60]

---

58. See Congar, *I Believe in the Holy Spirit*, 2: 39.
59. See Congar, *Sainte Église*, 183.
60. Yves Congar, "A Semantic History of the Term 'Magisterium,'" 297–313 in *Readings in Moral Theology No. 3: The Magisterium and Morality*, ed. Charles E. Curran and Richard A. McCormick (New York: Paulist Press, 1982).

and his work on the "forms" the magisterium has taken.[61] The objective here will not be to follow the historical understanding of the word and forms of the magisterium systematically —a work already done clearly and concisely by Congar himself—but to glean the theological nature of the magisterium as Congar articulates it from that history.

Though it would be anachronistic to use the word "magisterium" for the teaching function of the church in the first centuries—the meaning of the word as used today was only finally established in the eighteenth century[62]—Congar points to the foundation of the magisterial task in the apostolic mission entrusted by Christ to the apostles in Matthew 28:18-20. This foundation in "mission" will prove to be central in Congar's understanding of the very nature of the magisterium. Also in the New Testament, words such as *didaskalos* and *didaskalia* reveal the "fact" of "teaching" and a "teaching office" within the lives of the first Christian communities.[63] Behind the word magisterium are also phrases such as Irenaeus's *charisma veritatis certum*; *cathedra*, "the episcopal function, its continuity, succession, *doctrina*"[64]; and "[i]n almost all periods people have spoken of 'officium docendi.'" The word *magisterium* was used by Augustine, for whom its "first meaning refers to teaching; its second is most often reserved to God (to Christ), while men of the church have only a *ministerium*."[65]

In Congar's analysis of the magisterial function within the church he stresses its "apostolic" and "missionary" nature, which shows the "first function of the Magisterium [to be] one of witness."[66] Thus to speak of the magisterium is to speak of a *duty* and a *service*. It is the duty of the magisterium to proclaim the faith; that proclamation is its service to the faith itself and to that of the people. This again underscores the essential link within the tradition "between the magisterium and the faith of the Church."[67]

---

61. Yves Congar, "A Brief History of the Forms of the Magisterium," in *Readings in Moral Theology No. 3*, 314–31.

62. Yves Congar, "Theologians and the Magisterium in the West: From the Gregorian Reform to the Council of Trent," *Chicago Studies* 17 (1978): 210–24, at 210.

63. Congar, "A Semantic History," 297.

64. Congar, "A Brief History," 315.

65. Congar, "A Semantic History," 297, 298.

66. Yves Congar, *The Meaning of Tradition*, trans. A. N. Woodrow (New York: Hawthorn Books, 1964), 63.

67. Yves Congar, "Magisterium, Theologians, the Faithful, and the Faith," *Doctrine and Life* 31 (1981): 548–64, at 549, 552.

Congar insists that the principal character of the magisterium as mission shows its essence to lie not in defining doctrine or dogmas; rather, it is "to keep the deposit faithfully and to bear witness to its totality by respecting the balance of different parts."[68] Magisterium is here primarily "considered not as a juridical authority possessing as such a power to compel, but as a function through which the Church receives the faith inherited from the apostles."[69]

Congar, by emphasizing the "missionary" dimension of the magisterium, has given a renewed understanding of that reality from a broader reading of the tradition. The history of the church, and in particular the period of the eleventh and twelfth centuries, is decisive for how the term "magisterium" came to be understood and used. It is the development of "the schools and . . . a theological task of interpretation or systematization, of a rational type," that brought about a significant development in how the teaching office of the bishops was viewed.[70] Out of the development of the universities and scholasticism grew a distinction between a *magisterium cathedrae pastoralis* and that of a *magisterium cathedrae magistralis*. By the thirteenth century "[d]octors and universities acquired a position and a role of authority to make decisions or to call for submission" on crucial theological questions.[71] The historical fact that there existed in the church "different ways in which the Faith [was] regulated"[72] is expressed in the theological controversy surrounding Martin Luther. "In the case of Luther, there was condemnation of the theses by universities (Louvain, Paris), then preparation of a papal document (bull *Exsurge Domine*, 15.6.1520), by university documents (Cologne, Louvain) and by theologians (Eck, Cajetan)."[73] This duality of a *clavis scientiae* and a *clavis potestatis*[74] existed in various degrees of balance and tension up to the time of the French Revolution, at which time the "suppression of most faculties of theology . . . all those in France, thirteen of eighteen in Germany" brought this dynamic duality essentially to an end. The elimination of these centers of theology meant

---

68. Congar, *The Meaning of Tradition*, 64.
69. Congar, "A Brief History," 316. See also J. M. R. Tillard, *Church of Churches: The Ecclesiology of Communion*, trans. R. C. De Peaux (Collegeville, MN: Liturgical Press, 1992), 115.
70. Congar, "Theologians and the Magisterium," 212.
71. Congar, "A Brief History," 318, 319.
72. Congar, "Magisterium, Theologians," 563.
73. Congar, "A Brief History," 320.
74. Cf. Congar, *L'Église: de saint Augustin à l'époque moderne*, 47; idem, "A Semantic History," 302.

that the "problem of the 'cathedrae magistralis' [would] not arise again" as it had in the preceding centuries. When the theological faculties were restored in the nineteenth century this was done in large part by the papacy, and the faculties remained under its authority.[75]

Congar's analysis of this history identifies a significant development arising from the relationship between hierarchical authority and the "scholarly expertise" of the theologians. Because knowledge, throughout this period, increasingly gained "a value independently of power,"[76] hierarchical authority exerted its own teaching authority, its magisterium, by intervening to settle disputes. Here, Congar notes the significant distinction made by Gratian. "But there is a difference between deciding cases [*causas*] and diligently interpreting the scriptures. To decide cases learning is not enough, power, too, is needed."[77] This power to define doctrine, according to Gratian, rests with the hierarchy and, in the end, is to be preferred to theological exposition.[78]

This distinction between scholarship and teaching authority certainly represents the ancient tradition.[79] The climate within the church, however, in reaction to the Protestant Reformation and, later, the rise of rationalism in the eighteenth century, meant that this distinction "developed under the aegis of the affirmation of this authority. . . ."[80] This climate hardened the distinction between authority and scholarship, tending toward a view of authority isolated from reason and standing over faith. Within this context the important thing came to be not so much what (*quod*) was taught—the teaching itself—but the authority by which (*quo*) it was said: who is teaching.[81]

The classic distinction between the ordinary and extraordinary magisterium is helpful in showing the broader understanding of the magisterium from tradition. The ordinary magisterium is especially connected to the mission dimension of the hierarchical function: its day-to-day proclamation of the saving truths of revelation, which is certainly ac-

---

75. Congar, "A Brief History," 323.
76. Congar, "Theologians and the Magisterium," 214.
77. Aemilius Friedberg, ed., *Decretum Magistri Gratiani, Dictum* before canon I, Distinctio XX (Graz: Akademische Verlagsanstalt, 1959), col. 65. English translation by Ladislas Örsy, *The Church: Learning & Teaching* (Wilmington, DE: Michael Glazier, 1987), 68.
78. Congar, "Theologians and the Magisterium," 214–15. See also Thomas Aquinas, *Summa Theologiae*, II-II, q. 10, art. 12, c.
79. Congar, "Theologians and the Magisterium," 215.
80. Congar, "A Brief History," 322.
81. Congar, "Magisterium, Theologians," 554; idem, "A Brief History," 326.

companied by the authority of the episcopal office and the Spirit, an authority that is inherent even in the Word itself. In the extraordinary magisterium, however, a juridical aspect of this authority is added.

> When the pastoral Magisterium presents its testimony thus in the form of a "definition" or of dogmatic "canons," when it promulgates a "dogma," it endows a simple revealed truth, to which it bears witness, with a *legal* value, binding for the whole Church. It does this by exercising the *authority* which it has received to "feed" God's people, by teaching and governing it. At that precise moment, the pastors of the Church are more than witnesses, and even more than interpreters of the deposit; they do not merely state that those who accept such and such an interpretation have placed themselves outside the truth and the Church: they excommunicate them formally. In this way they exercise their power of ruling and jurisdiction.[82]

This function of the magisterium, however, is, just as the classic distinction shows, an "extraordinary" act, normally carried out when "forced to by the threat to the faith of the Church, brought about by a nascent heresy." The "ordinary" task of the magisterium remains "to keep the deposit faithfully and to bear witness" to it.[83]

The Second Vatican Council located the understanding of the magisterium within the greater tradition by recognizing as well the laity's share in Christ's prophetic function.

> Christ, the great prophet, who by the witness of his life and the power of his word, proclaimed the Father's kingdom, continues to carry out his prophetic task . . . not only through the hierarchy who teach in his name and by his power, but also through the laity whom he constitutes his witnesses and equips with an understanding of the faith and a grace of speech (see Ac 2, 17-18; Ap 19:10) precisely so that the power of the gospel may shine forth in the daily life of family and society. (*LG* 35)

*Lumen Gentium* goes on to say that the laity "[i]n accordance with the knowledge, competence or authority that they possess . . . have the right and indeed sometimes the duty to make known their opinion on matters which concern the good of the church" (*LG* 37).[84] Here, two essential

---

82. Congar, *The Meaning of Tradition*, 66.
83. Ibid., 64, 65.
84. See Congar, "Magisterium, Theologians," 555–56.

aspects of the entire Congarian synthesis on the magisterium are evident. First, the teaching function of the church is essentially related to that of Christ and, second, it is a function in which the whole people of God are engaged. The hierarchy have an added power for preserving and defining.

In summary, we see that the reality of a magisterial authority flows necessarily from the apostolic mission entrusted to the apostles for the proclamation of the Gospel. For Congar its essential task is safeguarding and handing on the faith as it has been once for all entrusted to the church by Christ through the apostles. It is by its very nature ordered to the service of the living faith, present and active in the life of the whole people of God. Faith itself, what Congar refers to as the *quod*, contains authority and demands the obedience of the disciple in the first order. That this *quod* might effectively call forth the obedience of faith, there is a *quo*, the magisterial mission that contains the necessary power and charism to fulfill that mission. Through *ordinary magisterium* it does so by proclaiming and teaching the faith. In the *extraordinary magisterium*—which Congar emphasizes is just that, extraordinary—it defines the faith in dogmas to safeguard it from error. In all cases the power connected to the magisterium's mission is intrinsically ordered to serving the faith and transmitting it authentically from one generation to the next.

### Service

"The notion that the hierarchy consists essentially in service is a theme that runs all through Christian tradition."[85] This central conviction of Père Congar, which also runs all through his theological reflection on authority, presents the justification for turning again, and in a more focused way, to the reality of hierarchical authority directed essentially to service.

Since we have already looked at Congar's analysis of authority as service in the New Testament (in chapter two), it will be adequate here simply to state his conclusion in this regard. "Jesus was not content simply to remind [people] of the spirit in which authority was to be exercised," he wrote, "or to transfer authority from the scribes and rabbis to the apostles, from the priesthood of Aaron to the ministers of the Gospel. He radically transformed the whole character and even the nature of authority."[86]

---

85. Yves Congar, *Power and Poverty*, trans. Jennifer Nicholson (Baltimore: Helicon Press, 1964), 17.
86. Ibid., 81.

The way in which Jesus transformed the nature of authority was to situate it entirely in "the spirit of the beatitudes . . . authority, in the Church, is 'not domination, does not impose itself by force, it is service, humility, unselfishness, self-sacrifice' " and entirely "relative to the living body of Christ, which is made up of the faithful."[87]

Congar moves from the scriptural testimony to that of the historical sources, where he identifies three particular terms or phrases that are used consistently in relation to authority and show that its nature is service.[88] The first of these is *praeesse-prodesse*, two words linked together in order to speak of the necessity of good works or benefits flowing from the one possessing preeminence in the church. Augustine offers the classic expression of this concept in his *City of God*. "[A] bishop who loves preeminence (*praeesse*), not good works (*non prodesse*), should understand that he is no bishop."[89] In short, positions of preeminence in the church are necessarily directed toward the good work to be produced on behalf of the whole people of God.

A second term Congar examines from history is that of *utilitas*.[90] Augustine linked *utilitas* with the word *vera*. "[W]hen Augustine uses *utilis* as a qualification of a good pastoral activity, the word has a very forceful sense: it concerns an activity that truly builds up the Church in charity."[91] Thus "we could say that on the Christian plane the common good is the salvation (that is to say the true and successful order in

---

87. Ibid., 81, 83.

88. Yves Congar, "Quelques expressions traditionnelles du service chrétien," 101–34 in *L'épiscopat et l'Église Universelle*, ed. Yves Congar and Bernard-Dominique Dupuy (Paris : Cerf, 1962), at 101–32.

89. Augustine, *City of God*, Book XIX, chap. 19. English translation by W. C. Greene, *Augustine, City of God*, LCL 6 (London: William Heineman, 1969), 203. For a further, and most direct, example of Augustine's sense of service as it relates to the episcopacy see his Sermon 340A, "At the Ordination of a Bishop," in *Sermons*, vol. 3/9, trans. Edmund Hill, ed. John E. Rotelle (Hyde Park, NY: New City Press, 1994). For instance, Augustine says there, "The man, you see, who presides over the people ought first of all to understand that he is the servant of many masters. And let him not disdain this role; let him not, I repeat, disdain to be the servant of many people, because the Lord of lords did not disdain to serve us," 295. Further, "[t]he one who enjoys his status more than the welfare and salvation of God's flock, who at this pinnacle of ministry *seeks his own advantage, not that of Jesus Christ* (Phil 2:21) [*sic*]. He's called a bishop, but he isn't a bishop; it's an empty name for him," 298. See also Thomas Aquinas, *Summa Theologiae*, II-II, q. 185, art. 1, c.

90. Congar, "Quelques expressions," 106–23.

91. Ibid., 114.

God and in creation) obtained for humanity in Jesus Christ."[92] A true or authentic good is that which is directed to the church, built up in love.[93]

A third series of terms Congar identifies as moving throughout the history of the church is *praepositus—rector—praelatus ecclesiae*. Clearly these terms designate within ecclesial history a position of pastoral authority with obligation to govern. Still, Congar points out, this authority is relative to the church, as these terms are most frequently encountered in connection with terms designating the church (i.e., *rectores ecclesiarum*, *praelati ecclesiae*). What these terms indicate, then, is that hierarchical authority is situated in relation to the ecclesial community and is not viewed in itself apart from this relation.[94]

In view of the testimony of the New Testament and that found throughout the theological tradition, Congar insists on the importance of not separating the hierarchical expression of authority from the rest of the community so that the hierarchy comes to possess "an autonomous status and value."[95] Rather, theological history testifies—and here again is encountered the ontology of grace—that it is only "within a whole people characterized by service as by its own proper form of existence that certain members are placed in a position of command which is, in the last analysis, a post of responsibility for service."[96] What is being emphasized here is the whole community as "ontologically qualified" by its nature of service and mission, out of which some are called to structure the service and mission of the whole Body of Christ.[97]

Congar points to Ephesians 4:11-12, to which he frequently has recourse,[98] to highlight the proper relationship between the hierarchical ministry and the whole Body. "The gifts he gave were that some would be apostles, some prophets, some evangelists, some pastors and teachers to equip the saints for the work of ministry, for building up the body of Christ." It is all the "saints" who are engaged in ministry, building up the Body of Christ, while certain particular ministries are raised up from within the whole to structure the task common to all.

---

92. Congar, *Blessed Is the Peace of My Church*, 60.
93. See Congar, "Quelques expressions," 119.
94. Ibid., 119, 128–29, 132.
95. Congar, *Ministères*, 34–35, 42.
96. Yves Congar, "The Church: The People of God," trans. Kathryn Sullivan, *Concilium* 1, ed. Karl Rahner and Edward Schillebeeckx, 11–37 (New York: Paulist Press, 1965), at 13.
97. Congar, *Ministères*, 39.
98. Cf. ibid.; Congar, "The Church: The People of God," 13; idem, *Christians Active in the World*, trans. P. J. Hepburne-Scott (New York: Herder & Herder, 1968), 22.

Congar emphasizes the relationship of this understanding of the hierarchical principle of authority as service to its nature as apostolic. Again, the authentic *regula fidei* is preserved within the whole Body of Christ as such, "whereas it is the pastoral *magisterium* which interprets, teaches and authentically formulates that Tradition."[99] This service to the truth of the Gospel is a result of a *charisma veritatis certum*, which the hierarchy possesses and carries out *in media ecclesiae*. The authority flowing from this charism unique to the hierarchical function within the church is directed to the building up of the Body of Christ, specifically in the truth of God's saving revelation.

To conclude this reflection on the hierarchical principle of authority in its essential nature as service, it is helpful to turn again to further comments by Congar on Ephesians 4. What is found in this passage, according to Congar, is that "the Church [is] a body alive in every part, in which the hierarchical functions of ministry are, precisely, organs of *movement*: joints, muscles, and tendons, for service. Every cell in the body is priestly, in order to offer to God the spiritual sacrifice of its own life, but the body as a whole is organized. It is also *organically* priestly, and by the will and animation of its head, our High Priest, it includes members qualified by a priesthood of service, functional, ministerial and hierarchical."[100]

Deeply characteristic of Congar's thought is the essential connection of ecclesiology and spiritual anthropology. Hierarchical authority is given as a gift of service to the church in order that the church might be built up as the living person of Christ Jesus, wholly offered to the Father, by the action of the Holy Spirit. It is the whole Body, made up of individual Christians, that is offered and offering and therefore priestly. Yet because this priesthood is only one—that of Christ himself—there is a hierarchical ordering of the Body, directed to the Body, that the Body might indeed exist in the essential unity of that one person, Jesus Christ. Hierarchical authority, in short, is directed toward spiritual anthropology, the service of building up the Body of Christ, and in this is viewed as a service entirely "relative to the living body of Christ, which is made up of the faithful."[101]

---

99. Yves Congar, *The Word and the Spirit*, trans. David Smith (San Francisco: Harper & Row, 1986), 181.

100. Yves Congar, *A Gospel Priesthood*, trans. P. J. Hepburne-Scott (New York: Herder & Herder, 1967), 96.

101. Congar, *Power and Poverty*, 83.

### *Mysterion* and *Sacramentum*

We have looked at the hierarchical principle of authority in its essential nature as apostolic, with a magisterium for authentically proclaiming and defining the faith and ordered to service. These aspects clearly reveal the functional or ministerial character of the hierarchy. To stop there, however, would neglect the essential nature of the hierarchy's place in the Christian economy. To speak of the sacrament of orders as essentially a ministry or service "conceals . . . a danger, that of dissolving the specific notion of *priesthood* into the larger reality of the *apostolate*, that one replaces a definition *of priesthood* by a description of what *priests* must do." Congar remains "convinced that one must define the priesthood by the quality authorizing a man to offer to God a sacrifice that is pleasing to him." He is further "persuaded that one is able to assume and situate all . . . under the condition of understanding well what the sacrifice of the New Testament is." In other words, "the true question is one of the original nature of the Christian cult."[102]

A full appreciation of the nature of Christian cult or worship is fundamental to understanding the nature of the hierarchical principle of authority. This places the hierarchical question within the broader sphere of the sacramentality of holy orders specifically, and its relationship more generally to the other sacraments and the nature of the church itself as sacrament.

Largely in dependence on the liturgical movement of the first half of the twentieth century, the Second Vatican Council benefited from significant theological studies on the sacramental reality.[103] These studies sought to highlight the biblical foundations of sacrament in the notion of mystery.[104] This reality of mystery, or *mysterion*, has its roots in the Old Testament, specifically in the writings of the Hellenistic period, where it carries "its profane sense, of 'secret': secret intentions, the secret design or plan of a king, of a leader of war, of a friend. In Daniel, the term is applied to divine decrees (cf. Dan 2:18, 19, 27-30, 47)." This mystery, in

---

102. Yves Congar, "Le sacerdoce du Nouveau Testament. Mission et culte," 233–56 in *Vatican II, Les prêtres. Formation, ministère et vie*, Unam Sanctam 62 (Paris: Cerf, 1968), at 242.

103. Yves Congar, *Un peuple messianique* (Paris: Cerf, 1975), 19. Particularly significant in this regard are the foundational works of Henri de Lubac, *Corpus Mysticum: L'Eucharistie et l'Eglise au moyen age*, 2d ed. (Paris: Montaigne, 1949), and Edward Schillebeeckx, *Christ the Sacrament of the Encounter with God*, rev. trans. Mark Schoof and Laurence Bright, 3d ed. (London: Sheed & Ward, 1965).

104. Ibid., 57–74. Cf. Tillard, *Church of Churches*, 45–53, for a recent study of the notion of mystery as it relates to an understanding of the nature of the church.

the gospels, is essentially linked to the kingdom of God (cf. Mark 4:11; Matt 13:11; Luke 8:10), where one sees that "the realization of the 'mystery' is inseparable from its revelation, from its knowledge and finally from its announcement."[105] For Congar this highlights the importance of seeing the sacraments not simply as ritual or sign but also as message. The content of the sacraments is "the Christ *proclaimed*." For St. Paul the mystery is the hidden plan of God for human beings and all creation, now revealed in the Christ (cf. Eph 1:9; 3:2, 5, 9; Col 1:26). It is the wisdom of God, inaccessible to human wisdom but made known in the wisdom of the cross (cf. 1 Cor 1:18-25; 2:6-8). The aspect of mystery as "manifestation" in Christ is found particularly in the captivity epistles (2 Tim 1:9-10; Titus 2:11; 3:4) where it is affirmed that "in Jesus Christ a decision, until then hidden in the eternity of God and which concerns the definitive destiny of all humanity and even all creatures, visible and invisible, has been all at once realized and manifested." Made explicit in this is the truth that "Christ is, therefore, the primary, essential and absolute sacrament of the design of grace born of the gracious love of God."[106]

The content expressed in the Greek notion of *mysterion* was taken over in Latin by the word *sacramentum* and, indeed, "[i]n Saint Augustine, *sacramentum* and *mysterium* are synonymous."[107] For Congar this renewed awareness of the basis of sacrament in the biblical notion of mystery carries the profound implication that a sacrament can again be viewed as fundamentally "an act of God having reference to the messianic work of Christ."[108] Sacrament refers to a "sign" (*sacramentum*) that is "expressive, dynamic, and realizing"[109] of the reality (*res*) that is the plan of God for humanity and all of creation contained in the mission, death, and resurrection of Christ.[110] Sacraments, in other words,

---

105. Ibid., 27–28. See also Aidan Nichols, *Yves Congar* (London: Geoffrey Chapman, 1989), 15–16, where Nichols describes the relationship between mystery and revelation in Congar's work as having "at once a *noetic* sense—a sense concerned with knowing—and a *liturgical* sense—a sense connected with the celebration of salvation. What is common to both the liturgically celebrated sacraments and the object of revelation is that, in each case, a hidden reality acts and discloses itself, while yet remaining concealed—and thus establishes a tension towards a definitive or eschatological fulfillment."

106. Ibid., 29–32.
107. Ibid., 48, 50.
108. Congar, *Ministères*, 46.
109. Congar, *Sainte Église*, 249.
110. Cf. ibid., 506; Congar, *L'Église: de saint Augustin à l'époque moderne*, 169.

are those realities that make present and effective the historical, saving action of God in Christ.

Seeing sacrament as based on this biblical notion of mystery makes it possible to understand how the church itself is the "universal sacrament of salvation," as it was called by the Second Vatican Council. "God has called together the assembly of those who look to Jesus in faith as the author of salvation and the principle of unity and peace, and he has constituted the church that it may be for one and all the visible sacrament of this saving unity" (LG 9). Congar finds it worthy of note that this sacramentality of the church is here placed within the context of *Lumen Gentium*'s discussion on the people of God. "It is the whole People of God that hears the Lord and which is the instrument of grace."[111] Again, recognition of the church as the supreme sacrament of Christ places the hierarchical principle in dynamic relationship with the whole community.

To appreciate Congar's sense of the church as sacrament it is again necessary to recall his deeply eschatological perspective on the Christian reality. Congar insists that the church occupies the "space between" Christ's ministry, death, resurrection, and ascension into heaven (Christ as Alpha) and his return in glory (Christ as Omega). "The Church is, in this space-between, the body of Christ, in which Christ lives in the world and 'completes' himself from the world's substance."[112]

The sacramental nature of the church further shows that the church is not simply created within itself but is given from outside and above itself. It is Christ who "makes" the church, specifically by means of the sacraments and the instituted ministry with the corresponding powers to effect those sacraments.[113] The episcopal and presbyteral priesthood is instituted precisely to show forth the reality that it is "Christ the Head who builds up His body."[114] The hierarchical principle, within the sacramental economy, is instituted in relation to this reality of Christ as Head of, and in this way transcendent to, the Body, the church. "[T]he profound reason for the being of the hierarchy in the Church is finally to safeguard *the unique mediation of Christ* and to make sensible and real at the same time this immense truth: in the Church, *all comes from on high*."[115] This principle shows the church to *be* not only the Body of

---

111. Congar, *Blessed Is the Peace of My Church*, 27.
112. Congar, *Lay People*, 70, 72.
113. Ibid., 165.
114. Congar, *Blessed Is the Peace of My Church*, 27. See also Walter Kasper, *Leadership in the Church*, trans. Brian McNeil (New York: Crossroad, 2003), 130–31.
115. Congar, *Sainte Église*, 218–19.

Christ (*réalité*) but also the *means* (*moyen*) through which it becomes the Body of Christ.[116]

If we return now to the nature of Christian cult or worship, we can explicate the Christian priesthood as such and explore its implications for the hierarchical principle of authority.[117] "The sacraments are only the bringing about of God's Sacrament which is the Christ, or of the 'mystery' in the Pauline sense of the word."[118] In the Eucharist in particular it is Christ himself in the offering of himself to the Father on the cross who is made sacramentally active and real. Christ is the reality (the *res*) of the sacraments. This is absolutely central to the nature of the Christian cult, which Congar refers to as the realization of the Old Testament's "prophetic program" with regard to sacrifice.[119] Within the Christian cult what is offered is not a *thing*, but a *person*, specifically Jesus Christ.[120] Here, Congar refers to Hebrews 10:5-6: "Sacrifice and offering you have not desired, but a body you have prepared for me; in burnt-offerings and sin-offerings you have taken no pleasure. Then I said, 'See, God, I have come to do your will, O God.'" It is, then, Jesus Christ who "fulfills perfectly the intention of the cult willed by God and who, beyond the whole legal system still linked to the immolation of exterior things, considered the only sacrifice that of man himself conforming his will lovingly to that of God." Congar refers to this as the Augustinian synthesis of the Eucharist,

---

116. Ibid., 252–53. See also Kasper, *Leadership in the Church*, 110.

117. Congar's framing of the question of "power" and priesthood in relation to Christian cult is well affirmed by Joseph A. Fitzmyer's commentary on Rom 15:16, where Paul describes the grace given him by God "to be a minister of Christ Jesus to the Gentiles in performing the priestly service of the gospel of God, so that the offering up of the Gentiles may be acceptable, sanctified by the holy Spirit." Fitzmyer comments: "Paul describes his role in liturgical language, using neither *diakonos*, 'servant,' as in 2 Cor 3:6, nor *oikonomos*, 'steward,' as in 1 Cor 4:1, but *leitourgos*, 'cultic minister.' In his mission to the Gentiles he sees his function to be like that of a Jewish priest serving in God's Temple. If all Christian life is to be regarded as worship paid to God (12:1), the spreading of Christ's gospel is easily compared to the role of a sacred minister in such worship. . . . Paul implies that the preaching of the word of God is a liturgical act in itself. If Clement of Rome (*Ad Cor.* 8:1) could look on the OT prophets as cultic ministers of God's grace, this can be applied even more to the apostles and prophets of the NT (cf. 11:13; 2 Cor 3:3; Phil 2:17)." Fitzmyer, "The Letter to the Romans," 830–68 in *The New Jerome Biblical Commentary*, ed. Raymond E. Brown, Joseph A. Fitzmyer, and Roland E. Murphy (Englewood Cliffs, NJ: Prentice Hall, 1990), at 866–67.

118. Congar, "Le sacerdoce," 254.

119. Cf. Hos 6:6; Amos 5:24-25; Isa 1:16-17; Micah 6:6-8.

120. Congar, "Le sacerdoce," 252.

106   *A Church Fully Engaged*

highlighting the three "senses" in which the body of Christ offered is understood. "Augustine shows that this body, the subject of sacrifice and object of Christ's priesthood, is at the same time the personal body of Christ, the communal (or 'mystical') body, that we form in him, and, making the living link of the second to the first, his sacramental or Eucharistic body."[121] Christian worship is the offering of Christ himself made in loving obedience to his Father by the action of the Holy Spirit. Christ, in offering his person, made possible the offering of all human persons to the Father. In the Eucharist what is offered is the personal body of Christ sacramentally present *and* his communal body, the faithful joined to him by baptism and Eucharist, which is the church.[122] The essential content of the Christian cult, then, is the offering to the Father of the Christ, in himself and in his Body the church.[123]

The hierarchical principle of authority can now be addressed specifically. Decisive here, for Congar, is Vatican II's clear affirmation that the fullness of the sacrament of holy orders is found in the episcopacy.[124] In declaring the episcopacy to be the "supreme priesthood" the council fathers revealed the explicit link between the power to consecrate the Eucharist and the power of governance and teaching,[125] the full expression of the connection between Christ's eucharistic body and his fellowship body, the church. This teaching of the council served as a corrective to those developments in the church, beginning decisively in the twelfth century—including absolute ordinations, private Masses, and the elaboration of treatises on the individual sacraments—that served to isolate the priesthood from the community by defining the priesthood strictly as a power to consecrate the Eucharist.[126] In the teaching of the Second Vatican Council concerning the sacramentality of the episcopacy the power to consecrate the Eucharist is intrinsically linked to the pastoral power of fashioning the people of God into Christ's Body, the church. In this way the teaching and governing functions are viewed sacramentally and in clear connection to the Eucharist, which is the end or goal of the entire ministry of the episcopacy and, by participation, the presbyterate.

---

121. Congar, *Sainte Église*, 246, 248.
122. Cf. Congar, *Lay People*, 36, where he defines the Christian as "a *fidelis*" who is "someone sacramentally incorporated in the ecclesial reality."
123. See Joseph Famerée, *L'Ecclésiologie d'Yves Congar avant Vatican II: Histoire et Église, Analyse et reprise critique* (Leuven: Leuven University Press, 1992), 302–3.
124. *Lumen Gentium* 21.
125. Congar, "Le sacerdoce," 243–44.
126. Ibid., 234. See also, Congar, *Ministères*, 35–36.

In short, it is not possible to isolate Christian cult, the Eucharist, from the building up of the Body of Christ that is the church.[127]

In summary, we see that the dynamic understanding of sacrament articulated by Congar implies a profoundly sacramental aspect in the hierarchical principle of authority. The apostles, and their successors the bishops, are given a *potestas sacra* in the command of our Lord "to do this in memory of me."[128] This power is essentially the power of Christ made present and active by the sacrament of holy orders in the bishop (and, in cooperation with him, the priest) by which Christ continues the offering of himself to the Father and draws all people into that same offering, joining their lives with his. Hierarchical authority is essentially directed to the community, to the building up of the Body of Christ. This sacramental understanding shows decisively that it is always Christ, transcending his Body, who is the principal *auctor* in the building up of this Body.[129] Authority is thus situated in the context of authentic Christian worship, the offering of the lives of the Christian faithful joined to the one Body of Christ in praise to the Father by the active presence of the Holy Spirit, working sacramentally through the hierarchical priesthood.

### Order and Jurisdiction

The discussion of the sacramental nature of hierarchical authority evokes difficult questions surrounding the nature of the *sacra potestas* within that authority. There are, at least functionally, three areas of authority typically ascribed to the hierarchy: teaching, sanctifying, and governing. What is unclear is whether this distinction is simply functional, with an essential unity underlying it, or if in fact the distinction itself is essential. Congar's writings do not contain a detailed or systematic treatment of the topic, though he alludes to it rather frequently in his more historical works. A brief look now at this issue will focus mainly on two articles by Congar written on the opposite ends of his theological career. The first is his 1933 article titled "Ordre et juridiction dans l'Église."[130] The second, written in 1983, is "Sur la trilogie: prophète—roi—prêtre."[131] Though these articles are separated by fifty years, and inevitably show a

---

127. Ibid., 256.
128. See Congar, *Lay People*, 165.
129. Cf. Congar, *Ministères*, 40.
130. This article was originally published in *Irénikon* 10 (1933): 22–31, 97–110, 243–52, 401–8, and was reprinted in *Sainte Église*, 203–37. The page numbering will be taken from the reprinted version.
131. *Revue des sciences philosophiques et théologiques* (*RSPT*) 67 (1983): 97–115.

significant evolution in thought, they provide a good sense of the direction of Congar's thought on this topic.

Joseph Ratzinger offers a helpful note on the historical basis for the distinction between order and jurisdiction: "From about the 12th century on, a distinction is made in the episcopal office between the *ordo* and *jurisdictio*, i.e., between the power of ordination and the power of governing. The power of ordination is, then, particularly related to the 'true Body of Christ' in the holy eucharist in which the priest, by virtue of the *ordo*, consecrates the bread in holy mass, while the power of jurisdiction is said to be related to 'the Mystical Body of Christ.'"[132] This distinction arose from the need to resolve the problem of the validity of the sacraments by ordained persons who had in one way or another separated themselves from the communion of the church, as well as the validity of absolute ordinations (that is, the validity of the sacramental acts of those ordained without jurisdiction).[133] At first this was simply a functional distinction, and the essential connection between the two was maintained: the power over the Mystical Body of Christ (jurisdiction) was seen as deriving from the fact that one possessed, through orders, power over the true Body of Christ (order).[134] By the thirteenth century, however, the distinction had hardened in such a way that the power of jurisdiction was viewed separately from and independent of sacramental power.[135]

Congar, in his 1963 article "Ordre et jurisdiction dans l'Église," holds rigidly to the distinction of hierarchical powers. He declares that "[o]ne generally distinguishes three powers in the Church: order, jurisdiction,

---

132. Ratzinger, "Pastoral Implications of Episcopal Collegiality," 57. Elsewhere Ratzinger says pointedly: "The most crucial event in the development of the Latin West was, I think, the increasing distinction between sacrament and jurisdiction, between liturgy and administration as such. . . . Fullness of power for the celebration of the Eucharist was no longer combined with that for administration. . . . The essential unity of Church and liturgical assembly, of Church and *communio*, was no longer evident." *Principles of Catholic Theology* (San Francisco: Ignatius Press, 1987), 254–55.

133. Cf. Eugenio Corecco, "Nature and Structure of the *Sacra Potestas* from the Point of View of Doctrine and in the New Code of Canon Law," trans. Lawrence Feingold, 190–221 in *Canon Law and Communio: Writings on the Constitutional Law of the Church* (Vatican City: Libreria Editrice Vaticana, 1999) (hereafter "Nature and Structure").

134. Cf. Congar, *L'Église: de saint Augustin à l'époque moderne*, 236.

135. Ibid., 148. Corecco, "Nature and Structure," shows the extent to which this distinction came to be drawn when he points out that in the late Middle Ages and even after the Council of Trent some bishop-princes would rule their dioceses "only in virtue of the power of jurisdiction. Without receiving episcopal consecration, they had auxiliary bishops substitute for themselves in the area of sacramental power" (p. 192).

and magisterium."[136] Fifty years later, in "Sur la trilogie," he identifies the "three powers" no longer as distinct *potestates* but as the "three competencies" or "functions" of Christ.[137] There are "in the Church, three competencies, or faculties or functions and two powers. Maybe even only one truly merits this name."[138]

If we are to appreciate the basis of Congar's ambiguity on the nature of the hierarchical power(s) we need to examine his definitions of the power of jurisdiction and the power of order.

> The power of jurisdiction or government is the power that the Church has to govern spiritually souls, to issue laws in the Christian society, to assure their execution thanks to a juridical power bolstered by a faculty of coercion. These powers belong to the Church as a social body and, although they are spiritual powers received from God as something exceptional, they make the whole Church similar to any human society juridically constituted.

The power of order is distinct from this; it gives to "the Church the charge and authority for continuing the redemptive work of Christ and for transmitting to each soul the benefits of the Passion of Christ by faith and the sacraments of faith."[139] For Congar the jurisdictional power of the hierarchy is shaped by the sacramental power of order.

In Congar's 1933 article "Ordre" the distinction between the "two powers" follows from the particular way in which each is "held" within the church. The power of order "claims and admits in the church only a power of pure ministry, instrumentality, which God uses to bring each soul into the degree of divine life and intimacy with himself that he has fixed." The power of jurisdiction, in contrast, is "formally a human power, although received from God, [which] can be handed over to the church in all the fullness of its property, in such a way that the church uses it with mastery and authority." The power of order is distinctly "sacramental" and has its effect by being the instrument of Christ's faithful and active power to bring salvation. The power of jurisdiction, however, is "a *vicarial* power received from Christ to act in his place."[140] Here one

---

136. Congar, "Ordre et juridiction dans l'Église," 203–38 in idem, *Sainte Église: Études et approches ecclésiologiques*, Unam Sanctam 41 (Paris: Cerf, 1963), at 203–4.

137. Yves Congar, "Sur la trilogie: prophète—roi—prêtre," *RSPT* 67 (1983): 107–9.

138. Ibid., 108.

139. Congar, "Ordre et juridiction," 211.

140. Ibid., 211–12, 220. See Jean-Pierre Torrell, "Yves Congar et l'Ecclésiologie de S. Thomas d'Aquin." *RSPT* 82 (1998): 201–42, esp. 225–40. Torrell contends that

notes a distinctly nonsacramental view of *vicariously* held power with which Congar takes issue throughout his later work; that view is no doubt compatible with this rigorous distinction between the power of jurisdiction and that of order.

Fifty years later Congar continues to hold this distinction, and from the same reasoning, because "[t]he two are possessed by the Church in a different manner," though the distinction is no longer so rigid. The hierarchical powers, though they can be distinguished, possess a fundamental unity based on the end of the pastoral endeavor, which is the building up of the Body of Christ.[141] In this we see the growing sense within Congar's thought of the unity of the *sacra potestas* flowing from his more profound eschatological sense and reflection on the teaching of the Second Vatican Council regarding the fullness of the sacrament of orders as existing in the episcopacy.

Congar's theological reflection tends toward the view that the essential unity of the *sacra potestas* is given in holy orders. This flows from his articulation of the sacramental nature of the hierarchical principle, as described above. In the episcopacy, as expressed in the documents of Vatican II, the power related to the eucharistic Body of Christ (*ordo*) is essentially connected to the power related to the ecclesial Body of Christ, (*jurisdiction*).[142] Congar's insistence on the ontology of grace and the nature of the church as essentially a communion of persons naturally leads to a vision of ecclesial power as unique and undivided.[143] "The question of 'powers' has been treated not long ago in the perspective of an ecclesiology of a perfect society that was . . . a hierarchology. It must be today [treated] in the perspective of an ecclesiology of communion."[144] It is to this *communio* that the *sacra potestas* is directed, whether expressed in the modality of governance or of teaching or sanctification. Though Congar was not able to clearly express the essential unity of the

---

Congar is imprecise about the nature of "secondary causality" when addressing the topic of jurisdiction in Thomas. Congar's insistence here on the nature of the power of order as a power of "mere instrumentality" seems also to lack precision regarding the full significance of the role played by the "instrument" of the divine action.

141. Congar, "Sur la trilogie," 110, 112.

142. Cf. Yves Congar, "Vision de l'Eglise chez Thomas d'Aquin," *RSPT* 44 (1960): 523–41, at 529.

143. Cf. Congar, "R. Sohm nous interroge encore," *RSPT* 57 (1973): 263–94, at 282–87.

144. Congar, "Sur la trilogie," 106. See also idem, "Bulletin d'ecclésiologie," *RSPT* 66 (1982): 87–119, at 95–97.

*potestas* entrusted to the hierarchy for the building up of the communion of the church, his theological efforts lead toward this vision.

Though this position possesses an inner coherence, it is important to note that the fundamental unity of the *sacra potestas* flowing from ordination is still a matter of theological debate. There remains the difficulty presented by certain historical realities connected with governance. For instance, bishops throughout history have often exercised jurisdictional authority upon appointment to office and before episcopal consecration. Further, within monasticism governance was often exercised by those without sacramental ordination. Today the positions, for example, of diocesan chancellor or financial officer, which can be invested with powers of governance, are being held by lay persons.[145]

Nonetheless, a reading of Congar shows that the three *munera* of teaching, governing, and sanctifying are all directed toward the one end of gathering all people into the one Body of Christ. Both jurisdiction and order serve the ontological constitution of the church, which is communion in the divine life. In the sacrament of orders the fullness of the *sacra potestas* is given to bishops. A juridical mandate, by which the church shapes its societal life, adds nothing to this power but, rather, effectively directs it to the building up of the communion of the church.

## *Defining the Hierarchical Principle of Authority*

Now that we have considered the various aspects of this principle as they appear in the writings of Père Congar, we can provide a useful and succinct definition, and by examining that definition we can summarize all that has been said in its regard. We may then conclude by indicating the significance of Congar's theological efforts regarding the hierarchical principle.

### The Hierarchical Principle of Authority

The hierarchical principle of authority is the authority of Christ, as transcendent Lord, acting sacramentally to build up the church. This he does by entrusting to the college of apostles and their successors, the college of bishops, the mission of service, with the power and charisms

---

145. Cf. Hugh Lawrence, "Ordination and Governance," 73–82 in *Authority in the Roman Catholic Church: Theory and Practice*, ed. Bernard Hoose (Burlington, VT: Ashgate, 2002). See also John Beal, "Lay People and Church Governance: Oxymoron or Opportunity," 103–29 in *Together in God's Service. Toward a Theology of Ecclesial Lay Ministry* (Washington, DC: United States Catholic Conference, 1998).

necessary for that mission, of building up the church in authentic faith and the sacraments of faith. Thus this authority contains a sacra potestas for teaching, governing, and sanctifying the people of God that serves to unite them in the unique offering of Christ to the Father by the action of the Holy Spirit.

To say that hierarchical authority is *the authority of Christ, as transcendent Lord* shows that the chief protagonist in the building up of the church is God the Father, acting in Christ his Son, by the power of the Holy Spirit. The essential purpose of the hierarchical principle in the church "is finally to safeguard *the unique mediation of Christ* and to make sensible to all times this immense truth, that in the Church, *all comes from on high.*"[146]

That hierarchical authority is Christ *acting sacramentally to build up the church* further highlights this "vertical" dimension of the church "being built up" by Christ but adds to it the "horizontal" dimension. Christ continues to abide in the church, throughout the course of history, in those structures established by him. His presence is no pure "spiritual presence" but an authentic human reality as well. The fundamental "incarnational principle" is at the heart of Christian revelation. The authority of Christ, a spiritual reality, continues to act in a "human way" throughout history by means of the *regula fidei*, the sacraments of faith, and the hierarchical ministry. In the hierarchical ministry this *sacramental* way means that it is authentically Christ acting through the mediation and instrumentality of human beings. Implicit here as well is Congar's emphasis on the historical nature of the life of the church. This historical dimension, though it does not detract from the theological reality in itself, does serve to relativize its cultural and time-specific expressions.

To say that *he does* [so] *by entrusting to the college of apostles and their successors, the college of bishops, the mission of service* roots the hierarchical principle of authority in a communion with the apostolic faith held within the whole people of God. Thus hierarchical authority is decidedly made relative to the faith and placed within the communion of the church. To possess authentic authority within the church is to embrace and proclaim the authentic faith of the church. This collegial nature of hierarchical authority excludes any individualistic or voluntaristic notions of holding and exercising authority.

Hierarchical authority as a *mission of service* encompasses all that has been said above about Congar's vision of authority as directed to an authentic spiritual anthropology and related explicitly to the Christ.

---

146. Congar, "Ordre et jurisdiction," 219; emphasis in original.

Hierarchical authority is never for the "self," but is always an act of service to the other, and most specifically to the Christ.

That this authority possesses *the power and charisms necessary for that mission, of building up the church in authentic faith and the sacraments of faith* is expressive of Congar's deep conviction that within the tradition is found a "principle of continuity" between God's saving action in Christ, accomplished once for all historically, and God's "covenantal presence" drawing the people of God throughout space and time to their faithful completion in Christ at the end of time. God abides, through the hierarchical principle, by "a covenant relation . . . to secure the unerring character of the Church (Mt 16:18), its indefectibility in that which bears specifically upon the substance of the covenant, and hence, the decisive acts which touch upon the preservation and interpretation of the deposit."[147] That this is accomplished by a power linked to charism reveals hierarchical authority's "rootedness" in the life of the community animated by the Holy Spirit.

The *sacra potestas for teaching, governing and sanctifying the people of God* is the concrete means by which God sustains this "covenant relation." The *sacra potestas* is the power specific to hierarchical authority, expressed in teaching, governing, and sanctifying, by which God assures the final building up of the church in authenticity and fullness of life.

This sacred power contained in the hierarchical principle, whether exercised in the function of teaching, governing, or sanctifying, always *serves to unite* [the people of God] *to the unique offering of Christ to the Father by the action of the Holy Spirit*. Here the essential unity of the *sacra potestas* is given expression. The fact of this unity is made explicit in Vatican II's clear teaching on the episcopacy as the fullness of the sacrament of holy orders. This recognition is a necessary consequence of viewing the proclamation of the Word and the governing of the church's life as social realities in direct continuity with its sacramental life. The unity of the *sacra potestas* further situates hierarchical authority within an understanding of the nature of Christian worship. All hierarchical authority is directed to the offering of the one sacrifice of the one High Priest, Jesus Christ. By means of the *sacra potestas* the whole people of God are made capable of joining their lives with the life of Christ in the one Body of Christ, offering praise and glory to God the Father. This is an expression of Congar's consistent emphasis on the ontology of grace. Hierarchical authority is essentially service to Christian anthropology, which is life lived in the communion of God: Father, Son, and Holy Spirit.

---

147. Congar, *Tradition and Traditions*, 312.

## Implications of Congar's Theology of the Hierarchical Principle

Congar's clear articulation of the hierarchical principle within the church is uniquely important for our day. The comments of Gerald Finnegan are helpful.

> Congar knows that today many would deny the reality of the "hierarchical fact" as a divinely given element of the Church's structure, and many more would deny even more strongly his interpretation of it as constituting a distinct sacramental priesthood. But for him the matter is clear. The existence of the "hierarchical fact" is proved by the community's recognition, from the very beginning, of a divinely constituted body of leaders first realized in the apostles and then in those chosen by them and their successors by means of the gesture of the laying on of hands.[148]

Finnegan continues by indicating the importance of the role of the hierarchy in Congar's synthesis as precisely that of showing Christ to be "in fact the author (*auctor*)" of the church's life.[149]

Hierarchical authority remains a particular "stumbling block" for persons of our own day. Certainly this is true for a number of philosophical, sociological, and historical reasons, in particular the "turn to the subject"—referred to in the conclusion to the previous chapter—and the Enlightenment philosophy of the eighteenth century. Immanuel Kant's definition of "enlightenment" is significant: "Enlightenment is man's leaving his self-caused immaturity. Immaturity is the incapacity to use one's intelligence without the guidance of another. Such immaturity is self-caused if it is not caused by lack of intelligence, but by lack of determination and courage to use one's intelligence without being guided by another. *Sapere Aude!* Have the courage to use your own intelligence! is therefore the motto of the enlightenment."[150] What is expressed here as an intellectual construct has become, in the succeeding centuries, a dominant psychological disposition in the minds of the persons of our age. Indeed, to live "without being guided by another" has become the underlying assumption persons take, often unconsciously, to be the path to authentic liberty and self-fulfillment.

---

148. Gerald F. Finnegan, SJ, "Ministerial Priesthood in Yves Congar," *Review for Religious* (July–August 1987): 523–32, at 525.

149. Ibid.

150. Carl J. Friedrich, ed. and trans., *The Philosophy of Kant: Immanuel Kant's Moral and Political Writings* (New York: Random House, 1949), 132.

How dramatically distinct from the Christian notion of "enlightenment" this truly is cannot be overstated. Jesus makes clear, in response to Peter's confession of faith, that Peter is "blessed" not based on enlightenment from "flesh and blood" but on a revelation coming from outside himself, from the "Father in heaven" (Matt 16:16-17). In the Christian tradition the source of enlightenment and "maturity" is precisely what is given "by another."

Congar was deeply aware of this "conflict" between the modern conception of fulfillment and liberty and that of Christian revelation. He saw clearly in the Enlightenment the radical "discovery of the point of view of the subject" and its implications for the church. In the world in which the church exists today, so dramatically different from the medieval world, "it is no longer institutions which make [people] Christians, but [people] who make institutions." For Congar this means that "now everything depends on individual consciences, and it is from the starting-point of the individual conscience that [the church] can hope, to some extent, to transform the institutions, the collective condition of life."[151] Congar recognized that authority simply must address the modern person from "within." This presents clear implications for the church's task.

> The future of religion depends on deep personal convictions. What is therefore necessary is to educate consciences, to educate lay apostles, [people] of faith and prayer. . . . What we need, then, is to carry out an educative work, to educate the religious conscience of our people, and first of all our own, as regards concrete facts, initiatives to be undertaken, responsibilities to be accepted. If we do not, we risk catastrophe; we shall be men who, in the hour of action, have no resource but to appeal to an authority which is absent and too far away, and is itself unable, because of its position, to provide the concrete solution. I think, then, that we are entering an age of secular Christendom, which obliges a priest to give educational activity a sort of primacy.[152]

In this analysis of the world in which Christianity finds itself today Congar's own articulation of the apostolicity and sacramentality of hierarchical authority is crucial, especially in its important recognition that the fullness of the sacrament of orders is found in the episcopacy. In this recognition the "authoritative word" proclaimed and taught is viewed in its authentic importance for the building up of the Body of Christ.

---

151. Congar, *A Gospel Priesthood*, 187, 185, 212.
152. Ibid.

Authority in relation to the sacraments (and specifically the Eucharist) demands a prior building up of individual Christians "from within" by means of the Word of God in such a way that they might be made capable of offering themselves for assimilation in the Eucharist to the saving offering of Christ on the cross to the Father.

Congar's analysis of hierarchical authority proves particularly decisive for the church of today. His articulation of the authentic tradition shows that in the church the hierarchical aspect serves as an essential reminder that the church, and indeed all humanity, finds its ultimate life in a gift that comes not of its own constructing but from outside and above. His clear insight into the nature of this authority as apostolic and sacramental serves to situate it in such a way that it may fruitfully address persons of this age by speaking a word that addresses and forms their interior consciences from within a fundamental relationship of unity flowing from the ontology of grace. Congar's analysis provides, in short, a way of understanding hierarchical authority that is both soundly based in tradition and profoundly responsive to the demands of the age.

Chapter Five

# A Trinitarian Logic of Authority

## *Introduction*

Yves Congar's enormous theological *opus*, when analyzed and brought to bear systematically on the question of ecclesial authority, yields rich insights and a profoundly constructive lens through which authority may be understood and lived within today's church. I have attempted to do this work of systematization, not inherent within Congar's work itself, while respecting the fundamental approach he takes to the study of questions of ecclesiology. It is Congar's approach that has made it necessary to articulate the reality of ecclesial authority under the dual principles of life and hierarchy, thus respecting the overall dialectical methodology of Congar's ecclesiology.

> In the measure that I advanced in the knowledge of this reality that is the Church, I better realized that one could hardly study its *structure* and not also speak of its *life*. This very distinction between life and structure appeared to me to permit the better posing of, and therefore clarification of, a large number of problems. The Church has its structure, from which it receives its constitutive elements; but, structured, it lives, and the faithful live in it, in unity. The Church is not solely a framework, a system, an institution; it is a communion.[1]

---

1. Yves Congar, *Vraie et fausse réforme dans l'Église,* Unam Sanctum 72, 2d ed. (Paris: Cerf, 1968), 7–8.

In this chapter I would like to give an overview of ecclesial authority as found within the work of Congar by drawing the two principles into a coherent whole. Relating these two principles exposes a certain weakness of Congar's use of a dialectical method. It will be necessary to identify the problems to which such a method is susceptible. Though there is this inadequacy within the overall framework of Congar's analysis of ecclesial authority, he has provided a sound foundation for and intimations of a more integral articulation of the question of authority in the church. To achieve this more integral articulation we must transpose the dialectic of hierarchy and life into a more truly trinitarian logic of authority. It is my intention to offer certain intimations toward such a trinitarian logic of authority as well.

## *Overview of Congar's Theology of Ecclesial Authority*

In a 1993 interview Congar was asked what is the essential reality of the faith, to which he responded directly: "The Resurrection. Without that, our faith would be in vain." He then went on to say, importantly, "[f]ocus on the essential allows us great freedom. I, for example, have often been described as a 'progressive.' That is absurd. I am also very conservative. I am totally on the side of the Tradition."[2] Congar found in the rigorous discipline of historical study the key to avoiding "the mistake of taking for 'tradition' that which is only recent and which has altered more than once in the course of time." The "conserving" of the church's history through study gave him a great freedom from "over-dramatizing anxieties aroused in us with evil consequence by new ideas and forms" and afforded him the liberty of finding "our true place in the present. . . ."[3] As a conservator of the tradition Congar was a theologian truly capable of advancing theological insights that serve the church with renewed vitality and the authentic authority of the Gospel in its progression through the present age into the future.

As we have already seen, one of the underlying motivations for Congar's ambition to retrieve the church's authentic tradition was his early sense of the needs facing the church in the modern world. "Everywhere we get a sense that, from the recovery of a large, rich, vital sense of the church, full of biblical and traditional vigor, much good would result in

---

2. Stefano M. Paci, "The Pope Also Obeys," *30 Days* 3 (1993): 24–29, at 29.
3. Yves Congar, "Church History as a Branch of Theology," trans. Jonathan Cavanagh, *Concilium* 57, ed. Roger Aubert, 85–96 (New York: Herder & Herder, 1970), at 88.

our ministry and for the spread of Christianity in the world."[4] As his work in this direction developed he came to the conclusion that this necessary theological *ressourcement* demanded a more fundamental retrieval. "[I]t is not only our idea and our presentation of the Church which must be renewed in its source, it is our idea of God as a *living* God, and in light of this, our idea of Faith."[5] This implies how "enormously important it is, for the truth of our relations in the church, to have very alive in the mind a trinitarian vision of God, the God in whose image we are, and of whom the church is the reflection."[6]

Over the course of more than fifty years of theological labor, the relentless search of the historical sources of the church's understanding and living of her identity allowed Congar to draw forth the multiple aspects of the church's nature which show her to be a dynamic and living reality, flowing from the dynamic, living reality of God, Father, Son, and Holy Spirit. He methodically employed the dialectic of structure and life, which runs throughout his ecclesiology, precisely as a "way" or "avenue" into the living dynamic, which is the church. Congar's methodology has been demonstrated in the previous chapters to indeed be effective in the holding together of the many significant issues surrounding the complex reality of ecclesial authority.

Specifically it underscores the essentially *theological* nature of authority by clearly showing God the Father as the chief architect who constructs the church through his "two hands," the Word and the Spirit (see Figure 1). While the *structural* side of the dialectic, an essentially christological principle, allows Congar to clearly articulate the nature of the church as a *given* reality, the *life* principle, essentially pneumatological, enables him to give clear and consistent articulation to the dynamic, organic reality of the church. Importantly, Congar's methodological approach makes it possible for him to give expression to the complex theological tradition, allowing the various distinct aspects of this tradition to interact in a dynamic whole, all in light of the rich, profound reality of the mystery of God, Father, Son, and Holy Spirit.

While firmly holding to the church's essential institutional nature as a reality profoundly established above and outside of itself by the transcendent action of God, Congar shows the reality of God's action of building

---

4. Yves Congar, "Pour une théologie de l'Église," *La Vie Spirituelle* 52 (1937): 97–99, at 98.

5. Yves Congar, "The Council in the Age of Dialogue," trans. Barry N. Rigney, *Cross Currents* (Spring 1962): 144–51, at 148.

6. Yves Congar, "La Tri-unité de Dieu et l'Église," *La Vie Spirituelle* 128/604 (1974): 687–703, at 701.

**GOD THE FATHER,**

**THROUGH HIS "TWO HANDS,"**

**THE SON AND THE SPIRIT, CONSTRUCTS**

↓

**THE CHURCH**

**People of God, Body of Christ, Temple of the Holy Spirit**

↓

| **STRUCTURE** | **LIFE** |
|---|---|
| ↓ | ↓ |
| *Christological Principle* | *Pneumatological Principle* |
| → *principle of exteriority* | → *principle of interiority* |
| → *church as "given" (donum)* | → *church as "task" (factum)* |
| ↓ | ↓ |
| **Hierarchal Principle of Authority** | **Life Principle of Authority** |
| ↓ | ↓ |
| **Aspects** | **Aspects** |
| Apostolicity | Ecclesiology of *communio* |
| → Apostles or "The Twelve" | Ontology of Grace |
| Apostolic Succession | Church and World Relationship |
| Collegiality | Charisms and Initiatives |
| Primacy of Peter and the Keys | Conciliarity |
| Magisterium | Reception and *Sensus Ecclesiae* |
| Service | |
| *Sacramentum/Mysterion* | |
| Order and Jurisdiction | |
| → *sacra potestas* | |

*Figure 1*

up the church, which takes place also very much from within, from the variety of charisms, initiatives, and the living faith of the whole people of God. The methodological use of dialectic was necessary in the climate of the pure "hierarchologies" that characterized the *De ecclesia* treatises he sought to correct. Congar was profoundly aware of two tendencies within people's perceptions of the church. There are those who see only the church's structure—the faith, sacraments of faith, and hierarchical ministry—and who therefore "have but one preoccupation: to guard everything, to reaffirm everything." Then again, there are those who possess only a dynamic view of the church and only "see the Church as called by and almost seized by the demands of the times."[7] For Congar the church must live from both perspectives. By gathering the various aspects of the church's constitution into a consistent framework of structure and life, always pointing to the essential interaction of the two principles, he provides an explicit theological framework that serves to hold these two perspectives in balance.

In short, the French Dominican's methodological dialectic of structure and life provided the means by which to articulate the central theological realities of eschatology, pneumatology, and anthropology forcefully in relationship to questions of ecclesiology. In this way ecclesial authority is shown to be a profoundly theological reality in which God the Father gathers his people into the one Body of Christ by the action of the Holy Spirit.

## The Inadequacy of the Dialectical Method

As Congar's thought developed he expressed certain misgivings about an overly rigid application of a dialectical approach to questions of ecclesiology. To distinguish too firmly between structure and life tends to isolate the various aspects of the church one from the other. "My intention [in employing a dialectical way of speaking] was to call attention to the truth and importance of the mission of the Holy Spirit as something more than a simple replacement for Christ. I worked, however, too exclusively in a context of dualism and made too radical a distinction between the institution as derived from Christ and free interventions on the part of the Spirit."[8]

---

7. Yves Congar, "How Christian Is the Christian Church?" trans. Matthias Craddock, *Listening* 2 (Spring 1967): 92–102, at 95, 96.
8. Yves Congar, *I Believe in the Holy Spirit*, trans. David Smith (New York: Seabury, 1983), 2: 1l.

A strict dialectic is susceptible to isolating certain aspects from each other and potentially setting up opposition where there is mutuality and interdependence. The French Thomist Jean-Pierre Torrell, in his own analysis of Congar's interpretation of St. Thomas's ecclesiology, contends that Congar seems at times to oppose the internal communion of the church to its external structure.[9] In light of his understanding of authority the two principles can certainly lend themselves to a clergy/laity opposition and a Spirit/hierarchy contrast.

Perhaps more significant is the question of the effectiveness of a dialectical method for properly articulating the nature of authority as a united, harmonious reality. It is necessary to ask whether in his attempt to effectively restore the proper primacy of the authentic authority flowing from the very life of the whole people of God engaged in the living out of the faith he has done so in an integral way, such that all the aspects of authority are held in balance and viewed from within their proper relationship.

It seems that Congar's dialectic of hierarchy and life is susceptible to several profound ambiguities and dualisms. For instance, relating the hierarchical principle to the christological dynamic in the church begs the question of the relationship of charism and initiatives to the foundational work of Christ in establishing the church. Do not initiatives frequently serve to prophetically call the church to a more dramatic and authentic embrace, in deeper purity, of its foundations in Christ? Further, relating the life principle of authority to the pneumatological dynamic may lead one to envision an opposition between the "established order of things" and the "truly new and vital." Is it not the case that the Father acts by means of his Holy Spirit in the hierarchy to make the Gospel always "new and vital" to every age, in every place? More fundamental, how is it possible to speak of charisms in any way other than as part of the very constitution of the church, as an aspect of its "givenness"? Certainly Congar's dialectical methodology opens itself to questions and ambiguities along these lines.

Awareness of the limitations of speaking dialectically never led Congar to abandon its use altogether. It is certainly true that his growing sense of a dynamic understanding of the trinitarian God, flowing from his increasing interest in pneumatology, encouraged a clearer sense of the church as a *communio* and in this sense provided a more integrated synthesis than did the pure dialectic of structure and life. Nevertheless,

---

9. Jean-Pierre Torrell, "Yves Congar et l'ecclésiologie de saint Thomas d'Aquin," *RSPT* 82 (1998): 201–42, at 221 n. 74.

he never achieved a full trinitarian synthesis and therefore continued to rely on a dialectical dualism in articulating his ecclesiology.

## Toward a Trinitarian Synthesis of Ecclesial Authority

In order to obtain a more ample appreciation of the implications of Congar's contributions to the question of authority in the church it is necessary to transpose his insights, articulated, as we have said, by means of a dialectical method, into a more authentic trinitarian logic. This can be aided by a consideration of the trinitarian pneumatology of the Benedictine Kilian McDonnell. McDonnell's approach to trinitarian theology, I am convinced, provides a sound framework for a richer expression of Congar's theological insights on authority in the church.

McDonnell proposes a trinitarian pneumatology, that is, one explicitly grounded in the Trinity and thereby shedding light on the understanding of the Trinity. Pneumatology must be so grounded because "[t]he Trinitarian mystery is the ultimate reality and the absolute hermeneutic."[10] When pneumatology and Christology are not maintained within the trinitarian dynamic, McDonnell insists, "they lose their primary location."[11] Both pneumatology and Christology demand a "specifically Trinitarian logic" by which both can be understood in an authentically Christian way. The Trinity must serve a "control function" in any specific discussion of either the Spirit or the Word, so that the one necessarily informs the other.[12]

When "[p]neumatology is taken as the point of departure for trinitarian reflection,"[13] it is both grounded in the Trinity and serves to enlighten our understanding of the Trinity. It does so, according to McDonnell, because the Spirit is the "sole possibility of any knowledge of the Father and the Son . . . [and] the locus of entry into the Christological and Trinitarian mystery." Along this same line McDonnell speaks of the Spirit as "the universal horizon determining the interpretation of all reality,"

---

10. Kilian McDonnell, "A Trinitarian Theology of the Holy Spirit?" *Theological Studies* 46 (1985): 191–227, at 206.
11. Kilian McDonnell, *The Other Hand of God: The Holy Spirit as the Universal Touch and Goal* (Collegeville, MN: Liturgical Press, 2003), 3.
12. McDonnell, "Trinitarian Theology," 208, 193.
13. Kilian McDonnell, "A Response to Bernd Jochen Hilberath," 295–301 in *Advents of the Spirit*, ed. Bradford E. Hinze and D. Lyle Dabney (Milwaukee, WI: Marquette University Press, 2001), at 295.

"the teaching subject, not the object taught,"[14] "a principle of identity,"[15] "a way of knowing" that gives "proportionality." All of this is to say that "pneumatology is to theology what epistemology is to philosophy . . . [it] determines the 'rules' for speaking about God."[16]

The Holy Spirit accomplishes this "epistemological role" by what McDonnell calls the Spirit's "touch function" or, more frequently, "contact function."[17] "God reaches through the Son, in the Spirit, to touch and transform the church and the world, and to lead them in the Spirit, through Christ, back to the Father."[18] By this "contact function" the Spirit acts as the "turning around point" in "the circular movement" of the saving economy initiated by the Father in the missions of Word and Spirit, that "point" at which "church and world are caught up into trinitarian life."[19]

McDonnell's way of speaking here of the Holy Spirit is clearly economical rather than ontological. Instead of employing philosophy in an attempt to articulate the nature of God in himself, One and Three, he takes his lead from the New Testament texts and patristic authors, which speak of the experience of the Son and the Spirit in the history of salvation. As McDonnell points out, however, for "Thomas Aquinas, a mission includes an eternal procession with something added, namely, a temporal effect."

> It is a given in trinitarian theology that each of the divine persons communicates the divine personhood to us freely, gratuitously, in a proper personal particularity and diversity unrepeated in the other two persons. The threefoldness of this self-communication is not to be understood as a merely verbally distinct communication. . . . In salvation history the distinction of this self-communication is "real."[20]

This draws us into the complex history of the theological formulation of the term *person* as applied to the Father, Son, and Holy Spirit. It will suffice here to offer a general indication of its significance. Joseph Ratzinger, in his article addressing the theological foundations of the notion

---

14. McDonnell, "Trinitarian Theology," 220, 212, 218.
15. McDonnell, *The Other Hand of God*, 193.
16. McDonnell, "Trinitarian Theology," 223, 222, 217.
17. McDonnell, *The Other Hand of God*, 110.
18. McDonnell, "Response," 298–99.
19. McDonnell, *The Other Hand of God*, 95, 103.
20. Ibid., 82, 199.

of person, says forcefully that when the term "person" is situated within the trinitarian dynamic it does not imply "a substance that closes itself in itself, but the phenomenon of complete relativity, which is, of course, realized in its entirety only in the one who is God, but which indicates the direction of all personal being."[21] The theological notion of person reveals the centrality of the concept of relation in God. In God relation is not accidental, but substantial. The persons in God are "subsisting relations" identical with the essence of God. As St. Thomas says clearly, "Relation really existing in God is really the same as His essence."[22] Because the Father is really related as Father to the Son, the Father is in fact distinctly personal (as the Son is distinctly personal because of the substantial reality of his relation as Son to the Father).[23] The notion of relation contains within itself both unity and diversity. For there to be relation there must exist at least two distinct subjects—subsisting relations. Relation simultaneously speaks of the unity or, better, the communion that grounds the diverse subjects. Within the economy of salvation, according to McDonnell, "[t]he three self-communications are the self-communication of the one God in the three relative ways in which God subsists."[24]

For McDonnell it is this "trinitarian rhythm"[25] of the divine relatedness, in which the absolute unity of the Godhead and distinctiveness of persons is maintained, that must be part of any discussion of the divine persons.[26] The notion of relation provides a means for speaking of both distinction of persons—Father, Son, and Holy Spirit—and absolute unity of divinity. Relation opens into the language of communion (*koinonia*).[27]

How to give articulation to the relations, however, is a perennial question of trinitarian theology. Again, speaking from the point of view of the economy of salvation, McDonnell says, "While insisting on the 'real' distinction between the two missions of the Word and Spirit, there is danger of conceiving them as two foci at the ends of an ellipse, thus:

---

21. Joseph Ratzinger, "Concerning the notion of person in theology," *Communio* 17 (Fall 1990): 439–545, at 445.
22. See *Summa Theologiae* I, q. 28, art. 2.
23. See Gilles Emery, "Essentialism or Personalism in the Treatise on God in Saint Thomas Aquinas?" trans. Matthew Levering, *Thomist* 64 (2000): 521–63, at 535. See Yves Congar, "La Tri-unité de Dieu et l'Église," 693.
24. McDonnell, "Trinitarian Theology," 209.
25. McDonnell, *The Other Hand of God*, 92.
26. See McDonnell, "Trinitarian Theology," 211.
27. McDonnell, *The Other Hand of God*, 106, 135.

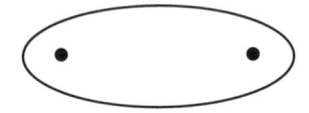

[Figure 2]

Such a conception . . . might lead to a kind of economic tritheism." This tendency can be seen in the Western theological tradition's inclination to take the Lukan Pentecost event as the "point of departure" for its pneumatology. "If pneumatology takes its point of departure only from the Pentecost event, the whole previous history is impoverished."[28] "First, it gives the impression that the Spirit was not operative before the day of Pentecost, in the people of Israel, and in the person and ministry of Jesus. Second, it adds the Spirit to an already existing body constituted in the first moment by Christ and only in a second moment vivified by the Spirit."[29] The New Testament accounts that envision the Spirit as dependant on Christ—"the mission of the Spirit is to make effective the work of Christ and to glorify Christ" (cf. John 14:26; 15:26; 16:7, 14)—must be balanced by the accounts that see the Spirit "out before" the Christ. "Through the prophets the Spirit announces the coming of Christ (Luke 24:27). The Spirit overshadows Mary (Luke 1:35; Matt 1:20), the Holy Spirit comes down on Christ in the Jordan and is the power of his ministry (Matt 3:16; Mark 1:12; Luke 3:22) . . . the Spirit (together with the Father) is the power of the resurrection." In short, pneumatology dependent on Christology must find its complement in a Christology dependant on pneumatology.[30]

What is of central importance, McDonnell insists, is the recognition that there exists only one unique economy of salvation "constituted by the missions of the Son and the Spirit, each of the missions being present and active at the interior of the other." What is to be emphasized here is that there can be no setting in opposition of these two missions, as if by placing an emphasis on pneumatology one might displace the Christ from the center of the Gospel proclamation. "The Son and the Spirit do not stand 'alongside' each other, or parallel to one another."[31]

To articulate the distinction between the missions of the Son and the Spirit McDonnell enlists the vocabulary of the Orthodox theologian Nikos

---

28. Ibid., 199–200, 60.
29. Ibid., 198.
30. Ibid., 83–84, 110, 193.
31. Ibid., 193, 227.

Nissiotis, who says that the Spirit is the "How" of the gospel while the Son is the "What."[32] To refer to Christ as the "what" is to highlight his saving mission as the "material center" of the Gospel. This is fundamental, according to McDonnell, because "neither the NT nor the theological tradition makes the Holy Spirit the central content of the gospel or the principal topic of theological reflection."[33] Still, this "material center" "is formed and informed by the Spirit," which is what is meant by calling the Spirit the "how." There is with the Spirit what McDonnell refers to as a "divine immediacy." It is in the Spirit, acting as the "how," that "the 'what' [Jesus Christ] is effected in history." While the objective content of the saving mystery is the life, death, and resurrection of Christ, this one, unique mystery is "operative and effective only in the mission of the Spirit ('through Christ in the Spirit')."[34] In light of this it must be emphasized again that there can be no "positing of two centers" (as in Figure 2) in which these missions are viewed as existing side by side or one following from another.[35] Rather, they exist in a *perichoretic* fashion—"the interpenetrating dance of the persons of the Son and the Spirit—the mutual interpenetrating of their missions, equal missions that remain unmixed and without confusion." The Spirit and the Son both occupy the same "space" at the heart of the saving plan of God the Father, related as the teaching subject—the "how"—to the object taught—the "what."[36]

To summarize, McDonnell's trinitarian pneumatology clearly demonstrates the necessary "trinitarian logic" that must underlie all pneumatology and Christology. He shows the necessity of seeing the missions of the Son and the Spirit in their full equality, both existing at the "center" of the saving plan of God the Father. This essential equality of mission, however, does not obscure their distinctiveness. The mission of the Son is the material object of the Gospel, or the "what," while the mission of the Spirit serves an epistemological function as the mediation of the saving work of the mediator, or the "how." Both the source and the end of the two missions are identical, that is, the Father. Indeed, it is the very intent of the missions to draw humanity into the very life of the divine Trinity, doing so in an utterly trinitarian way. "The Spirit operates as the

---

32. Ibid., 88 n. 15.
33. Ibid., 212.
34. McDonnell, *The Other Hand of God*, 227, 114, 210.
35. McDonnell, "Trinitarian Theology," 212.
36. McDonnell, *The Other Hand of God*, 87, 218.

reality of the exalted Son, not alongside Christ but in Christ, in movement from the Father and back to the Father."[37]

## *Transposing Congar's Dialectic into a Fuller Trinitarian Logic*

Kilian McDonnell's trinitarian pneumatology yields three fundamental theological principles that can be effectively applied to the systematic work done on Congar's treatment of ecclesial authority. Foundationally, McDonnell expresses the necessity for a "specifically trinitarian logic" that must be present at the interior of any theological question. Specifically, his trinitarian pneumatology shows the necessity of allowing the trinitarian doctrine to serve a "control function" in the very way ecclesial authority is conceived. Importantly, this "control function" of trinitarian theology is not merely an exemplar or a heuristic model for speaking of authority. Authority in the church is the authority of God acting through the instrumentality of human beings. By its very nature, then, ecclesial authority must possess the particular trinitarian "movement" that is from the Father through the Son in the Spirit. This movement is unique and undivided while at the same moment dynamically effected in the diversity of the three divine persons. Congar might describe this trinitarian movement as the "doxological movement." "To you, Father, through Jesus Christ, in the unity of the Holy Spirit, all honor and all glory. The Father is the end, as he is the absolute Source; the Christ-Son is our Priest and Mediator; the Spirit makes us the temple of this spiritual cult."[38] In light of this, ecclesial authority must be lived and given concrete forms such that its fundamental unity flowing from the Father and, at the same moment, its dynamism of diversity of persons and functions are given faithful expression in the life of the whole people of God.

Second, McDonnell clearly brings out the theological principle that the essential singularity of the divine economy necessitates the envisioning of the two missions of the Son and the Spirit in a way that does not separate the two, as if they stand side by side or in a temporal succession. The two missions exist in a relationship of mutual interiority. There can be no discussion of the activity of the Son that is not accompanied by the presence of the Holy Spirit. The action of the Spirit, in turn, must always be expressed "directionally" as flowing from and moving toward

---

37. Ibid., 119.
38. Yves Congar, *Esprit de l'homme, Esprit de Dieu* (Paris: Cerf, 1983), 42–43.

the Son and, ultimately, the Father. This mutual interiority of the divine missions possesses enormous implications for the way in which the hierarchical and life principles of authority must be envisioned. Both the Son and the Spirit exist at the center of each principle, highlighting the one same source and end of each, which is God the Father. There is only one saving economy, the fulfillment of which is an accomplishment of the one authority of God the Father.

Finally, by showing that the Spirit acts, economically, as the "contact" or "touch function" within the economy of salvation, McDonnell expresses the reality of the distinctive persons of the Son and the Spirit while at the same time establishing this "distinctiveness" radically within the trinitarian rhythm. As the Spirit is active in the mission of the Son, so too the Spirit is active in the whole people of God, uniting all things in the Son, to the glory and honor of the Father. The Spirit works at the interior of the hierarchy, making it effective in the proclamation and administration of the grace of Jesus Christ. The same Spirit is active at the interior of the life principle, conforming the whole people of God to the Christ. Both principles of authority are radically related equally to the Son and the Spirit. They are so related in a dynamically trinitarian way. Authority, which is radically one in its source and goal, is actively communicated to the whole people of God by the Spirit so that all creation might be drawn into union with the Son unto the Father.

The essential difficulty of Congar's dialectic between structure and life, resulting in the dialectic between hierarchy and life, is that it fails to place the various and certainly distinct aspects of the church within an authentic trinitarian dynamic. In his attempt to highlight the very real influence of those aspects of the life of the church outside the hierarchy, Congar's reliance on a dialectical methodology forces him to speak by way of distinction and contrast. While this method does indeed reveal the true diversity that exists in various aspects of the church, it threatens to diminish the essential unity of the divine economy. The central deficiency of Congar's analysis is found in the inability of a dialectical methodology to articulate the trinitarian logic of the church. Through its emphasis on two very real and distinct aspects of the ecclesial reality, the dialectical methodology forces opposition and separation on a reality that ought to show forth, as we might say, the harmony that flows from distinctiveness working in concert from one same musical score (the economy of salvation).

The implications of transposing Congar's dialectical methodology to a trinitarian logic can be concretely demonstrated by turning briefly again to the nature of the *charismata*. In an analysis of Paul's teaching

130  *A Church Fully Engaged*

to the church at Corinth (1 Cor 12:4-6), where Paul "is dealing with the underlying unity in the diversity of the charisms," McDonnell articulates what can be referred to as the directionality of the Spirit working by way of the charisms that progress "from the charism of the Spirit to the service of Christ to the ultimate origin and creative force, God."[39] Here, charisms are viewed as "the concrete way in which the Spirit" is active in constructing the Body of Christ to the honor and glory of God the Father.[40] Such a view of charisms underscores the truth that "[t]here is no passive membership in the body of Christ. Every Christian stands equipped and ready for service."[41] The view of charisms as the concrete expression of the "touch" of the Spirit, through which the Body of Christ is built up to the glory of God, underlines the truth of Leonardo Boff's claim that "[a]ll charisms, not only some of them, are constitutive of the Church."[42]

That all charisms in general are constitutive of the church does not imply, according to Ernst Käsemann's interpretation of Paul's theology of charisms, a flat egalitarianism. "Ecclesiastical egalitarianism is . . . ruled out of court [in the theology of St. Paul]. . . . There is differentiation in the divine generosity, whether in the order of creation or of redemption. Equality is not for Paul a principle of Church order."[43] It is necessary, when speaking of the charisms, to recognize the presence of an "order" to the charisms. "[T]here is obviously a hierarchy among them, according to the needs of the Church. There are some more necessary charisms."[44] Clearly, one can speak of the hierarchy itself as imbued with charismatic character.

> For it is evident that ultimately speaking the gifts of the Spirit can only be regulated by a gift of the Spirit. In other words any attempt to regard the official and the charismatic elements as simply opposed to one another would be totally at variance with the real situation. It is perfectly reasonable to suppose that some of the charismata as such are destined for the official functionaries of the Church such

---

39. McDonnell, *The Other Hand of God*, 93.
40. Leonardo Boff, *Church: Charism & Power: Liberation Theology and the Institutional Church*, trans. John W. Diercksmeier (New York: Crossroad, 1985), 159. See also Ernst Käsemann, *Essays on New Testament Themes*, trans. W. J. Montague (London: SCM Press, 1964), 73.
41. Käsemann, *Essays*, 73.
42. Boff, *Church: Charism & Power*, 160.
43. Käsemann, *Essays*, 76.
44. Boff, *Church: Charism & Power*, 159.

that without them these functionaries could not rightly perform their duties.[45]

This expresses the mutual interiority of the missions of the Son and the Spirit found analogously in the church: the hierarchical and life principles occupy the one same center, which is the church built up into the Body of Christ, without either charism losing its distinctive functions, a distinction found in the multiplicity of gifts as the concrete expression of the active presence of the Holy Spirit. In short, the charisms—of the hierarchical or life variety—are the concrete expressions of the Holy Spirit communicating the authority of the Father for the building up of the Body of Christ.

Within a full trinitarian logic, ecclesial authority is envisioned in the essential unity grounded in its ultimate source and goal, the God and Father of all. The direction or aim of the Father's authority is the building up of Christians as the various stones of the one Temple, the distinct parts of the one Body. Everywhere, every way this "building up process" is accomplished, it is done by the one authority of the Father who communicates his authority to his people in the Holy Spirit, drawing them through Christ to himself.

This trinitarian logic underscores the essential unity of ecclesial authority while honoring the diversity of functions and roles that make up an authentic communion of persons. The German theologian Michael Welker writes: "the unity of the body [of Christ] that arises consists in the interplay of a differentiated diversity that cannot be reduced to a simple unity (1 Cor 12:14ff.)."[46] All the diverse aspects of the hierarchical principle and the life principle within the Congarian framework, as articulated in chapters two and three, continue in their distinction and diversity. The trinitarian logic, however, overcomes the opposition and false tension created within a dialectical methodology by placing them, in all their diversity, within the one, unique, trinitarian rhythm, as aspects of the one authority of God the Father communicated through Christ in the Holy Spirit and now communicated by the Holy Spirit (expressly as charisms) for the building up of the Body of Christ to the glory of God the Father.

---

45. Karl Rahner, "Observations on the Factor of the Charismatic in the Church," trans. David Bourke, 81–97 in Rahner, *Theological Investigations* 12 (New York: Crossroad, 1974), at 86.

46. Michael Welker, *God the Spirit*, trans. John F. Hoffmeyer (Minneapolis: Fortress Press, 1994), 23.

Firmly grounded within the Trinity, the hierarchical and life principles are both decisively rooted in the mission of the Son and therefore equally correspond to the "structure," the foundation of the church. It is impossible to see any separation between the aspects that flow from the life principle of authority and the essential, saving mission, death, and resurrection of Christ in the founding of the church. Charisms and initiatives, reception and the *sensus ecclesiae*, councils and mission to the world, all relate to the proclamation and bringing forth of the kingdom of God. All the aspects of the life principle of authority have as their source and aim the one same mission of the Christ. Further, both the hierarchical and life principles are equally imbued with the Spirit who enlivens and animates them in the diverse ways in which they share in the construction of the church, the people of God, specifically demonstrating the impossibility of envisioning the hierarchical principle of authority apart from the animating action of the Holy Spirit. Apostolicity, magisterium, service to the Body of Christ, its sacramental nature, and the *sacra potestas* found in order and jurisdiction exist within and are made effective by the action of the Holy Spirit.

A trinitarian logic, applied to ecclesial authority, transposes the authentic differences in the roles of the hierarchy and the lay faithful by situating them in an authentic relationship of a communion of persons marked, as in the Trinity, by the call to love, generosity, and receptivity. Authority within the church is entirely of God, communicated in diversely rich ways to the whole people of God, for the one aim of drawing all who "were once estranged" from him into the reconciliation achieved for us by the death of Christ so that all may be presented to God "holy and blameless and irreproachable" (Col 1:21-22). Just as there is a certain order (*taxis*) in the Godhead, authority within the church possesses an order, the reality of which enables, and indeed demands, the existence of authentic diversity within which a true communion of love and reciprocity can develop. Within a trinitarian framework, unity demands multiplicity and reveals the true nature of living life in God as the exchange of gifts in love from which unity, *communio*, arises. A trinitarian logic of authority demands that all within the church, as Timothy Radcliffe puts it, "acknowledge and respect the authority that each brother [and sister] has, and refuse to absolutise any single form of authority."[47]

---

47. Timothy Radcliffe, *Sing a New Song: The Christian Vocation* (Springfield, IL: Templegate, 1999), 92.

## Conclusion

Père Congar's life project of restoring a more richly biblical, more deeply traditional and vital conception of the church led him on a profound journey of inquiry into the historical sources of the church's self-understanding and the actual practice of its ecclesial life. His historical survey of these sources led him to the conviction that in order to speak authentically of the nature of the church one must in some way give expression to its actual life beyond its hierarchical dimensions. He frequently engaged a dialectical methodology that enabled him to highlight the two poles of the church, its structure and its life, its nature as a reality given and one that is at the same time a task to be lived.

This dialectic allowed Congar to express the full spectrum of God's saving action in the life of the church. By highlighting the nature of the church under the rubric of a life principle alongside the hierarchical aspect of the church, he was able to speak of the church as a communion of persons, to show the essential significance of the ontology of grace, to give expression to the church's missionary dimension toward the world, and to highlight the effective reality of charisms and initiatives, councils, reception, and the *sensus ecclesiae* as means by which God acts to build up his church. In doing so Congar laid the theological groundwork that has made it impossible today to conceive of the saving activity of God—the authority of God—as limited to the hierarchical domain.

This fundamental accomplishment of illuminating the understanding of the church, with all the rich diversity of its tradition, by means of the dialectic of structure and life accentuates the need to speak in a vital, theological way of the church as a reality living as the image of God who is a Trinity of persons. There is, in other words, a crucial "interchange" throughout the work of Congar between theology strictly speaking and his ecclesiological understanding. The need to accentuate the life principle, in all its various historical manifestations, is deeply connected to Congar's growing awareness of the need for a renewal of pneumatology within theology. Indeed, he became utterly convinced that the building up of the church can only be conceived as an act accomplished in a trinitarian way: by the two hands—the Son and the Spirit—of the Father. Because of this he spoke of the structure and hierarchical principle of the church as corresponding to the saving mission of Christ the Son presently acting from outside and above the church, and the various aspects of the life principle as the ways in which the Spirit continues to work from within the church. In so doing Congar articulated a truly dynamic understanding of God's action within all members of the church while still giving due weight to the truly distinct ways in which God does so act.

The dialectical methodology Congar employed, though effective in bringing the rich theological tradition into a clear and coherent whole, ultimately does not reach a truly full theological synthesis. For a genuinely theological understanding of ecclesial authority the dialectical method must be transposed to a fully trinitarian logic. The distinction and opposition created by a dialectical method are contrary to the very nature of the Trinity. A trinitarian logic replaces distinction by diversity and opposition, the mutual giving and receiving of the diverse charisms and functions in the communion of persons that is the church.

Ecclesial authority is therefore the authority of God the Father made present and concretely active in the life of the church in the Holy Spirit, expressed in charisms of a hierarchical and a life variety, for the building of the Temple of the Holy Spirit, the Body of Christ.

# Conclusion

## Introduction

Yves Congar sought throughout his theological work to move the church's self-presentation beyond the mere "hierarchologies" of post-Tridentine ecclesiology to the vital, organic reality he knew it to be, both theologically and personally. The retrieval of the church's authentic tradition, and in particular the biblical and patristic testimony, was most significant. Throughout his long theological journey he gained profound perspective on the inherent difficulty met by concepts and ideas once they are proposed. In reflecting on the crisis the church faced following the Second Vatican Council some twenty years after that remarkable event he offered this very circumspect observation:

> You will know that there are sixteen documents [of the Second Vatican Council]. . . . These are texts, i.e. collections of ideas. But the ideas still have to be applied in a specific way. Obviously these ideas themselves have a dynamic of their own. And I believe that the Council really does have a dynamism in this sphere. The fact that some of the ideas may perhaps have been abused does not mean that there was not a real vitality in the Council. But it would be dangerous to think that the composition of texts was all that there was to it. At this point in a way I am making a criticism of myself, since this is a tendency that I can note in my own life: I have often worked as if once one has put forward ideas, that's that. But that is not true: the ideas then have to be put into practice.[1]

---

1. Yves Congar, *Fifty Years of Catholic Theology: Conversations with Yves Congar*, ed. Bernard Lauret, trans. John Bowden (Philadelphia: Fortress Press, 1988), 6.

Congar's self-critique is significant and suggests a certain caution that ought to be exercised in drawing conclusions from this present study of ecclesial authority. What has been examined here, in large measure, is a set of "ideas" gleaned from the tradition concerning ecclesial authority. Their concrete application will be neither self-evident nor automatic.

Congar's introspection, however, should not be interpreted as a dismissal of either the foundational importance or the authentic dynamic of ideas. Ladislas Örsy stresses that "we need a correct vision before we can undertake a prudent action—if we do otherwise, we shall end up in an erratic process. We must know our theological values before we create practical norms to serve them."[2] The fact that the French Dominican did not foresee or draw out explicitly all the practical implications of his theological efforts is hardly worthy of criticism. The work he accomplished is enormous and there is no one person or group who could possibly be expected to effect the change of minds, hearts, and structures necessary to perfectly conform practice to the broad ideas Congar put forward. Further, it is the very process of searching out practice based on ideas that clarifies theory and illustrates the viability of practical applications. Within this dynamic it was Père Congar's essential role to envision a theology that gives rise to an authentic *raison d'agir*.

In this conclusion I would like to present, briefly, three significant and relatively concrete implications from all that has been looked at in the preceding pages. There is no claim that these are the only implications and I will not attempt to draw out their full consequences. I simply offer them as certain possible "dynamics" toward which the "ideas" move.

## *Declericalization of Authority*

This study reveals the necessity for a reframing or "broadening out" of the word "authority" as it is understood and used within the church. By means of charisms, through the inspiration of authentic initiatives, in the active reception of the faith, all the baptized, animated by the Holy Spirit, can be actively engaged in the building up of the church to the praise of God the Father and in loving service to the world. The Spirit truly empowers all disciples, each uniquely, for the reception and carrying forth of the gospel through space and time. When these theological realities are placed firmly within a trinitarian rhythm, the authentic unity

---

2. Ladislas Örsy, "The Church of the Third Millennium: In Praise of *Communio*," 229–52 in *Common Calling: The Laity & Governance of the Catholic Church*, ed. Stephen J. Pope (Washington, DC: Georgetown University Press, 2004), at 235.

of authority flowing from its principle in God the Father is maintained within the rich diversity of the "many" who make up the Body of Christ fully acting, fully empowered for the work of constructing the kingdom of God. Neither authority's essential unity as grounded in the Father nor its diversity in all the members of the church is compromised. As the unity of the Trinity arises from the communion of persons, so the essential unity of ecclesial authority is found in the communion of love among the persons of the church precisely because each is animated by the one same Spirit who gathers all into the one Body of Christ to the praise of the God and Father of all. Further, the truth that this essential unity of the Trinity does not exclude, but presupposes, a very specific order, a *taxis*, inherently conditions authority in the church as a reality possessing a necessary order. Just as the *taxis* within the Trinity is what gives rise to the distinctiveness of the divine persons, so too order within the church serves to protect not simply its unity, but its authentic diversity.

Just as with Congar's enormous contribution to restoring a concept of priesthood not limited simply to the ordained but including the common priesthood of all the faithful and his lifelong effort to restore the understanding of the church as the whole people of God and not simply the hierarchy, *so too does the treatment of his theology of ecclesial authority call for an expansion of how authority is understood*. What this analysis of authority in Congar's work clearly implies is that "*all* have authority, of different and complementary kinds, within the one body, or should have, for the body's health."[3]

The essential "declericalization of the idea of the church"[4] necessitates the declericalization of the idea of authority—the idea that spiritual authority is purely the domain of the clergy. Congar's theological labors reveal the inadequacy of the envisioning of authority as limited to the clergy without in any way denying the latter's unique position. In many of Congar's own writings one finds the strictly narrow sense of ecclesial authority as limited to the hierarchical principle.[5] Yet this broader understanding is a clear outgrowth of his much larger theological effort

---

3. Paul McPartlan, "The Same but Different: Living in Communion," in *Authority in the Roman Catholic Church: Theory and Practice*, ed. Bernard Hoose, 149–67 (Burlington, VT: Ashgate, 2002), at 160; emphasis in original.

4. Yves Congar, "L'Avenir de l'Église," 207–21 in *Avenir et éternité*, ed. M. Olivier Lacombe (Paris: Librairie Arthème Fayard, 1964), at 213.

5. Cf. Yves Congar, "Authority, Initiative & Co-responsibility," in idem, *Blessed Is the Peace of My Church*, trans. Salvator Attanasio (Denville, NJ: Dimension Books, 1973), 57–90; idem, *Laity, Church and World*, trans. Donald Attwater (Baltimore: Helicon Press, 1960).

that shows ecclesial authority to be essentially God's saving activity on behalf of humanity. This authority is concretely expressed in the diverse charisms of all the baptized, each within her or his own unique capacity. *Ecclesial authority, in short, is the ordered responsibility of each of the baptized, with the corresponding spiritual power to build up the Body of Christ.*

## *Priority of Conversion over Structures*

Not infrequently, when the issue of authority in the church is raised, the discussion quickly goes to a perceived need for "structural changes."[6] People within the church are said to be "dissatisfied with certain forms, structures and expressions of authority."[7] There is the claimed "unwillingness of the hierarchy . . . to begin the process of restructuring the church in such a way as to promote genuine collaboration between clergy and laity in all aspects of Roman Catholic ministry."[8] Richard Gaillardetz suggests the need for "[r]evised structures for theological consultation at the local and universal levels."[9] In the United States the recent crisis involving the sexual abuse of children by clergy has proven, according to James Post, to be "too deep and profound to be resolved without undertaking significant change in the structures, systems, and culture that produced it."[10]

Without in any way denying the significance of structures and a necessary reform of those structures, a presentation of Congar's understanding of ecclesial authority transposed to a fully trinitarian logic places the fundamental Gospel call to conversion at the very heart of any renewal of the understanding and practice of authority. Père Congar is explicit: "Among the Church's tasks and pastoral undertakings I would give the formation of Christian [persons] precedence over organizations and systematic groupings."

---

6. Terence L. Nichols, "Participatory Hierarchy," 111–26 in *Common Calling*, ed. Stephen J. Pope, at 123.

7. Bernard Hoose, "Preface," ix–xii in idem, ed., *Authority in the Roman Catholic Church*, at ix.

8. R. Scott Appleby, "From Autonomy to Alienation: Lay Involvement in the Governance of the Local Church," 87–109 in *Common Calling*, ed. Stephen J. Pope, at 105.

9. Richard R. Gaillardetz, "What Can We Learn from Vatican II?" 80–95 in *The Catholic Church in the 21st Century: Finding Hope for Its Future in the Wisdom of Its Past*, ed. Michael J. Himes (Liguori, MO: Liguori Publications, 2004), at 94.

10. James E. Post, "The Emerging Role of the Catholic Laity: Lessons from Voice of the Faithful," 209–28 in *Common Calling*, ed. Stephen J. Pope, at 227.

The broad understanding of ecclesial authority flowing from the systematic treatment of Congar's theological work demands an "adult Christianity," that is, "conscious Christians, whose faith is alive and personal, penetrating their whole being."[11] Harvard University professor Mary Jo Bane, in addressing the need for a more deliberative approach to decision making in the church, offers an important cautionary note: "Though contemporary American Catholics are the best-educated generation of laity in the church's history, few are well educated in scripture and theology, few are practiced in prayer, and few are engaged in service or evangelization."[12]

Congar's articulation of the life principle of authority expresses the aspect of authority that flows from the divine life active within the faithful by the action of the Holy Spirit through the sacraments of baptism and confirmation. Such authority depends on intentional engagement on the part of the Christian with the life of the Spirit. This is precisely the point of Congar's connecting the life principle to the aspect of the church that calls for action (*factum*); it explicitly highlights the necessary engagement of the faithful with the "givenness" of God's saving activity. There is, in other words, no guarantee of such authority apart from the active sharing in divine life that comes from the ongoing embrace of God's saving revelation and the consequent living of life from that revelation. Unlike the hierarchical principle, which carries with it the assurance of God's saving authority on behalf of his people within particular contexts—for instance, the sacraments and the defining of doctrine—the authority indicated in the life principle speaks of the mysterious dialogue between God's activity and free engagement with God's grace by individuals or groups of Christians.[13] It is not enough simply to speak of the authority present within all the faithful for the building of the kingdom of God without at the same moment being fully aware of the inherent demands required for the authentic living out of this authority or, even more, the actual presence of such authority. The broad notion of authority presented here requires the profound intellectual and spiritual conversion of all the faithful.[14]

---

11. Congar, *Laity, Church, and World*, 26, 24, 39.

12. Mary Jo Bane, "Voice and Loyalty in the Church: The People of God, Politics, and Management," 181–94 in *Common Calling*, ed. Stephen J. Pope, at 190–91.

13. Cf. Thomas F. O'Meara, *Theology of Ministry*, rev. ed. (New York: Paulist Press, 1999), 208–9.

14. For a helpful analysis of this demand for both intellectual and spiritual conversion among all the faithful, see Hermann J. Pottmeyer, "The Actualization of Vatican II," *Theology Digest* 49 (Summer 2002): 145–50, at 147.

## An Adult Ministerial Priesthood

The formation of the adult Christian that Congar sees as the central pastoral task for today's church likewise demands an adult ministerial priesthood. "Only an adult priesthood can increase the number of adult lay people."[15] For Congar this "adulthood," both of the laity and of the priest, is characterized by freedom. It is the very nature of freedom that demands a new level of maturity in the priesthood. "Freedom calls for open discussion and frank give-and-take: it is therefore a threat to dogmatism (I do not say 'to dogma'!). Freedom involves the acceptance sometimes of uncertainties and hazards; these are things that alarm a short-sighted authority, or one that is too self-conscious, an authority that is inclined to 'paternalism.'"[16]

The broad understanding of authority found within the fullness of the tradition demands a rejection of this "paternalism" and a recognition that hierarchical authority possesses a "spiritual paternity [that] does not beget sons, it begets brothers because it leads to communion with the same good and the same life, in dependence on the same true Father (cf. Matt 23:9; Eph 3:15)."[17] Again, Congar's constant emphasis on the primacy of the ontology of grace is present here and is given very concrete implications for the hierarchical reality within the church. The essential unity of the church is found in the ontology of grace. Because this unity is a sharing in the very unity of the Trinity it cannot be viewed "solely as a unity of obedience *sub uno*, but as a unity of communication, of exchange, of personal participation, and, all said, of communion."[18] Hierarchical authority is exercised from within this "logic of fraternal communion" in which "[c]o-responsibility inheres."[19] Hierarchical authority must recognize the authentic authority present in the diverse charisms animated by the Holy Spirit that are possessed by all the baptized and must seek ways to nurture and lead all the faithful in the building up of the Body of Christ.

---

15. Congar, *Laity, Church, and World*, 25.

16. Ibid., 27.

17. Congar, *Blessed Is the Peace of My Church*, 75. In this regard it is worth noting that when the Holy Father addresses an assembly of Christians he most frequently begins with the words, "My dear brothers and sisters in Christ. . . ." Even here, at the level of supreme apostolic authority, the "holy father" stands in the midst of brothers and sisters, not sons and daughters.

18. Yves Congar, "Initiatives locales et normes universelles," *La Maison-Dieu* 112 (1972): 54–69, at 67.

19. Congar, *Blessed Is the Peace of My Church*, 82.

## Conclusion

During the course of the church's history there has been a repeated tendency, at times, to self-definition based on secular notions of how a society functions and on a juridical conception of the church's authority. This tendency has occurred "each time . . . the [church's] leaders have been involved in conflict with secular powers and have translated their reaction in terms of power against power." The result has been that "biblical themes, which are fundamentally spiritual, have been translated into juridical terms. . . ."[20] Congar's enormous *ressourcement* of the church's great tradition has given today's church the possibility of speaking, and, one hopes, acting from a more fully *evangelical* conception of the authority present within it.

This study of ecclesial authority has exhibited this particular contribution of Congar, which provides the church with evidence of the richly theological, anthropologically grounded, and profoundly evangelical nature of its authority. Ecclesial authority is seen to be a *theological* reality that has its ultimate principle in God the Father, who builds up the Body of his Son by the action of the Holy Spirit. Because authority in the church is a theological reality, it is at the same time profoundly *anthropological* in that it engages persons as subjects with a diversity of charisms in the fundamental plan of God, which is the building up of the Body of Christ and the growth of the kingdom of God. Ecclesial authority's *evangelical* nature is revealed in the necessary call for conversion addressed to all who seek to be disciples of Christ and in its ultimate direction of the construction of the Body of Christ and the advancement of the kingdom of God. Because ecclesial authority is theological, anthropological, and evangelical in its very nature it far transcends any purely secular expression and practice of authority. Ecclesial authority exists "only within the fundamental religious relationship of the Gospel," which will always demand of Christians nothing less than "radical conversion."[21]

In the end, all that has been said reveals the ultimate *doxological* character of authority within the church. Ecclesial authority within the writings of Père Congar, transposed into a fully trinitarian logic, is ultimately from God the Father in Christ the Son through the Holy Spirit and back again by the diversity of charisms inspired by the Holy Spirit

---

20. Yves Congar, *Power and Poverty in the Church*, trans. Jennifer Nicholson (Baltimore: Helicon Press, 1964), 97. See also idem, *Fifty Years*, 42.

21. Congar, *Power and Poverty*, 98–99.

uniting all the faithful into the one Body of Christ for the praise and adoration of God the Father.[22] The absolute goal of ecclesial authority, whether in its hierarchical or its life expression, is life in and praise of the living God, Father, Son, and Holy Spirit.

---

22. Yves Congar, *Esprit de l'homme, Esprit de Dieu* (Paris: Cerf, 1983), 42–43.

# Selected Bibliography

## *Works by Congar*

### Books

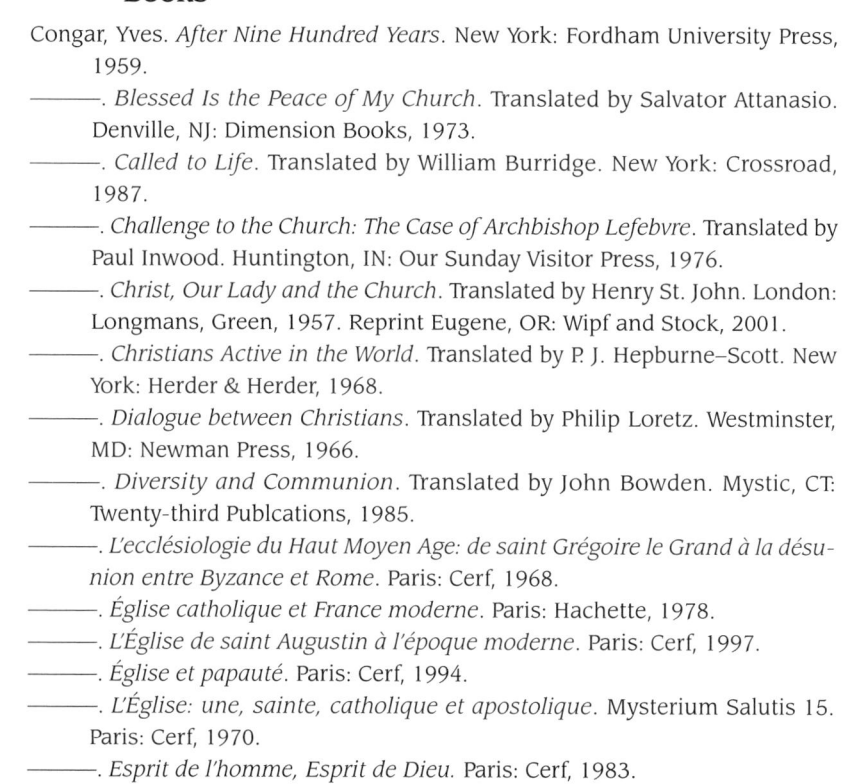

Congar, Yves. *After Nine Hundred Years*. New York: Fordham University Press, 1959.

———. *Blessed Is the Peace of My Church*. Translated by Salvator Attanasio. Denville, NJ: Dimension Books, 1973.

———. *Called to Life*. Translated by William Burridge. New York: Crossroad, 1987.

———. *Challenge to the Church: The Case of Archbishop Lefebvre*. Translated by Paul Inwood. Huntington, IN: Our Sunday Visitor Press, 1976.

———. *Christ, Our Lady and the Church*. Translated by Henry St. John. London: Longmans, Green, 1957. Reprint Eugene, OR: Wipf and Stock, 2001.

———. *Christians Active in the World*. Translated by P. J. Hepburne–Scott. New York: Herder & Herder, 1968.

———. *Dialogue between Christians*. Translated by Philip Loretz. Westminster, MD: Newman Press, 1966.

———. *Diversity and Communion*. Translated by John Bowden. Mystic, CT: Twenty-third Publcations, 1985.

———. *L'ecclésiologie du Haut Moyen Age: de saint Grégoire le Grand à la désunion entre Byzance et Rome*. Paris: Cerf, 1968.

———. *Église catholique et France moderne*. Paris: Hachette, 1978.

———. *L'Église de saint Augustin à l'époque moderne*. Paris: Cerf, 1997.

———. *Église et papauté*. Paris: Cerf, 1994.

———. *L'Église: une, sainte, catholique et apostolique*. Mysterium Salutis 15. Paris: Cerf, 1970.

———. *Esprit de l'homme, Esprit de Dieu*. Paris: Cerf, 1983.

143

———. *Faith and Spiritual Life*. Translated by Aelfric Manson and Lancelot C. Sheppard. New York: Herder & Herder, 1968. Originally published as part of *Les Voies du Dieu Vivant*. Paris: Cerf, 1962.

———. *Fifty Years of Catholic Theology: Conversations with Yves Congar*. Edited by Bernard Lauret. Translated by John Bowden. Philadelphia: Fortress Press, 1988.

———. *A Gospel Priesthood*. Translated by P. J. Hepburne-Scott. New York: Herder & Herder, 1967.

———. *I Believe in the Holy Spirit*. 3 volumes. Translated by David Smith. New York: Seabury, 1983.

———. *Jalons pour une théologie du laïcat*. Paris: Cerf, 1953.

———. *Jesus Christ*. Translated by Luke O'Neill. New York: Herder & Herder, 1966.

———. *Journal d'un théologien, 1946–1956*. Paris: Cerf, 2000.

———. *Laity, Church and World*. Translated by Donald Attwater. Baltimore: Helicon Press, 1960.

———. *Lay People in the Church*. Translated by Donald Attwater. Westminster, MD: Newman Press, 1957. Reprint Westminster, MD: Christian Classics, 1985.

———. *Martin Luther: sa foi, sa réforme*. Paris: Cerf, 1983.

———. *The Meaning of Tradition*. Translated by A. N. Woodrow. New York: Hawthorn Books, 1964.

———. *Ministères et communion ecclésiale*. Paris: Cerf, 1971.

———. *Mon journal du Concile*. 2 volumes. Paris: Cerf, 2002.

———. *The Mystery of the Church*. Translated by A. V. Littledale. London: Geoffrey Chapman, 1965.

———. *The Mystery of the Temple*. Westminster, MD: Newman Press, 1962.

———. *Un peuple messianique*. Paris: Cerf, 1975.

———. *Power and Poverty in the Church*. Translated by Jennifer Nicholson. Baltimore: Helicon Press, 1964.

———. *The Revelation of God*. Translated by Aelfric Manson and Lancelot C. Sheppard. New York: Herder & Herder, 1968.

———. *Sainte Église. Études et approches ecclésiologiques*. Paris: Cerf, 1963.

———. *Tradition & Traditions*. Translated by Michael Naseby and Thomas Rainborough. Needham Heights, MA: Simon & Schuster, 1966.

———. *Vraie et fausse réforme dans l'Eglise*. Unam Sanctum 72. Second edition Paris: Cerf, 1968. English translation: *True and False Reform in the Church*. Translated by Paul Philibert. Collegeville, MN: Liturgical Press, 2010.

———. *The Wide World, My Parish*. Translated by Donald Attwater. Baltimore: Helicon Press, repr. 1962.

———. *The Word and the Spirit*. Translated by David Smith. San Francisco: Harper & Row, 1986.

## Articles

Congar, Yves. "The apostolic college, primacy, and episcopal conferences." *Theology Digest* 34 (Fall 1987): 211–15.

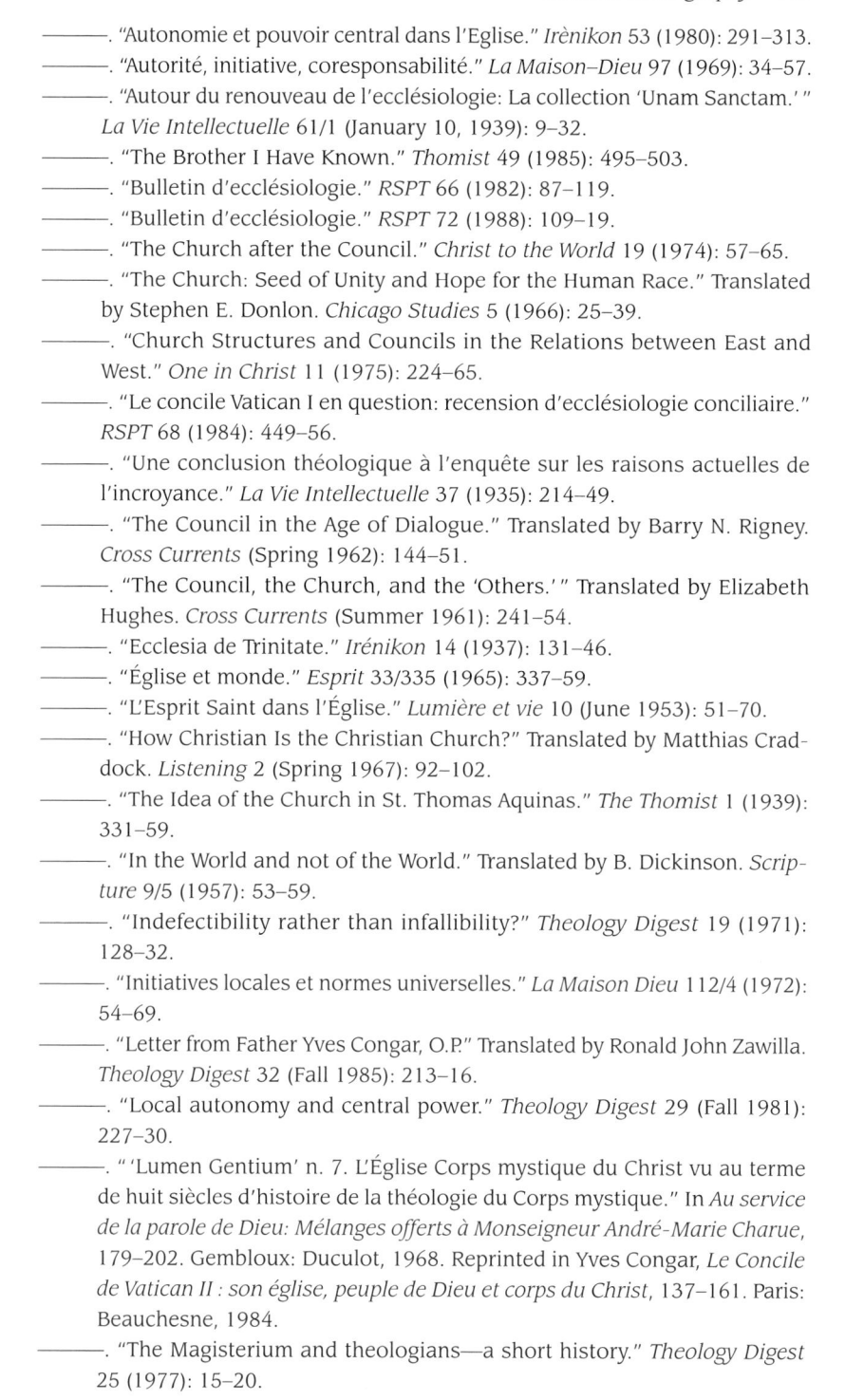

———. "Autonomie et pouvoir central dans l'Eglise." *Irènikon* 53 (1980): 291–313.

———. "Autorité, initiative, coresponsabilité." *La Maison–Dieu* 97 (1969): 34–57.

———. "Autour du renouveau de l'ecclésiologie: La collection 'Unam Sanctam.'" *La Vie Intellectuelle* 61/1 (January 10, 1939): 9–32.

———. "The Brother I Have Known." *Thomist* 49 (1985): 495–503.

———. "Bulletin d'ecclésiologie." *RSPT* 66 (1982): 87–119.

———. "Bulletin d'ecclésiologie." *RSPT* 72 (1988): 109–19.

———. "The Church after the Council." *Christ to the World* 19 (1974): 57–65.

———. "The Church: Seed of Unity and Hope for the Human Race." Translated by Stephen E. Donlon. *Chicago Studies* 5 (1966): 25–39.

———. "Church Structures and Councils in the Relations between East and West." *One in Christ* 11 (1975): 224–65.

———. "Le concile Vatican I en question: recension d'ecclésiologie conciliaire." *RSPT* 68 (1984): 449–56.

———. "Une conclusion théologique à l'enquête sur les raisons actuelles de l'incroyance." *La Vie Intellectuelle* 37 (1935): 214–49.

———. "The Council in the Age of Dialogue." Translated by Barry N. Rigney. *Cross Currents* (Spring 1962): 144–51.

———. "The Council, the Church, and the 'Others.'" Translated by Elizabeth Hughes. *Cross Currents* (Summer 1961): 241–54.

———. "Ecclesia de Trinitate." *Irénikon* 14 (1937): 131–46.

———. "Église et monde." *Esprit* 33/335 (1965): 337–59.

———. "L'Esprit Saint dans l'Église." *Lumière et vie* 10 (June 1953): 51–70.

———. "How Christian Is the Christian Church?" Translated by Matthias Craddock. *Listening* 2 (Spring 1967): 92–102.

———. "The Idea of the Church in St. Thomas Aquinas." *The Thomist* 1 (1939): 331–59.

———. "In the World and not of the World." Translated by B. Dickinson. *Scripture* 9/5 (1957): 53–59.

———. "Indefectibility rather than infallibility?" *Theology Digest* 19 (1971): 128–32.

———. "Initiatives locales et normes universelles." *La Maison Dieu* 112/4 (1972): 54–69.

———. "Letter from Father Yves Congar, O.P." Translated by Ronald John Zawilla. *Theology Digest* 32 (Fall 1985): 213–16.

———. "Local autonomy and central power." *Theology Digest* 29 (Fall 1981): 227–30.

———. "'Lumen Gentium' n. 7. L'Église Corps mystique du Christ vu au terme de huit siècles d'histoire de la théologie du Corps mystique." In *Au service de la parole de Dieu: Mélanges offerts à Monseigneur André-Marie Charue*, 179–202. Gembloux: Duculot, 1968. Reprinted in Yves Congar, *Le Concile de Vatican II : son église, peuple de Dieu et corps du Christ*, 137–161. Paris: Beauchesne, 1984.

———. "The Magisterium and theologians—a short history." *Theology Digest* 25 (1977): 15–20.

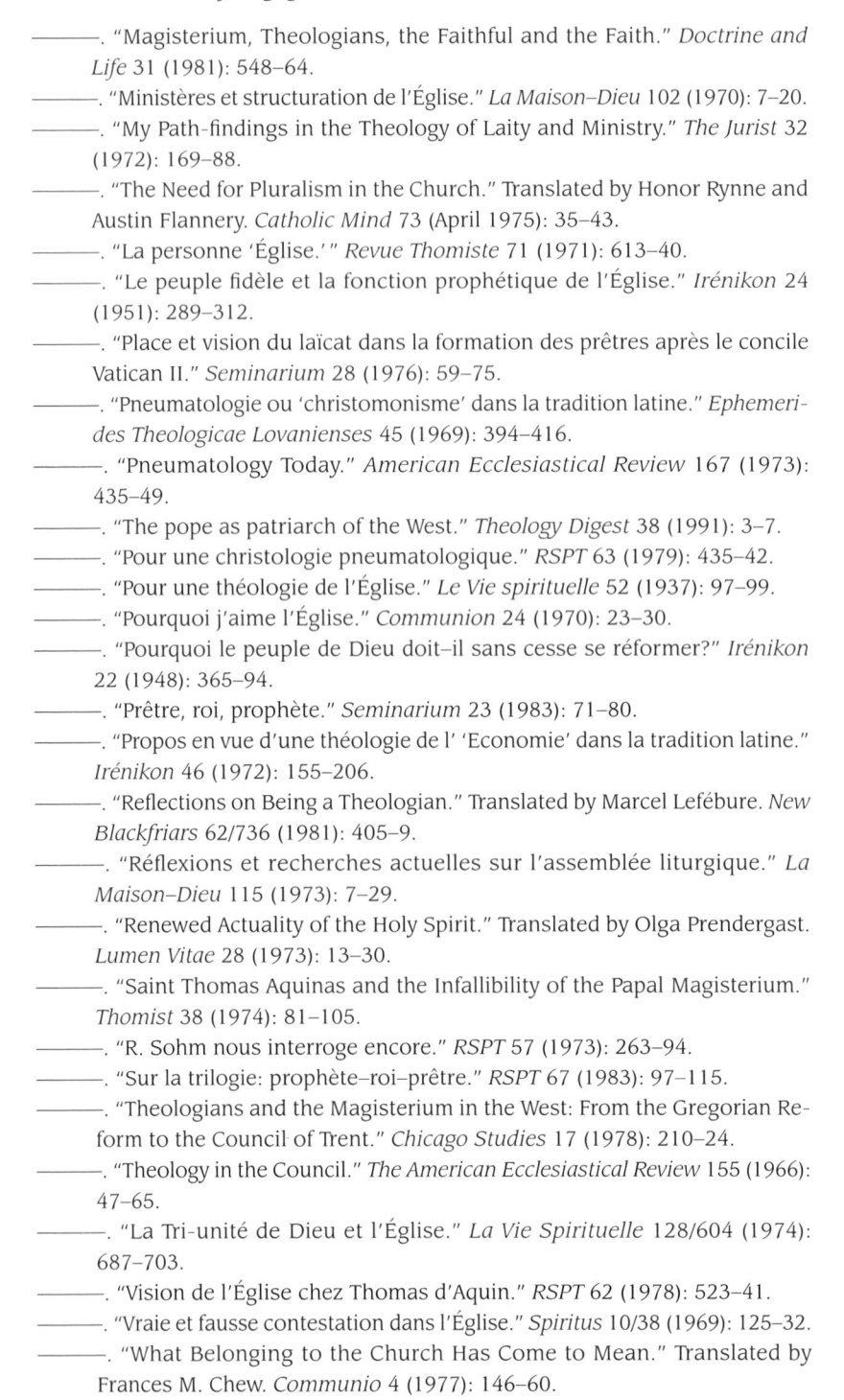

———. "Magisterium, Theologians, the Faithful and the Faith." *Doctrine and Life* 31 (1981): 548–64.
———. "Ministères et structuration de l'Église." *La Maison–Dieu* 102 (1970): 7–20.
———. "My Path-findings in the Theology of Laity and Ministry." *The Jurist* 32 (1972): 169–88.
———. "The Need for Pluralism in the Church." Translated by Honor Rynne and Austin Flannery. *Catholic Mind* 73 (April 1975): 35–43.
———. "La personne 'Église.'" *Revue Thomiste* 71 (1971): 613–40.
———. "Le peuple fidèle et la fonction prophétique de l'Église." *Irénikon* 24 (1951): 289–312.
———. "Place et vision du laïcat dans la formation des prêtres après le concile Vatican II." *Seminarium* 28 (1976): 59–75.
———. "Pneumatologie ou 'christomonisme' dans la tradition latine." *Ephemerides Theologicae Lovanienses* 45 (1969): 394–416.
———. "Pneumatology Today." *American Ecclesiastical Review* 167 (1973): 435–49.
———. "The pope as patriarch of the West." *Theology Digest* 38 (1991): 3–7.
———. "Pour une christologie pneumatologique." *RSPT* 63 (1979): 435–42.
———. "Pour une théologie de l'Église." *Le Vie spirituelle* 52 (1937): 97–99.
———. "Pourquoi j'aime l'Église." *Communion* 24 (1970): 23–30.
———. "Pourquoi le peuple de Dieu doit-il sans cesse se réformer?" *Irénikon* 22 (1948): 365–94.
———. "Prêtre, roi, prophète." *Seminarium* 23 (1983): 71–80.
———. "Propos en vue d'une théologie de l' 'Economie' dans la tradition latine." *Irénikon* 46 (1972): 155–206.
———. "Reflections on Being a Theologian." Translated by Marcel Lefébure. *New Blackfriars* 62/736 (1981): 405–9.
———. "Réflexions et recherches actuelles sur l'assemblée liturgique." *La Maison–Dieu* 115 (1973): 7–29.
———. "Renewed Actuality of the Holy Spirit." Translated by Olga Prendergast. *Lumen Vitae* 28 (1973): 13–30.
———. "Saint Thomas Aquinas and the Infallibility of the Papal Magisterium." *Thomist* 38 (1974): 81–105.
———. "R. Sohm nous interroge encore." *RSPT* 57 (1973): 263–94.
———. "Sur la trilogie: prophète–roi–prêtre." *RSPT* 67 (1983): 97–115.
———. "Theologians and the Magisterium in the West: From the Gregorian Reform to the Council of Trent." *Chicago Studies* 17 (1978): 210–24.
———. "Theology in the Council." *The American Ecclesiastical Review* 155 (1966): 47–65.
———. "La Tri-unité de Dieu et l'Église." *La Vie Spirituelle* 128/604 (1974): 687–703.
———. "Vision de l'Église chez Thomas d'Aquin." *RSPT* 62 (1978): 523–41.
———. "Vraie et fausse contestation dans l'Église." *Spiritus* 10/38 (1969): 125–32.
———. "What Belonging to the Church Has Come to Mean." Translated by Frances M. Chew. *Communio* 4 (1977): 146–60.

## Contributions

Congar, Yves. "1274–1974. Structures ecclésiales et conciles dans les relations entre Orient et Occident." In *Droit ancien et structures ecclésiales*, 355–90. London: Variorum Reprints, 1982.

———. "Autorité et liberté dans l'Eglise." In *À temps et à contretemps*. Edited by Jacques Loew et al., 7–39. Paris: Cerf, 1969.

———. "L'avenir de l'Église." In *Avenir et éternité*. Edited by M. Olivier Lacombe, 207–21. Paris: Librairie Arthème Fayard, 1964.

———. "A Brief History of the Forms of the Magisterium and Its Relations with Scholars." In *Readings in Moral Theology No. 3: The Magisterium and Morality*. Edited by Charles E. Curran and Richard A. McCormick, 314–31. New York: Paulist Press, 1982.

———. "Cephas—Céphalè—Caput." In *Études d'ecclésiologie médiévale*, 5–42. London: Variorum Reprints, 1983.

———. "Christ in the Economy of Salvation and in Our Dogmatic Tracts." In *Concilium* 11, 5–25. New York: Paulist Press, 1965.

———. "The Church: People of God." Translated by Kathryn Sullivan. In *Concilium* 1. Edited by Karl Rahner and Edward Schillebeeckx, 11–37. New York: Paulist Press, 1965.

———. "Church History as a Branch of Theology." Translated by Jonathan Cavanagh. *Concilium* 57. Edited by Roger Aubert, 85–96. New York: Herder & Herder, 1970.

———. "Classical Political Monotheism and the Trinity." Translated by Paul Burns. In *Concilium* 143. Edited by Johannes–Baptist Metz and Edward Schillebeeckx, 31–36. New York: Seabury, 1981.

———. "Clercs et laïcs au point de vue de la culture au Moyen Age: 'laicus' = sans lettres." In *Études d'ecclésiologie médiévale*, 309–32. London: Variorum Reprints, 1983.

———. "De la communion des Églises à une ecclésiologie de l'Église universelle." In *L'épiscopat et l'Église universelle,* Unam Sanctum 39. Edited by Yves Congar and Bernard-Dominique Dupuy, 227–60. Paris: Cerf, 1962.

———. "The Conciliar Structure or Regime of the Church." Translated by Francis McDonagh. In *Concilium* 167, 3–9. New York: Seabury , 1983.

———. "The council as an assembly and the church as essentially conciliar." In *One, Holy, Catholic, and Apostolic*, ed. Herbert Vorgrimler, 44–88. London: Sheed & Ward, 1968.

———. "The Crucial Question." In *Problems Facing the Church Today*. Edited by Frank Fehmers, 8–14. New York: Newman Press, 1969.

———. "Ecclesia ab Abel." In *Études d'ecclésiologie médiévale*, 79–108. London: Variorum Reprints, 1983.

———. " 'Ecclesia' et 'populus (fidelis)' dans l'ecclésiologie de S. Thomas." In *St. Thomas Aquinas, 1274–1974, Commemorative Studies*. Edited by Armand Maurer, et al., 159–73. Toronto: Pontifical Institute of Medieval Studies, 1974.

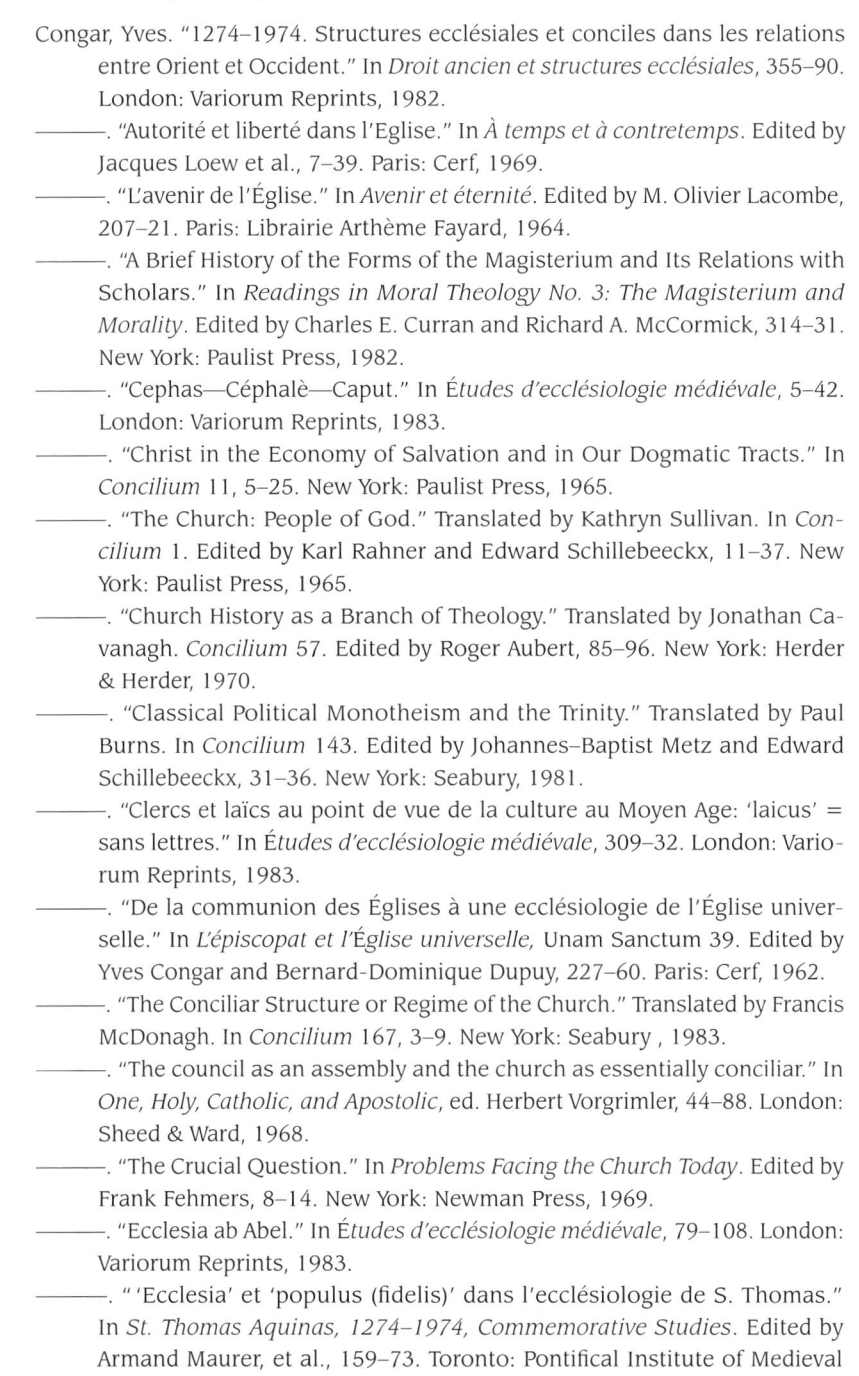

———. "L'ecclésiologie de la Révolution française au Concile du Vatican, sous le signe de l'affirmation de l'autorité." In *L'ecclésiologie au XIX siècle,* Unam Sanctam 34, 77–114. Paris: Cerf, 1960.

———. "L'ecclésiologie de S. Bernard." In *Études d'ecclésiologie médiévale*, 136–90. London: Variorum Reprints, 1983.

———. "Église et monde dans la perspective de Vatican II." In *Vatican II: L'Église dans le monde de ce temps*, 3: 15–41. Paris: Cerf, 1967.

———. "Les fausses décrétales, leur réception, leur influence." In *Église et papauté*, 81–92. Paris: Cerf, 1994.

———. "Fondements théologiques de l'Esprit œcuménique d'après Vatican II." In *Le schisme: Sa signification théologique et spirituelle*, 11–60. Lyon: Xavier Mappus, 1967.

———. "The Historical Development of Authority in the Church: Points for Christian Reflection." In *Problems of Authority*. Edited by John M. Todd, 119–56. Baltimore: Helicon Press, 1962.

———. "Histoire dogmatique." In *Encyclopédie de la foi*. Edited by Heinrich Fries, 1: 421–42. Paris: Cerf, 1965.

———. "Les implications christologiques et pneumatologiques de l'ecclésiologie de Vatican II." In *Les Églises après Vatican II: Dynamisme et prospective*. Edited by Giuseppe Alberigo, 117–30. Paris: Beauchesne, 1981.

———. "Institutionalized Religion." In *The Word in History*. Edited by T. Patrick Burke, 133–53. New York: Sheed & Ward, 1966.

———. "The Laity." In *Vatican II: An Interfaith Appraisal*. Edited by John H. Miller, 239–49. Notre Dame, IN: University of Notre Dame Press, 1966.

———. "A Last Look at the Council." In *Vatican II: By Those Who Were There*. Edited by Alberic Stacpoole, 337–58. London: Geoffrey Chapman, 1986.

———. "Ministères et laïcat dans les recherches actuelles de la théologie catholique romaine." In *Ministères et laïcat*, 127–48. Taizé: Les Presses de Taizé, 1964.

———. "Le moment 'économique' et le moment 'ontologique' dans la *Sacra Doctrina* (Révélation, théologie, *Somme Théologique*)." In *Mélanges offerts à M.-D. Chenu*, 135–85. Paris: Librairie philosophique J. Vrin, 1967.

———. "Moving Towards a Pilgrim Church." In *Vatican II: By Those Who Were There*, 129–54. London: Geoffrey Chapman, 1986.

———. "Notes sur le destin de l'idée de collégialité épiscopale en Occident au Moyen Age (VII–XVI Siècles). In *La Collégialité épiscopale: Histoire et théologie,* Unam Sanctam 52, 99–129. Paris: Cerf, 1965.

———. "Ordre et jurisdiction dans l'Église." In *Sainte Église: Études et approches ecclésiologiques,* Unam Sanctum 41, 203–38. Paris: Cerf, 1963.

———. "The People of God." In *Vatican II: An Interfaith Appraisal* (1996), 197–207.

———. "Pneumatologie dogmatique." In *Initiation à la pratique de la théologie*. Edited by Bernard Lauret and Francois Refoulé, 2: 485–516. Paris: Cerf, 1982.

———. "Pneumatologie et théologie de l'histoire." In *La théologie de l'histoire: herméneutique et eschatologie*, 61–70. Paris: Éditions Montaigne, 1971.

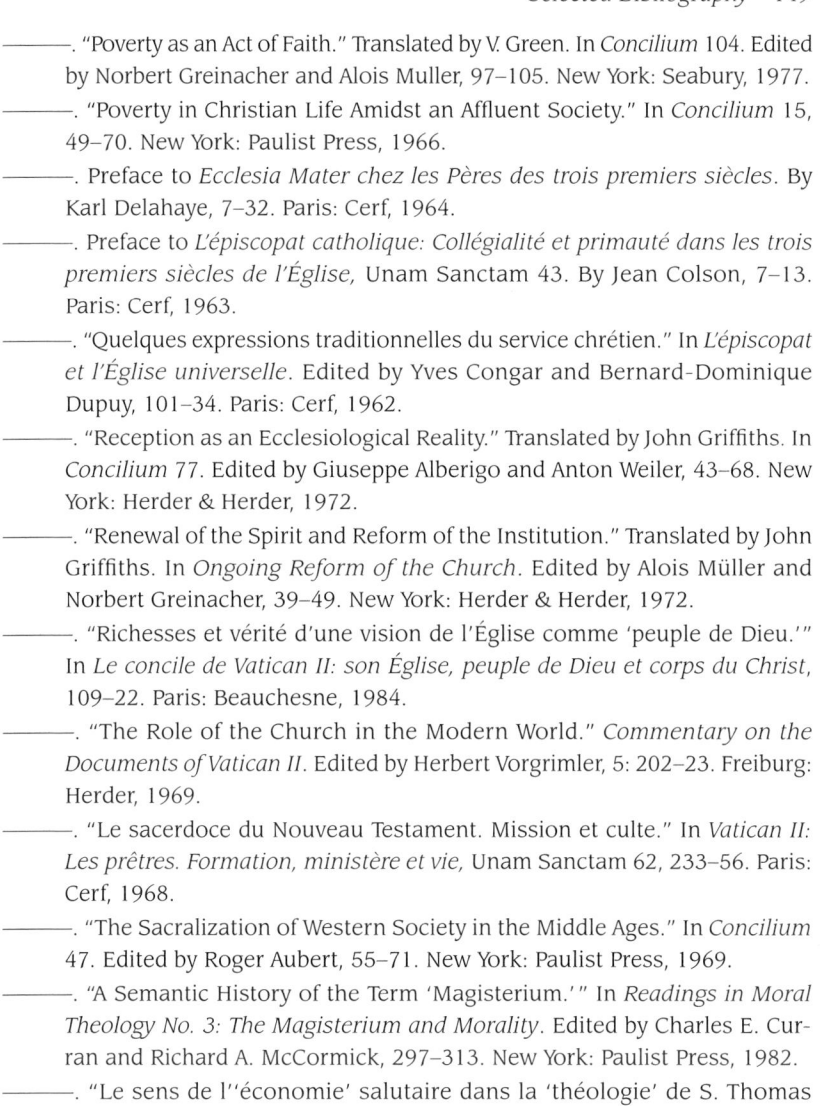

———. "Poverty as an Act of Faith." Translated by V. Green. In *Concilium* 104. Edited by Norbert Greinacher and Alois Muller, 97–105. New York: Seabury, 1977.

———. "Poverty in Christian Life Amidst an Affluent Society." In *Concilium* 15, 49–70. New York: Paulist Press, 1966.

———. Preface to *Ecclesia Mater chez les Pères des trois premiers siècles*. By Karl Delahaye, 7–32. Paris: Cerf, 1964.

———. Preface to *L'épiscopat catholique: Collégialité et primauté dans les trois premiers siècles de l'Église,* Unam Sanctam 43. By Jean Colson, 7–13. Paris: Cerf, 1963.

———. "Quelques expressions traditionnelles du service chrétien." In *L'épiscopat et l'Église universelle*. Edited by Yves Congar and Bernard-Dominique Dupuy, 101–34. Paris: Cerf, 1962.

———. "Reception as an Ecclesiological Reality." Translated by John Griffiths. In *Concilium* 77. Edited by Giuseppe Alberigo and Anton Weiler, 43–68. New York: Herder & Herder, 1972.

———. "Renewal of the Spirit and Reform of the Institution." Translated by John Griffiths. In *Ongoing Reform of the Church*. Edited by Alois Müller and Norbert Greinacher, 39–49. New York: Herder & Herder, 1972.

———. "Richesses et vérité d'une vision de l'Église comme 'peuple de Dieu.'" In *Le concile de Vatican II: son Église, peuple de Dieu et corps du Christ*, 109–22. Paris: Beauchesne, 1984.

———. "The Role of the Church in the Modern World." *Commentary on the Documents of Vatican II*. Edited by Herbert Vorgrimler, 5: 202–23. Freiburg: Herder, 1969.

———. "Le sacerdoce du Nouveau Testament. Mission et culte." In *Vatican II: Les prêtres. Formation, ministère et vie,* Unam Sanctam 62, 233–56. Paris: Cerf, 1968.

———. "The Sacralization of Western Society in the Middle Ages." In *Concilium* 47. Edited by Roger Aubert, 55–71. New York: Paulist Press, 1969.

———. "A Semantic History of the Term 'Magisterium.'" In *Readings in Moral Theology No. 3: The Magisterium and Morality*. Edited by Charles E. Curran and Richard A. McCormick, 297–313. New York: Paulist Press, 1982.

———. "Le sens de l'"économie' salutaire dans la 'théologie' de S. Thomas d'Aquin (*Somme Théologique* )." In *Festgabe Joseph Lortz*. Edited by Erwin Iserloh and Peter Manns, 2: 73–122. Baden–Baden: Burno Grimm, 1957.

———. "Théologie." In *Dictionnaire de théologie catholique*. Edited by Alfred Vacant, Eugène Mangenot, and Émile Amann, cols. 314–502. Paris: Letouzey et Ané, 1946. English: *A History of Theology*. Translated by Hunter Guthrie. Garden City, NY: Doubleday, 1968.

———. "Théologie historique." In *Initiation à la pratique de la théologie*, Tome I: Introduction. Edited by Bernard Lauret and Francios Refoulé, 233–62. Paris: Cerf, 1994.

———. "Towards a Catholic Synthesis." Translated by John Maxwell. In *Concilium* 148, 68–80. New York: Seabury, 1981.

———. "Travail théologique et Communion." In *Communio sanctorum*, 19–24. Paris: Labor et Fides, 1982.

———. "Where Are We in the Expression of the Faith?" Translated by Dinah Livingstone. In *Concilium* 170. Edited by Edward Schillebeeckx, Paul Brand, and Anton Weiler, 85–87. New York: Seabury, 1983.

## Works on Yves Congar

### Books

Dunne, Victor. *Prophecy in the Church: The Vision of Yves Congar*. New York: Peter Lang, 2000.

Famerée, Joseph. *L'Ecclésiologie d'Yves Congar avant Vatican II: Histoire et Église, Analyse et reprise critique*. Leuven: Leuven University Press, 1992.

Flynn, Gabriel. *Yves Congar's Vision of the Church in a World of Unbelief*. Burlington, VT: Ashgate, 2004.

Groppe, Elizabeth Teresa. *Yves Congar's Theology of the Holy Spirit*. New York: Oxford University Press, 2004.

Jossua, Jean-Pierre. *Yves Congar: Theology in the Service of God's People*. Translated by Mary Jocelyn. Chicago: Priory Press, 1968.

Nichols, Aidan. *Yves Congar*. Outstanding Christian Thinkers. Edited by Brian Davies. Wilton, CT: Morehouse-Barlow, 1989.

Puyo, Jean. *Yves Congar: Une vie pour la vérité*. Paris: Le Centurion, 1975.

### Dissertations

Henn, William. *The Hierarchy of Truths according to Yves Congar, O.P.* STD diss. Roma: Editrice Pontificia Università Gregoriana, 1987.

MacDonald, Timothy I. *The Ecclesiology of Yves Congar: Foundational Themes*. New York: University Press of America, 1984.

Quinn, James Patrick. *The Two Hands of the Father: The Role of the Holy Spirit Along with Christ as the Co-instituter of the Church in the Writings of Yves Congar*. STD diss. Roma: Editrice Pontificia Università Gregoriana, 1997.

### Articles

Dulles, Avery. "Yves Congar: In Appreciation." *America* (July 15, 1995): 6–7.

Famerée, Joseph. "L'ecclésiologie du Père Yves Congar." *RSPT* 76 (1992): 377–419.

Finnegan, Gerald F. "Ministerial Priesthood in Yves Congar." *Review for Religious* (July/August 1987): 523–32.

Flynn, Gabriel. "Book Essay: *Mon journal du Concile*: Yves Congar and the Battle for a Renewed Ecclesiology at the Second Vatican Council." *Louvain Studies* 28 (2003): 48–70.

———. "The Role of Affectivity in the Theology of Yves Congar." *New Blackfriars* 83: 977/978 (July/August 2002): 347–64.

Fouilloux, Étienne. "Friar Yves, Cardinal Congar, Dominican: Itinerary of a Theologian." Translated by Christian Yves Dupont. *U.S. Catholic Historian* 17 (Spring 1999): 63–90.

Groppe, Elizabeth Teresa. "The Contribution of Yves Congar's Theology of the Holy Spirit." *Theological Studies* 62 (2001): 451–78.

Henn, William. "Yves Congar, O.P. (1904–1995)." *America* 173 (August 12, 1995): 23–25.

McBrien, Richard. "Church and ministry: the achievement of Yves Congar." *Theology Digest* 32 (Fall 1985): 203–11.

Nichols, Aidan. "An Yves Congar Bibliography 1967–1987." *Angelicum* 66 (1989): 422–66.

O'Meara, Thomas. "'Raid on the Dominicans': The Repression of 1954." *America* 170/4 (February 5, 1994): 8–16.

Paci, Stefano M. "The Pope Also Obeys." *30 Days* 3 (1993): 24–29.

Pellitero, Ramiro. "Congar's Developing Understanding of the Laity and Their Mission." *The Thomist* 65 (2001): 327–59.

Philibert, Paul J. "Yves Congar: Theologian, Ecumenist, and Visionary," *U.S. Catholic Historian* 17 (Spring 1999): 116–20.

Torrell, Jean–Pierre. "Yves Congar et l'ecclésiologie de saint Thomas d'Aquin." *RSPT* 82 (1998): 201–42.

Wedig, Mark. "The Fraternal Context of Congar's Achievement: The Platform for a Renewed Catholicism at *Les Éditions du Cerf* (1927–1954)." *U. S. Catholic Historian* 17 (Spring 1999): 106–15.

Wicks, Jared. "Yves Congar's Doctrinal Service of the People of God." *Gregorianum* 84 (2003): 499–550.

———. "Theologians at Vatican II: Ways and Means of Their Contribution to the Council." Unpublished article, February 2004.

Winter, Michael M. "Masters in Israel: VI. Yves Congar." *Clergy Review* 55 (1970): 275–88.

## Contributions

Capitani, Ovidio. "Congar et l'ecclésiologie du haut Moyen Age." In *Cardinal Yves Congar, 1904–1995*. Edited by André Vauchez, 41–50. Paris: Cerf, 1999.

Doyle, Dennis M. "Communion, Mystery, and History: Charles Journet and Yves Congar," 38–55 in idem, *Communion Ecclesiology: Vision and Versions*. Maryknoll, NY: Orbis Books, 2000.

Famerée, Joseph. "Formation et ecclésiologie du 'premier' Congar." In *Cardinal Yves Congar, 1904–1995*. Edited by André Vauchez, 51–70. Paris: Cerf, 1999.

———. "Y.M.-J. Congar: Un théologien de la catholicité." In *Le christianisme: Nuée de témoins—beauté du témoignage*. Edited by Guido Vergauwen, OP, 15–31. Fribourg: Éditions Universitaires, 1998.

Flynn, Gabriel. "Appendix: An Yves Congar Bibliography 1987–1995, with Addenda: 1996–2002." In idem, *Yves Congar's Vision of the Church in a World of Unbelief*, 229–33. Burlington, VT: Ashgate, 2004.

Granfield, Patrick. "Yves Congar." In idem, *Theologians at Work*, 243–62. New York: Macmillan, 1967.

O'Meara, Thomas F. "Beyond 'Hierarchology': Johann Adam Möhler and Yves Congar." In *The Legacy of the Tübingen School: The Relevance of Nineteenth–Century Theology for the Twenty–First Century*. Edited by Donald J. Dietrich and Michael J. Himes, 173–91. New York: Crossroad, 1997.

Quattrocchi, Pietro. "General bibliography of Yves Congar." In *Yves Congar: Theology in the Service of God's People*. By Jean-Pierre Jossua. Translated by Mary Jocelyn, 189–241. Chicago: Priory Press, 1968.

## *Works by Others*

### Books

Boff, Leonardo. *Church: Charism & Power: Liberation Theology and the Institutional Church*. Translated by John W. Diercksmeier. New York: Crossroad, 1985.

Campenhausen, Hans von. *Ecclesiastical Authority and Spiritual Power in the Church of the First Three Centuries*. Translated by J. A. Baker. Peabody, MA: Hendrickson, 1997.

Chenu, Marie-Dominique. *Faith and Theology*. Translated by Denis Hickey. New York: Macmillan, 1968.

Clément, Olivier. *You Are Peter: An Orthodox Theologian's Reflection on the Exercise of Papal Primacy*. Translated by M. S. Laird. New York: New City Press, 2003.

Duffy, Eamon. *Faith of Our Fathers. Reflections on Catholic Tradition*. New York: Continuum, 2004.

———. *Saints & Sinners: A History of the Popes*. New Haven: Yale University Press, 1997.

Dulles, Avery. *Models of the Church*. Expanded Edition. New York: Doubleday Image Books, 2002.

Dupré, Louis. *Passage to Modernity*. New Haven: Yale University Press, 1993.

———. *Religious Mystery and Rational Reflection*. Grand Rapids, MI: Eerdmans, 1998.

———. *The Enlightenment & the Intellectual Foundations of Modern Culture*. New Haven: Yale University Press, 2004.

Emery, Gilles. *Trinity in Aquinas*. Ypsilanti, MI: Sapientia Press, 2003.

Fedwick, Paul Johnathan. *The Church and the Charisma of Leadership in Basil of Caesarea*. Pontifical Institute of Mediaeval Studies, 1979. Reprinted Eugene, OR: Wipf and Stock, 2001.

Forte, Bruno. *La Chiesa della Trinità. Saggio sul mistero della Chiesa comunione e missione*. Milan: San Paolo, 1995.

———. *The Church: Icon of the Trinity*. Translated by Robert Paolucci. Boston: St. Paul Books & Media, 1991.

Gaillardetz, Richard R. *By What Authority? A Primer on Scripture, the Magisterium, and the Sense of the Faithful.* Collegeville, MN: Liturgical Press, 2003.

———. *Teaching with Authority: A Theology of the Magisterium in the Church.* Collegeville, MN: Liturgical Press, 1997.

Käsemann, Ernst. *Essays on New Testament Themes* Translated by W. J. Montague. London: SCM Press, 1964.

Kasper, Walter. *Leadership in the Church.* Translated by Brian McNeil. New York: Crossroad, 2003.

———. *Theology & Church.* Translated by Margaret Kohl. New York: Crossroad, 1989.

Lakeland, Paul. *The Liberation of the Laity: In Search of an Accountable Church.* New York: Continuum, 2003.

Lafont, Ghislain. *Imagining the Catholic Church: Structured Communion in the Spirit.* Translated by John J. Burkhard. Collegeville, MN: Liturgical Press, 2000.

Lambert, Malcolm. *Medieval Heresy: Popular Movements from the Gregorian Reform to the Reformation.* 3d ed. Oxford: Blackwell, 2002.

Loew, Jacques, and Michel Meslin, eds. *Histoire de l'Église par elle–même.* Paris: Fayard, 1978.

Logan, F. Donald. *A History of the Church in the Middle Ages.* New York: Routledge, 2002.

Lubac, Henri de. *Corpus Mysticum: L'Eucharistie et l'Église au moyen age.* 2d ed. Paris: Montaigne, 1949.

McDonnell, Kilian. *The Baptism of Jesus in the Jordan: The Trinitarian and Cosmic Order of Salvation.* Collegeville, MN: Liturgical Press, 1996.

———. *The Other Hand of God: The Holy Spirit as the Universal Touch and Goal.* Collegeville, MN: Liturgical Press, 2003.

Meyendorff, John. *Byzantine Theology: Historical Trends and Doctrinal Themes.* New York: Fordham University Press, 1979.

Möhler, Johann Adam. *Unity in the Church or the Principle of Catholicism Presented in the Spirit of the Church Fathers of the First Three Centuries.* Translated by Peter C. Erb. Washington, DC: Catholic University of America Press, 1996.

Morrison, Karl F. *Tradition and Authority in the Western Church, 300–1140.* Princeton, NJ: Princeton University Press, 1969.

Newman, John Henry. *On Consulting the Faithful in Matters of Doctrine.* Edited by John Coulson. New York: Sheed & Ward, 1961.

Nichols, Aidan. *The Shape of Catholic Theology.* Collegeville, MN: Liturgical Press, 1991.

Nichols, Terence L. *That All May Be One. Hierarchy and Participation in the Church.* Collegeville, MN: Liturgical Press, 1997.

Oakley, Francis. *Council Over Pope? Towards a Provisional Ecclesiology.* New York: Herder and Herder, 1969.

Oakley, Francis, and Bruce Russet, eds. *Governance, Accountability, and the Future of the Catholic Church*. New York: Continuum, 2004.

O'Gara, Margaret. *Triumph in Defeat: Infallibility, Vatican I, and the French Minority Bishops*. Washington, DC: The Catholic University of America Press, 1988.

O'Malley, John W. *Trent and All That: Renaming Catholicism in the Early Modern Era*. Cambridge, MA, and London: Harvard University Press, 2000.

O'Meara, Thomas F. *Theology of Ministry*. rev. ed. New York: Paulist Press, 1999.

Örsy, Ladislas. *The Church: Learning and Teaching*. Wilmington, DE: Michael Glazier, 1987.

Pottmeyer, Hermann J. *Towards a Papacy in Communion: Perspectives from Vatican Councils I & II*. Translated by Matthew J. O'Connell. New York: Crossroad, 1998.

Prusak, Bernard P. *The Church Unfinished: Ecclesiology through the Centuries*. New York: Paulist Press, 2004.

Radcliffe, Timothy. *Sing a New Song: The Christian Vocation*. Springfield, IL: Templegate, 1999.

Rahner, Karl. *The Church and the Sacraments*. Translated by W. J. O'Hara. New York: Herder & Herder, 1963.

Ratzinger, Joseph. *Called to Communion. Understanding the Church Today*. Translated by Adrian Walker. San Francisco: Ignatius Press, 1996.

———. *Principles of Catholic Theology*. Translated by Mary Frances McCarthy. San Francisco: Ignatius Press, 1987.

Rush, Ormond. *The Reception of Doctrine: An Appropriation of Hans Robert Jauss' Reception Aesthetics and Literary Hermeneutics*. Tesi Gregoriana, Serie Teologia 19. Rome: Editrice Pontificia Università Gregoriana, 1997.

Scheeben, Matthias Joseph. *Le Mystère de l'Église et de ses sacrements*. Unam Sanctam 15. 2d ed. Paris: Cerf, 1956.

Schillebeeckx, Edward. *Christ the Sacrament of the Encounter with God*. 3d ed. Revised translation by Mark Schoof and Laurence Bright. London: Sheed & Ward, 1965.

———. *Ministry: Leadership in the Community of Jesus Christ*. New York: Crossroad, 1981.

———. *The Layman in the Church and Other Essays*. New York: Alba House, 1963.

Schnackenburg, Rudolf. *The Church in the New Testament*. Translated by W. J. O'Hara. London: Burns & Oates, 1974.

Stagaman, David J. *Authority in the Church*. Collegeville, MN: Liturgical Press, 1999.

Sullivan, Francis A. *Creative Fidelity: Weighing and Interpreting Documents of the Magisterium*. Dublin: Gill & Macmillan, 1996.

———. *Magisterium: Teaching Authority in the Catholic Church*. Mahwah NJ: Paulist Press, 1983. Reprinted Eugene, OR: Wipf and Stock, 2002.

———. *From Apostles to Bishops: The Development of the Episcopacy in the Early Church*. New York: Newman Press, 2001.

Thomas Aquinas. *Summa Theologiae*. Translated by Fathers of the English Dominican Province. New York: Benziger Brothers, 1947.

Tierney, Brian. *Foundations of the Conciliar Theology. The Contribution of the Medieval Canonists from Gratian to the Great Schism*. London: Cambridge University Press, 1955.

Tillard, J. M. R. *The Bishop of Rome*. Translated by John de Satgé. Wilmington, DE: Michael Glazier, 1983.

———. *Church of Churches: The Ecclesiology of Communion*. Translated by R. C. De Peaux. Collegeville, MN: Liturgical Press, 1992.

Ullmann, Walter. *A Short History of the Papacy in the Middle Ages*. 2d ed. London: Routledge, 2003.

Volf, Miroslav. *After Our Likeness: The Church as the Image of the Trinity*. Grand Rapids, MI: Eerdmans, 1998.

Welker, Michael. *God the Spirit*. Translated by John F. Hoffmeyer. Minneapolis: Fortress Press, 1994.

Wood, Susan K. *Sacramental Orders*. Collegeville, MN: Liturgical Press, 2000.

Zizioulas, John D. *Being as Communion*. Crestwood, NY: St. Vladimir's Seminary Press, 1985.

## Articles

Dulles, Avery. "The Papacy for a Global Church." *America* 183 (July 15–22, 2000): 6–11.

———. "What Constitutes Authentic Church 'Reform'?" *Our Sunday Visitor* (September 7, 2003): 11–14.

———, and Ladislas Örsy. "In Dialogue: Avery Dulles and Ladislas Örsy Continue Their Conversation about the Papacy." *America* 183 (November 25, 2000): 12–15.

Emery, Gilles. "Essentialism or Personalism in the Treatise on God in Saint Thomas Aquinas?" Translation by Matthew Levering. *The Thomist* 64 (2000): 521–63.

FitzGerald, Thomas. "Conciliarity, Primacy, and the Episcopacy." *St. Vladimir's Theological Quarterly* 38 (1994): 17–43.

McDonnell, Kilian. "Does Origen Have a Trinitarian Doctrine of the Holy Spirit?" *Gregorianum* 75 (1994): 5–35.

———. "A Trinitarian Theology of the Holy Spirit?" *Theological Studies* 46 (1985): 191–227.

———. "The Ratzinger/Kasper Debate: The Universal Church and Local Churches." *Theological Studies* 63 (2002): 227–50.

Morerod, Charles. "Trinité et unité de l'Église." *Nova et Vetera* 77/3 (2002): 5–17.

Örsy, Ladislas. "The Papacy for an Ecumenical Age: A Response to Avery Dulles." *America* 183 (October 21, 2000): 9–15.

Pottmeyer, Hermann J. "The Actualization of Vatican II." *Theology Digest* 49 (Summer 2002): 145–50.

———. "Primacy in Communion." *America* 182 (June 3, 2000): 15–18.

156   A Church Fully Engaged

———. "Reception and Submission." *The Jurist* 51 (1991): 269–92.
———. "Refining the Question about Women's Ordination." *America* 175 (October 26, 1996): 16–18.
———. "The Traditionalist Temptation of the Contemporary Church." *America* 168 (September 5, 1992): 100–4.
Ratzinger, Joseph. "Concerning the notion of person in theology." *Communio* 17 (Fall 1990): 439–545.
Zizioulas, John D. "The pneumatological dimension of the Church." *Communio* 1 (1974): 142–58.

## Contributions

Appleby, R. Scott. "From Autonomy to Alienation: Lay Involvement in the Governance of the Local Church." In *Common Calling: The Laity & Governance of the Catholic Church*. Edited by Stephen J. Pope, 87–109. Washington, DC: Georgetown University Press, 2004.
Bane, Mary Jo. "Voice and Loyalty in the Church: The People of God, Politics, and Management." In *Common Calling: The Laity & Governance of the Catholic Church* (2004), 181–94.
Beal, John. "Lay People and Church Governance: Oxymoron or Opportunity." In *Together in God's Service. Toward a Theology of Ecclesial Lay Ministry*, 103–29. Washington, DC: United States Catholic Conference, 1998.
Corecco, Eugenio. "A Juridical–Insitutional Reflection on the Common Priesthood and the Ministerial Priesthood." Translated by Lawrence Feingold. In *Canon Law and Communion: Writings on the Constitutional Law of the Church*. Edited by Graziano Borgonovo and Arturo Cattaneo, 124–65. Vatican City: Libreria Editrice Vaticana, 1999.
———. "Nature and Structure of the *Sacra Potestas* from the Point of View of Doctrine and in the New Code of Canon Law. Translated by Lawrence Feingold. In *Canon Law and Communion* (1999), 190–221.
Coreth, Emerich. "Hegel, Georg Wilhelm Friedrich." In *New Catholic Encyclopedia*, 2d ed. Executive editor Berard L. Marthaler, 6: 704–9. New York: Gale, 2003.
Dulles, Avery. "Catholic Ecclesiology since Vatican II." *Concilium* 188. Edited by Giuseppe Alberigo and James Provost, 3–13. Edinburgh: T & T Clark, 1986.
Fitzmyer, Joseph. "The Letter to the Romans." In *The New Jerome Biblical Commentary*. Edited by Raymond E. Brown, SS, Joseph A. Fitzmyer, SJ, and Roland E. Murphy, OCarm, 830–68. Englewood Cliffs, NJ: Prentice Hall, 1990.
Gaillardetz, Richard R. "What Can We Learn From Vatican II?" In *The Catholic Church in the 21st Century: Finding Hope for Its Future in the Wisdom of Its Past*. Edited by Michael J. Himes, 80–95. Liguori, MO: Liguori Publications, 2004.
Henn, William. "The Normativity of Tradition." In *Sapere teologico e unità della fede: Studi in onore del Prof. Jared Wicks*. Edited by Carmen Aparicio Valls, Carmelo Dottolo, and Gianluigi Pasquale, 125–48. Rome: Editrice Pontificia Università Gregoriana, 2004.

Hinze, Bradford E. "Releasing the Power of the Spirit in a Trinitarian Ecclesiology." In *Advents of the Spirit*. Edited by Bradford E. Hinze and D. Lyle Dabney, 347–81. Milwaukee: Marquette University Press, 2001.

Hoose, Bernard. Preface to idem, *Authority in the Roman Catholic Church: Theory and Practice*, ix–xii. Burlington, VT: Ashgate, 2002.

Lawrence, Hugh. "Ordination and Governance." In *Authority in the Roman Catholic Church: Theory and Practice* (2002), 73–82.

———. "Spiritual Authority and Governance: A Historical Perspective." In *Authority in the Roman Catholic Church: Theory and Practice* (2002), 37–57.

McDonnell, Kilian. "A Response to Bernd Jochen Hilberath." In *Advents of the Spirit* (2001), 295–301.

McPartlan, Paul. "The Same but Different: Living in Communion." In *Authority in the Roman Catholic Church: Theory and Practice* (2002), 149–67.

Moeller, Charles. "History of *Lumen Gentium's* Structure and Ideas." In *Vatican II: An Interfaith Appraisal* (1996), 123–52.

Nichols, Terence L. "Participatory Hierarchy." In *Common Calling: The Laity & Governance of the Catholic Church* (2004), 111–26.

O'Gara, Margaret. "Understanding Infallibility." In *Sapere teologico e unità della fede* (2004), 519–34.

Örsy, Ladislas. "The Church of the Third Millennium: In Praise of *Communion*." In *Common Calling: The Laity & Governance of the Catholic Church* (2004), 229–52.

Philibert, Paul J. Introduction to *Aquinas and His Role in Theology*. By Marie-Dominique Chenu, v–viii. Collegeville, MN: Liturgical Press, 2002.

Pope, Stephen J. "Introduction: The Laity and the Governance of the Church Today." In *Common Calling: The Laity & Governance of the Catholic Church* (2004), 1–23.

Post, James E. "The Emerging Role of the Catholic Laity: Lessons from Voice of the Faithful." In *Common Calling: The Laity & Governance of the Catholic Church* (2004), 209–28.

Rahner, Karl. "Observations on the Factor of the Charismatic in the Church." Translated by David Bourke, 81–97. In Rahner, *Theological Investigations* 12. New York: Crossroad, 1974.

Ratzinger, Joseph. "The Pastoral Implications of Episcopal Collegiality." In *Concilium* 1. Edited by Karl Rahner and Edward Schillebeeckx, 39–67. New York: Paulist Press, 1964.

Ryan, Christopher. "The Theology of Papal Primacy in Thomas Aquinas." In *The Religious Roles of the Papacy: Ideals and Realities, 1150–1300*. Edited by Christopher Ryan, 193–225. Toronto: Pontifical Institute of Medieval Studies, 1989.

Sullivan, Francis A. "The Sense of Faith: The Sense/Consensus of the Faithful." In *Authority in the Roman Catholic Church: Theology and Practice* (2002), 85–93.

Tierney, Brian. "Church Law and Alternative Structures." In *Governance, Accountability, and the Future of the Catholic Church* (2004), 49–61.

Volf, Miroslav. "Trinity, Unity, Primacy: On the Trinitarian Nature of Unity and Its Implications for the Question of Primacy." In *Petrine Ministry and the Unity of the Church*. Edited by James F. Puglisi, 171–84. Collegeville, MN: Liturgical Press, 1999.

# Index of Names

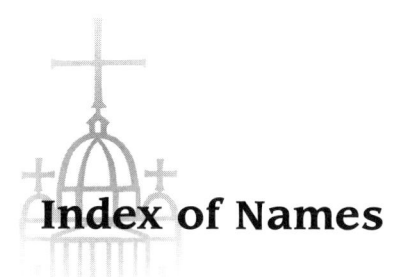

Augustine 19, 52, 62, 94, 99, 103, 106

Bane, Mary Jo 139
Basil the Great 47–48
Bellarmine, Robert 30, 51–52
Berengarius of Tours 52
Boff, Leonardo 130

Calvin, John 29
Chenu, Marie-Dominique 4–5
Corecco, Eugenio 108n135
Cyprian 17, 18, 66, 87, 91n52

Dominic 25–26
Doyle, Dennis M. 11–12
Dulles, Avery 1, 9
Dupré, Louis 32n102, 77–78

Finnegan, Gerald 114
Fitzmyer, Joseph A. 105n117
Francis of Assisi 25–26

Gaillardetz, Richard 138
Gregory VIII, pope 22–24

Henry of Ghent 27
Hippolytus 17

Ignatius of Antioch 17
Ignatius Loyola 30
Irenaeus 14, 17, 85–86, 94

John XXIII, pope 2, 8, 55
John Paul II, pope ix–x, 9

Kant, Immanuel 114
Käsemann, Ernst 130
Kasper, Walter ix, 104n114, 105n116
Küng, Hans 43

Lawrence, Hugh 23n55, 111n145
Leo, pope 69
Luther, Martin 29, 95

McDonnell, Kilian 123–30
Möhler, Johann Adam 59

Nissiotis, Nikos 127

Origen 17
Örsy, Ladislas 136

Pius IX, pope 31, 55, 65n88, 72
Pius XII, pope 6, 36, 59, 65n88, 72
Post, James 138
pseudo-Isidore 92

159

Ratzinger, Joseph 84–85, 87n30, 108, 124–125

Thomas Aquinas 4, 47–48, 71, 96n78, 99n89, 122, 124, 125
Torrell, Jean-Pierre 122

Welker, Michael 131
William of Ockham 27

Zizioulas, John 66
Zwingli, Huldrich 29

# Index of Subjects

Anthropology 16, 36, 42, 50–53, 54–55, 64–65, 73, 76–79, 101, 112–13, 121, 141
Apostolicity 38, 82–93, 115, 120, 132
Assumption 65n88, 72
*Auctor* 14, 74, 107, 114
*Auctoritas* 13, 14

Bishops 15, 17, 18, 20, 24, 27–28, 38, 40, 49, 63, 65, 66–67, 85–89, 93, 95, 107, 111

Canon Law 23
*caput—corpus* 92
*cephality* 89–93
Charism of truth 85, 86, 94, 101, 113
Charisms 14, 16, 18, 20, 36, 39, 42, 43–44, 46, 48, 53, 58–63, 74, 76, 78, 85–86, 93, 98, 113, 120, 122, 129–32, 133, 134, 136, 138, 140, 141
Church
　as Body 13, 14, 15, 16, 17, 18, 22, 36, 38, 39, 40, 42, 48–50, 52–53, 57, 58, 59, 60, 62, 63, 71, 72, 74, 76, 78, 81, 88, 92, 99, 100–101, 104, 107, 108–11, 113, 120, 130–32, 137
　as *communio* ix–xi, 24, 38, 46–50, 51, 58, 62, 64, 75, 81, 89, 92, 108n132, 110–11, 117, 120, 122, 125, 131, 132, 133, 137, 140
　and the Holy Spirit x, 11, 14, 18, 32, 42, 48–50, 59, 63, 64, 67, 71, 72, 74, 86, 101, 106, 113, 120, 121, 124, 131
　as the messianic people of God 57–58
　and mission 38, 46, 49, 56–57, 76, 78, 85, 93, 94–98, 100
　as people of God 37–38, 40, 48–50, 57, 60, 71, 73, 76, 78, 93, 98, 104, 106, 120, 129, 132, 137
　and sacramentality 13, 24, 52–53, 82, 87, 102–7, 120, 132
　as Temple 15, 17, 42, 44, 52, 53, 120, 128, 131, 134
　and Trinity ix, 37, 47, 50, 56, 65, 67, 87, 123–34, 137, 140
　and world 4, 12, 16, 17, 20, 21, 32, 40, 41, 46, 49, 53–58, 75–76, 77–78, 104, 115, 118, 120

162  *A Church Fully Engaged*

Collegiality 1, 2, 38, 41, 86–89, 120
Conciliarity 63–67, 75, 87, 120
Councils
   in general 18, 19, 23, 27, 43, 46, 63–67, 68, 69, 75
   Chalcedon 69
   Constantinople I 69
   Ferrara-Florence 70
   Nicaea 69
   Orange 69
   Trent 30, 58, 69, 108
   Vatican I 31, 51, 55, 69, 70
   Vatican II ix, x, 1, 2, 8, 34–39, 41, 50, 53, 54, 55, 59, 62, 70, 78, 86, 97, 102, 104, 106, 110, 113, 135

*Decretum Gratiani* 23
Democracy 33, 35, 39
Development of doctrine 48, 68, 72, 73
*Dictatus papae* 23, 24
*Donation of Constantine* 21, 55

Ecumenism xiii, 1–3, 5, 6, 45
Enlightenment, the 33, 41, 114–15
Epiclesis 76
Eschatology 49, 50, 55, 57, 76, 93, 103n105, 104, 110, 121
Eucharist 3, 52, 62, 64, 105–7, 108, 110, 116

*False Decretals* 92
Feudalism 20
*Filioque* 70

Gregorian Reform 22, 28, 28n86, 40

Hierarchology 31, 110
Hierarchy 14, 27, 28, 31, 33, 37, 39, 44, 50, 59, 61, 68, 70, 73, 78, 82, 87, 92, 96, 97, 98, 100, 101, 104, 107, 109, 111, 114–16, 118, 122, 129, 130, 132, 137

History and theology 11–12, 35, 37, 38, 40, 49, 50, 55, 69, 82, 83, 93, 96, 118, 124, 127
*Humani generis* 6

Iconoclast crisis 19
Immaculate Conception 65n88, 72
Incarnation 37, 47, 57, 112

Keys, power of the 19, 82, 89–93, 120

*Laetentur coeli* 70
Laity 1, 2, 16, 21, 29, 38, 40, 41, 43, 44, 45, 57, 97, 122, 138, 139, 140
Lay investiture 22, 40
Liturgical movement xiii, 36, 102

Magisterium 30–31, 37, 71, 92, 93–98, 101, 109, 120
Modernity 77, 79
Monasticism 17–21, 40, 111
Monothelite heresy 19
*Mysterion* 102–107, 120
*Mystici Corporis* 36, 59

Obedience 23, 25, 26, 32, 40, 68, 72, 73, 98, 106, 140
Ontology of grace 38, 46, 49, 50–53, 62, 63, 76, 78, 100, 110, 113, 116, 120, 133, 140
*Ordo* 88–89, 93, 108, 110

papacy, papal office x, 21, 23, 26, 31, 41, 83 96
Peace of Constantine 17, 20 22, 40
*Perichoresis* 47
*plenitudo potestatis* 92
*praeesse-prodesse* 99
Prophecy 60, 61
Protestant Reformation 22, 29–34, 41, 51, 78, 96

Reception 67–74, 78, 120, 132, 136

*regula fidei* (rule of faith) 19, 26, 29, 30, 43, 69, 82, 93, 101, 112
*Respublica Christiana* 20, 91, 92
*ressourcement* x, 45, 78, 82, 119, 141
Roman Empire 16

Sacraments 13, 24, 37, 38, 39, 52–53, 82, 87, 89, 102–107, 108n132, 109–11, 112, 1115, 139
Sacred Scripture 26–30, 33, 39, 41, 69, 83, 84
Secularization 33, 34, 39, 41
*sensus ecclesiae* 66, 67–74, 78, 132, 133
service 15–17, 19, 37, 39, 40, 42, 53, 58, 59, 60, 82, 94, 98–101, 111–13, 120, 130, 136

Simony 23
*sobornost* 88
Social history 61–62
Spiritual movements (anti-ecclesial movements) 22, 24–27, 28, 29, 31–32, 41, 78
*Synodality* 89

*théologie nouvelle* 6
Tradition 19, 26, 30–31, 39, 71, 73, 83, 93, 101, 118–19

Vicar of Christ 24, 92, 109–10

Worker Priest Movement 5, 6
World Council of Churches 36